INSTITUTIONAL ARRANGEMENTS
AND THE
INFLATION PROBLEM

355-2
13

CARNEGIE - ROCHESTER CONFERENCE SERIES ON PUBLIC POLICY

A supplementary series to the Journal of Monetary Economics

Editors

KARL BRUNNER
ALLAN H. MELTZER

Production Editor

GAIL McGUIRE

VOLUME 3

NORTH-HOLLAND PUBLISHING COMPANY
AMSTERDAM · NEW YORK · OXFORD

INSTITUTIONAL ARRANGEMENTS AND THE INFLATION PROBLEM

Editors

KARL BRUNNER

Graduate School of Management
The University of Rochester

ALLAN H. MELTZER

Carnegie-Mellon University

1976

NORTH-HOLLAND PUBLISHING COMPANY
AMSTERDAM · NEW YORK · OXFORD

ISBN North-Holland for this volume: 0 7204 0525 4

Publishers:

NORTH-HOLLAND PUBLISHING COMPANY
AMSTERDAM • NEW YORK • OXFORD

Distributors for the U.S.A. and Canada:

ELSEVIER / NORTH HOLLAND, INC.
52 VANDERBILT AVENUE
NEW YORK, N.Y. 10017

Library of Congress Cataloging in Publication Data

Main entry under title:

Institutional arrangements and the inflation problem.

   (Carnegie-Rochester conference series on public policy ; v. 3)
      1. Inflation(Finance)--Congresses. 2. Foreign exchange--Congresses. I. Brunner, Karl, 1916-
II. Meltzer, Allan H. III. Series: Carnegie-Rochester conference series ; v. 3)
HG229.I58   332.4'1   76-25052

PRINTED IN THE NETHERLANDS

INTRODUCTION TO THE SERIES

The Carnegie-Rochester Conference on Public Policy was initiated several years ago through the efforts of the Center for Research in Government Policy and Business at the University of Rochester and the Center for the Study of Public Policy at Carnegie-Mellon University. This book is the third volume in a new series which presents the papers prepared for the conferences, plus the comments of discussants and participants.

Policies depend not only on theories and evidence, but on the structure of policymaking bodies and the procedures by which policies are made, implemented and changed. The conferences direct the attention of economists to major problems of economic policy and institutional arrangements. We hope that the papers and the conferences will encourage further research on policy and on the effects of national agencies and international institutions on the choice of policies.

The Carnegie-Rochester Conference is an open forum. Participants are united by their interest in the issues discussed and by their belief that analysis, evidence and informed discussion have lasting effects on the public and its institutions.

This third volume of the series, offered as a supplement to the Journal of Monetary Economics, contains papers presented at the November 1974 conference. Additional volumes will be mailed to subscribers as a supplement to the journal. The editor of the journal will consider for publication comments on the papers published in the supplement.

K. BRUNNER

A.H. MELTZER

Editors

CONTENTS

INSTITUTIONAL ARRANGEMENTS
AND THE INFLATION PROBLEM

Karl Brunner
University of Rochester

Allan H. Meltzer
Carnegie-Mellon University

The institutions under which we live and the rules by which we govern, and are governed, do not emerge in a haphazard way. They are, to a considerable extent, a reflection of past experiences and attempts to avoid repetition of the past.

The worldwide depression of the thirties left many marks on domestic and international institutions and decisively altered monetary arrangements. Worldwide inflation in the past decade is a consequence of those arrangements. And, just as the experience with worldwide depression replaced old arrangements with new, the decade of worldwide inflation will reshape institutions and replace old practices with new.

Some changes have occurred. The worldwide inflation shattered the international monetary system erected at Bretton Woods and institutionalized in the International Monetary Fund. A fall in the relative price of oil contributed to the formation of the oil producers' cartel known as OPEC. In the United States, Germany and Switzerland, policies to control a stock of "money" replaced or supplemented policies to control interest rates.

Six papers on aspects of the problems of inflation and rising prices were presented at Carnegie-Rochester Conferences in 1974. The papers address three distinct but interrelated issues of public policy: the problem of domestic and international monetary arrangements, the nature of the inflation process, and some consequences of U.S. energy policies. All of the papers are concerned with the responses induced by particular institutional arrangements and the contributions of the institutions to inflation or higher prices.

I. DOMESTIC POLICY ARRANGEMENTS

The inflationary experience of the past ten years directed increased attention to domestic monetary arrangements and the procedures by which monetary policy is executed. Critics argue frequently that the Federal Reserve's efforts to smooth short-term fluctuations in interest rates reduces monetary control.

William Poole considers the "Benefits and Costs of Stable Monetary Growth," an old and much discussed issue. Throughout its history, the Federal Reserve has been concerned about the "flow of credit" and the prevention of "disorderly credit markets." Operations in the open market are often conducted solely for the purpose of smoothing short-run changes in interest rates. Short-run stabilization of interest rates implies greater variability of monetary growth.

Poole divides his paper into two major parts. First, he considers the relationship of short-run fluctuations in money growth to short-run fluctuations in interest rates. The usual argument is that short-run fluctuations in money growth are a desirable way of reducing short-run fluctuations of interest rates. Second, Poole considers the effects on GNP of short-run fluctuations in money growth.

Poole notes two traditional objections advanced by critics of interest rate smoothing. Critics argue that private speculators would smooth interest rates in the absence of intervention. Also, critics claim that, in practice, the rate of growth of money has not averaged out to appropriate levels over periods of several quarters or more.

Poole advances a new criticism. He claims that the model of interest rate fluctuations relied upon by proponents of smoothing is incorrect. Equation (1) of his paper is his interpretation of the model used by proponents of smoothing.

$$(1) \quad R_t = R_t^e + u_t .$$

R_t is the nominal rate of interest in time period t; R_t^e is the underlying equilibrium rate, and u_t is a random disturbance. The evidence assembled by Richard Roll (1970) on the time series properties of changes in Treasury bill rates casts doubt on this model. Other evidence discussed by Poole suggests to him that, for the purposes of short-run monetary management, movements in short-term interest rates should be treated as if they followed a random walk. Poole's equation (5) introduces an alternative model.

$$(5) \quad R_t - R_{t-1} = u_t .$$

A policy of interest rate smoothing changes equation (5) to (5') (not explicitly in the text) supplemented by equations (6) and (7).

$$(5') \quad R_t = R_{t-1} + w_t .$$

$$(6) \quad w_t = -\lambda \Delta M_t + u_t , \quad \lambda > 0 .$$

$$(7) \quad \Delta M_t = \beta w_t , \quad \beta > 0 .$$

The random term u_t describes the underlying stochastic process, whereas w_t describes the actually observed random change partly conditioned by a "defensive" adjustment of the money stock designed to offset the disturbance u. The change ΔM_t describes the "defensive" monetary operation as a deviation from a known trend. Suppose further that all "defensive operations" of period t are reversed in period t + 1. The reversal is shown as Poole's equation (7a).

(7a) $\Delta M_t = -\Delta M_{t-1}$.

Following Poole, we assume that desired money growth is achieved in period 0. The variance of the interest rate R implied by the combination of defensive and subsequent offsetting operations can then be expressed as follows:

(for period 1) $\sigma_{w_1}^2 = (\frac{1}{1 + \lambda\beta}) \sigma_u^2 < \sigma_u^2$;

(for period 2) $\sigma_{w_2}^2 = \sigma_u^2 [1 + (\frac{\lambda\beta}{1 + \lambda\beta})] > \sigma_u^2$.

The variance of ΔM resulting from defensive operations is given for both periods by the expression

$$(\frac{2\beta}{1 + \lambda\beta}) \sigma_u^2.$$

The smoothing operation, subject to boundaries on monetary growth expressed by equation (7a), redistributes the variability of interest rates over time. The gain from reducing the variance of the first period below the variance σ_u^2 of the underlying stochastic process is achieved at the cost of raising the variance above σ_u^2 in the second period. Moreover, lengthy stretches of "defensive operations" defined by equations (5'), (6) and (7) produce a variance of the cumulative sum of monetary growth $\sum_{t = 0}^{n} \Delta M_t$ that increases proportionately with the length of the time period not subject to a boundary control over monetary growth. Delayed control and offsetting distribute the increased variance of interest rates into the future and over a longer period.

The analysis leads Poole to question the effectiveness of interest rate smoothing. He argues that smoothing increases the instability of interest rates. In his judgment, the policy of interest rate smoothing has become increasingly counterproductive because participants in the financial markets have learned that the Federal Reserve responds to marked deviations in the rate of monetary expansion. He concludes his examination with the tentative judgment that short-run variability in money market rates might be lower if the Federal Reserve adopted a bank reserve target and did not smooth the Federal funds rate.

3

The second theme developed in Poole's paper reveals the difficulties in any determined empirical assessment of the short-run effects of fluctuations in money growth on economic activity. He finds the evidence thoroughly ambiguous and inconclusive. The large seasonal factor in the quarterly changes of GNP dominates the variability of historical monetary growth. Under the circumstances, it is impossible to obtain reliable estimates of the distributed lag in the relation between growth of money and GNP unless we observe some transitory changes in money growth that are large relative to past seasonal patterns. Poole finds no evidence to sustain the policy of using short-run fluctuations in money growth to smooth short-run fluctuations in interest rates. But neither is there any evidence that short-run erratic movements of money are damaging. The author cautions, however, that errors in controlling money have often been positively correlated and regretted after the fact.

II. INTERNATIONAL MONETARY ARRANGEMENTS

Charles Kindleberger and Ronald McKinnon were asked to present the best possible argument on behalf of a system of fixed exchange rates and to critique the floating exchange rate system as it operated after February 1973. Gottfried Haberler also comments on the alternative exchange rate systems in his study of inflation.

Kindleberger summarizes his argument in the introduction to his paper. His five main points are the following.

(1) The dollar exchange system was mismanaged and could have worked satisfactorily.

(2) Floating has not produced the sought-for changes in current accounts because of low exchange rate elasticities of imports and exports.

(3) Short-term capital movements were frequently destabilizing and required intervention by central banks.

(4) The absorption model of balance of payments adjustment is more useful than the elasticity and monetary approaches.

(5) If capital movements continue under floating, as has been the case, a single country cannot achieve monetary autonomy.

By early 1970, several European countries and Japan had become unwilling to adjust their domestic monetary growth to the requirements imposed by the fixed rate system and U.S. monetary and fiscal policies. Kindleberger presents two reasons for the breakdown. Triffin and Rueff argued that the fixed rate system was unstable because the reserve currency country misused its position and issued an excess supply of international money. Samuelson argued

4

that there had been competitive devaluation. The dollar was a reserve currency that could not be adjusted, whereas every other currency could be depreciated against the dollar.

Largely missing from this account is a discussion of the diversity of independent fiscal and monetary policies pursued by many countries. The breakdown involved more than a readjustment of par values relative to the dollar. The relative position of the mark, Swiss franc, French franc, pound sterling and Italian lira changed. Kindleberger emphasizes, in passing, that floating did not improve the Italian balance of payments, without mentioning the domestic monetary and exchange rate policies pursued by the Italian authorities.

The "Experience Under Floating" is surveyed by Kindleberger in section III of his paper. He finds little support for the economic theory set out by proponents of flexible exchange rates. Trade in goods and services failed to respond "to exchange-rate changes as contemplated by the normal theory plus elasticity optimism." Floating apparently did not hinder international capital movements, and, Kindleberger argues, capital flows were mostly "destabilizing." Moreover, "floating exchange rates did not effectively separate capital markets, and hence did not provide monetary autonomy to the several countries in the system."

A recent statement by Otmar Emminger, Deputy Governor of the Bundesbank, (1975, pp. 2-3) presents a very different view of monetary policy under the fixed and floating rate systems.

"In the Bundesbank we consider March 1973, when we went over to floating, to have been a sort of watershed not only in international but also in domestic monetary affairs. In the 3 1/4 years from the beginning of 1970 to March 1973, we were obliged under the Bretton Woods system of fixed exchange rates to take in $23 billion worth of foreign exchange, and to convert these foreign exchange inflows into DMarks, which led to a runaway increase in our money supply. As central bankers, we were no longer independent agents but were at the mercy of these destabilizing international money movements. We had to spend a large part of our time and energy in trying to avert or reduce these inflows and to counteract their inflationary impact on our monetary system. But whatever we did in order to sterilize these funds inevitably attracted additional money from abroad. And recycling the funds via the central bank, e.g., through swap credits, did not undo their initial inflationary impact; it merely increased the potential for ever more such disruptive flows.

"Our country was not the only one to be submerged by the inflationary effects of the huge money flows under the fixed rate system. In the three years from 1970 to 1972 the major industrial countries other than the U.S. had to contend with an increase in their money stocks (M1) of 51 per cent. . . .

"After the suspension of this inflation-prone system the Bundesbank quickly regained control over domestic money supply: in the 2 1/2 years from April 1973 to September 1975 our money supply increased on the average at an. annual rate of 7 per cent (central bank money stock) to 8 per cent (M1), i.e., about one half of the rate in 1972, the last year of the fixed rate system. This deceleration was not achieved without a temporary sharp increase in interest rates in the summer of 1973. But since the autumn of 1974 we have been able to pursue an expansionary policy as concerns both the money stock and interest rates. The fall in interest rates, both long and short term, since then has been very pronounced in Germany. This has demonstrated once again that the best way to attain lower interest rates over the longer-run is a determined counter-inflationary policy" (italics in the original).

In "Lessons for Theory," section IV, Kindleberger discusses the elasticity, absorption and monetary approaches to the balance of payments and expresses a preference for the absorption approach. The discussion is limited to very specialized versions of the three approaches. Analysis of the absorption approach yields the result that a devaluation permanently raises the balance of current account. This result contrasts with the transitory effect on the current account implied by the monetary approach. But the result requires the traditional Keynesian disregard of feedbacks from balance of payments (or government budget) to financial stock variables.

In his comment, Michael Mussa emphasizes that elasticity considerations, absorption aspects, and a monetary approach can be effectively integrated in a unified framework applicable to explanations of floating and devaluation. In Mussa's interpretation of exchange rates, the foreign exchange market is viewed as part of an ongoing portfolio adjustment similar to the adjustment in the market for equities. Changes in information are immediately reflected in adjustments of exchange rates. The large changes in exchange rates observed in the first three years of floating are the immediate and unavoidable consequence of persistent uncertainties about the budgetary and monetary policies of the major countries of the world. These uncertainties would also have operated under a fixed rate system with corresponding changes in international reserve flows and large shifting pressures on domestic monetary positions.

In the last paragraph of his paper, Kindleberger recognizes "the difficulties of harmonizing policies and Phillips curves sufficiently to sustain" a fixed-rate system. He "nonetheless insists that a system of permanently fixed rates adjusted only when policies go wrong and not from time to time as a regular device, plus the adoption of monetary and fiscal policies to make them work, is a first-best solution, attainable perhaps only in the very long run . . . ." This conclusion will easily find acceptance even among those who believe that floating rates should remain.

Ronald McKinnon's paper, "Floating Foreign Exchange Rates 1973-74," starts by noting that a "return to a parity system of fixed rates is out of the question, unless it were preceded by domestic monetary reforms and international monetary cooperation of a far-reaching kind." But McKinnon raises some issues about the operating characteristics of the system of floating rates and particularly the unexpected costs emerging in this system. He notes that scholars espousing floating rates during the 1950s or 1960s did not correctly predict some characteristics of the present system such as the large variability of rates over short time periods, the widening of bid-ask spreads in the spot and forward markets, the poor predictor quality of forward rates with respect to future spot rates, severe exchange losses suffered by banks and continued central bank intervention at a high level. McKinnon notes that "floating exchange rates are recognized as a necessity at the present time," but past theorizing "failed to comprehend the present 'disordered' and high-cost state of the markets for foreign exchange . . . ."

McKinnon mentions, first, the possibly increasing frequency of real shocks and (arbitrary?) interventions by central banks in foreign exchange markets. Mussa, in his comment, develops this analysis. McKinnon assigns more importance to a second explanation, the inadequate supply of capital to finance net positions of foreign currency. He describes several limitations on speculative positions.

When the central banks withdrew their parity commitment, the currency risk of exchange rate changes shifted to private speculators but was accompanied by an increase in banking risk (insolvency) that was not anticipated. The increase in banking risk reduced the supply of capital available for currency speculation. Moreover, banking regulations limit a bank's operations in foreign currency markets. Multinational corporations responded with similar caution to the new exchange regime. McKinnon notes a pronounced reluctance on the part of multinationals to take net positions.

Spot trading seems to have substituted to some extent for forward trading. "(T)he threat of default from either currency risk or banking risk effectively shortens the term structure of forward financing in the foreign exchanges . . . . (T)he heightened uncertainty has increased the capital requirements of both banks and their customers and restricted the scope of their operations."

An additional reason is offered to explain the limited supply of speculative capital and the general unwillingness to take net positions. "Private uncertainty about the future of national monetary policies" seems an important additional strand in a complete explanation of erratic and large movements of exchange rates. McKinnon notes that "private speculation is rendered more

difficult in the absence of any recognized international money that could otherwise act as a stable and liquid international store of value. <u>Speculators need a
haven, a relatively riskless asset, from which they can operate</u>" (italics in the
original).

The relation between a "safe international" asset and the supply of speculative capital reflects costs of information. A secure international money allows
speculators to restrict their knowledge to specific currencies and the conditions
underlying the currency's value. In McKinnon's view, "the potential supply of
speculative capital for the smoothing of foreign exchange markets in 1973-74 is
much reduced by the decline in the United States dollar as a stable international
money."

The last section of the paper explores the effect of floating rates on prices
and trade. McKinnon compares prices, stated in dollars, in various countries and
considers the possibility of "false trading" at price-cost relations not reflecting
the underlying pattern of comparative advantage. He finds that, under the old
regime of fixed rates, strong forces operated to align national price levels (trans-
lated in dollars). He finds also that cumulative "disalignments" can be used to
predict how exchange rates changed subsequently. But this state of affairs seems
to have changed after 1970 or 1971. "The sharp appreciations of European
currencies against the dollar in 1971 seem mildly surprising. And their further
relative appreciations in 1973 seem completely inexplicable to a theorist relying
on some notion of purchasing-power parity." The "very instability of exchange
rates in the 1973-74 period militates against a pure price-alignment view. . . . The
sharp fluctuations in exchange rates . . . continually disaligned real cost structures." The disalignments direct attention to the possibility of "false trading,"
when "goods move according to transitory price-cost relationships that do not
accurately reflect long-run comparative advantage."

III. ASPECTS OF THE INFLATION PROBLEM

Haberler introduces his paper on "Some Currently Suggested Explanations
and Cures for Inflation" with the widely accepted statement that "inflation is
a monetary phenomenon in the sense that there has never been a serious inflation without an increase in the quantity of money." Furthermore, "a serious
inflation cannot be slowed or stopped without restrictions on monetary
growth." The reader is cautioned, however, to penetrate beyond monetary
growth and analyze the economic, social and political forces that determine
changes in the money stock.

Haberler refers to a number of political-social changes in the postwar
period: the rise of "Keynesian thinking," the expansion of the public sector, the

8

rising monopoly power of labor unions, preoccupation with "full employment," and a pronounced unwillingness to accept comparatively high rates of unemployment. All these developments affect inflation, in Haberler's judgment, but "the important thing is to identify the channels through which they exert the inflationary pressure." The channel he chooses is their effect on the rate of monetary expansion. The argument is elaborated in three sections, one on "Demand Inflation and Cost Inflation," another on the role of "Special Factors," and the last on "International Aspects."

A criterion is necessary to distinguish between "demand inflation" and "cost inflation." Haberler takes a suggestion from Keynes' Treatise on Money. A demand inflation exists whenever "prices stay ahead of wages, salaries, and often costs so that profits continue to rise." Using this criterion, Haberler recognizes the operation of a demand inflation in 1973 and a cost-push inflation in 1974.

Haberler's position on the role of labor unions and other monopolies is the same as the position advanced by Lutz, v. Hayek and Giersch. Labor unions are "a major inflationary force." Haberler notes, however, that it is generally agreed "that a wage-push inflation requires permissive monetary policy" and "that the recent militancy of unions, in Great Britain and elsewhere, is largely a consequence of inflation . . . ."

A main disagreement about the effect of monopoly is whether increased monopoly power raises the price level persistently or only once. Haberler believes there is a persistent effect and attributes the persistence to a host of institutional changes, including unemployment or welfare benefits to strikers, court decisions and administrative rulings by agencies, and other changes of the same kind that gradually strengthened union positions and labor monopolies. He argues, also, that the cumulative effect of postwar institutional changes raised the equilibrium rate of unemployment above "politically acceptable" levels. The combination of political forces determines a permanent budget and monetary expansion leading to inflation. Increasing government regulation, in Haberler's view, adds to inflationary forces. He believes, however, that the real effects of inflation vanish with the adjustment of the economy to an inherited course of inflation.

The role of labor unions sketched by Haberler affects his evaluation of anti-inflationary policies. He sympathizes with v. Hayek's view that inflation can be "successfully" stopped "only in collaboration with the unions," or with Lutz' more pessimistic view that inflation is incurable without abolition of the monopoly powers accumulated by labor unions. These positions emerge whenever one believes that the political process and the search for "full employment" places the money supply process under the power and implicit decisions of the labor unions. The articulate case offered by Haberler, nevertheless, does not explain repeated waves of deceleration of the price level during the past twenty years in countries with powerful labor unions.

The second section of Haberler's paper discusses the special factors operating in 1973 and 1974. "Special factors" can aggravate the inflation problem by lowering the domestic supply of goods and services. The major real factors operating at the time, in Haberler's judgment, were the increase in oil prices and the reduction in agricultural output relative to demand. These factors undoubtedly raised the general price level for a given monetary policy. Haberler argues, however, that their impact "in a trillion dollar economy is small compared with the other . . . inflationary factors." He concludes that the impact of special factors has been exaggerated. Special factors contributed little more, in his judgment, than two or three percentage points to the inflation rate in 1974. The excellent comments prepared by Franco Modigliani offer some qualifying assessments of this conclusion.

A range of international aspects is discussed in the third section of the paper. Haberler first examines the impact of the dollar devaluation on the U.S. inflation in 1972-74. The devaluation operated like a real shock or "special factor." The effect of currency depreciation does not cause him to change his estimate of the role of special factors. Their combined effect remains below three percentage points.

Next, Haberler considers the Mundell-Laffer thesis that floating exchange rates increase inflation. The opposite conclusion seems better validated. "World inflation . . . makes floating necessary." Haberler asks, "How can exchange rates remain fixed when prices rise by close to 20 per cent in the United Kingdom and Italy, 15 percent in France, less than 7 percent in Germany, and 24 percent in Japan . . .?" Furthermore, "countries which have been more successful in holding down inflation than their neighbors are fully aware that they could not do it with fixed rates."

The paper concludes with a list of policy recommendations and a postscript on policy added half a year after the Conference in November 1974. Haberler proposes restrained and stable monetary growth, adequate control of the government budget, substantial deregulation, indexation of income taxes and continued floating. Wage policy appears in his view as the major problem and uncertainty. Haberler wonders whether the problem is as intractable as v. Hayek believes.

Benjamin Klein is not concerned with the causes and cures of inflation. In "The Social Costs of the Recent Inflation: The Mirage of Steady 'Anticipated' Inflation," Klein discusses the rationale of anti-inflationary policies. The social cost of such policies seems well established, and it is often argued that costly attempts to lower the rate of inflation should be abandoned.

Klein takes a broad historical view of the predictability of inflation. The variability of inflation is first measured by deviation of the annual rate of price change for the period 1880-1972. The measure gives some information about the unpredictability of price changes and the associated cost of uncertainty. Klein notes with interest that his measure clearly shows that the unpredictability of price changes was much lower in the past fifteen years than earlier. He then compares his first measure, the moving standard deviation, to a moving standard deviation of absolute rates of price change for the same 92 year period. The two series move closely together until 1955, then diverge. "This unprecedented separation is produced by the combination of two historically unique characteristics of our present monetary situation: a relatively high level in the average rate of change of prices and a very low variability of price change around that level." The data presented seem to suggest a comparatively steady and possibly anticipated inflation without serious problems and costs of unpredictability.

Klein pursues the issue. Three subperiods are selected: the gold standard period, a transition period covering the interwar and postwar years until 1955, and the period 1956-1972. The transition period has the largest average of the moving standard deviation of actual rates of price change. More importantly, the moving standard deviation for the most recent period is only about one-third of the value observed for the gold standard period, 1880-1916. In Klein's opinion this comparison is somewhat misleading. "The post-1952 period contains only positive price changes while the earlier time period contains positive and negative price changes." For the gold standard period, the moving standard deviation of absolute price changes was almost three percent on average but measured almost zero for the average of moving standard deviations of actual price changes.

The presence of systematic reversals of the direction of price change is shown also by an examination of the autocorrelation between annual rates of price change. The autocorrelations are negative in the gold standard period (or approximately zero) and positive in the most recent period. The gold standard produced changes in the direction of price changes; the postwar period produced uni-directional changes in prices and a rising mean rate of change. The author sees the separation between the two moving averages of standard deviations after 1955 as an "historically unique" phenomenon. He concludes that we are not "experiencing a predictable price movement, but . . . have moved fully to a new monetary standard where the long-term trend in prices is not expected to be zero and where large price changes in one direction are not expected to be reversible."

11

The theme of fundamental change in the monetary standard and its gradual recognition by economic agents is elaborated in substantial detail. The argument leads the author to an examination of the longer-term predictability of price movements. Klein believes that long-term unpredictability rose during the postwar period relative to the measures of short-term variability he considered. The evidence supporting the conclusion that long-term unpredictability has increased is relatively modest.

IV. ENERGY POLICY

There is substantial and perhaps universal agreement that a large increase in the price of energy contributed to the rate of price change in 1973-74. Disagreement centers on the relative size of the contribution and on the role of past government policies. Domestic oil and gas production and pricing are regulated by state and federal governments.

In "Policy Conflicts in the Separate Control of Quantity and Price in the Energy Industries," Paul MacAvoy analyzes the relation between government and the markets for energy. He first shows that a main effect of state regulation of oil has been to lower production and raise prices. This is accomplished by a system under which the state restricts the rate of output from each well. State regulation has also had the effect of reducing inventories of reserves. State regulation of natural gas, coal and electric utilities has had much smaller effects than regulation of oil, according to MacAvoy.

Federal regulation of energy became increasingly important in the late 1950s and early 1960s. Import controls on petroleum were supported by two groups, one concerned about secure supplies, the other concerned about falling prices. MacAvoy argues that the quota placed on oil imports during the 1960s did not achieve the aims of either group of supporters. Federal regulation of natural gas prices also began during the 1950s. Controls on gas were accompanied by favorable Federal tax treatment. Coal was the only major source of energy not affected by controls at the national level.

The legacy of the controls is cogently summarized. The macroscopic effects included limited expansion of production as relative prices declined and the quantity demanded by domestic consumers increased. The price freeze on natural gas reduced exploratory activities and resulted in substantial reductions in new reserves during the last half of the 1960s. MacAvoy observes that "the gas industry was in effect 'selling short' by meeting substantial additional demands out of existing stocks."

12

U.S. energy policy increased vulnerability to the international oil cartel. The "legacy of the 1960s was a set of markets unable to respond flexibly to abrupt changes in foreign supply conditions. Foreign supply had become the market clearing source." Significant shortages of natural gas had developed earlier, in 1970-71. Price controls and production constraints lowered the accumulation of oil reserves. Since there was little chance of substantial expansion of coal production because of the limitations imposed by safety regulation, a rapid expansion of imports of fuels was unavoidable.

MacAvoy also considers the welfare consequences of a policy of complete independence. This policy implies larger welfare losses than those reasonably to be expected from intermittent embargoes imposed on the USA by OPEC, according to his analysis.

Continuation of past policies, whether they are labelled "independence policy" or otherwise, "does not seem a productive path to amelioration of energy crises. . . ." Freezing prices reduces supplies in domestic markets. MacAvoy argues that unfreezing prices would be followed by substantially increased gas discoveries within the United States. Similarly, allowing domestic oil prices to rise to the level of import prices would have some of the same effects. Further, he believes that eliminating state wide "pro-ration" controls would also increase the growth of the domestic market. The author concludes his survey of U.S. energy policy with the observation: "The sum total of these policy changes would be to replace the growth in imports with domestic production."

U.S. vulnerability to potential real shocks administered by OPEC would be reduced if state and federal regulation and control were reduced. The direct and positive welfare effects of MacAvoy's policy proposals appear to outweigh the cost of removing controls. The reader should note with some interest the effects of government policy-making since 1974. We continue and even augment controls on energy prices.

REFERENCES

1. Emminger, Otmar, "The Role of the Central Banker," Remarks to the World Banking Conference, London, December 1975.

2. Roll, Richard. The Behavior of Interest Rates. New York: Basic Books, 1970.

BENEFITS AND COSTS OF STABLE MONETARY GROWTH
William Poole*
Brown University

There are now few macro theorists who dispute the contention that the rate of money growth is an important determinant of the paths of real income and the general price level in business cycle and secular contexts. There are, however, lively disagreements about how important money growth is relative to other factors and whether short-run fluctuations in money growth - - fluctuations month by month and quarter by quarter - - are of any particular importance. This second dispute is the subject of this paper.

Instability of money growth has sometimes been defended on the ground that it is not possible for the Federal Reserve to control the money stock very accurately in the short-run. This argument, however, has nothing to do with the issue of the benefits and costs of more stable monetary growth; if more stable growth is desirable, then there is much the Federal Reserve can and should do to improve the accuracy of its control over the money stock. [1] The issue to be explored here is whether the Fed would find the benefits of reforming its control procedures worth the cost.

If short-run fluctuations in money growth are costly, then historical experience appears to provide ample cause for concern. Shown in Figures 1 and 2 are annual rates of growth of M1 and M2 over three and twelve month spans based on standard Federal Reserve seasonally adjusted data. Many - - perhaps most - - economists would feel that marked changes in money growth over twelve-month spans matter and should occur only for good reason, while instability over three-month spans matters relatively little. This paper is devoted to an analysis of the short-run fluctuations, not because they are more important than the long-run fluctuations, but because their significance has been less thoroughly studied and debated.

The paper has two major sections. In the first the relationship of short-run fluctuations in money growth to short-run fluctuations in interest rates is explored. The usual argument is that short-run fluctuations in money growth serve the useful purpose of reducing short-run fluctuations in interest rates. Regardless of the merits of the goal of reducing interest rate fluctuations, it is found that, except for seasonal interest rate fluctuations, it appears that fluctuations in money growth do not in fact smooth interest rates. The claimed benefit

* At the time this paper was written the author was Adviser, Federal Reserve Bank of Boston. Thanks are due to Ruth Kupfer for handling the computer work and to Redenta de Leon for preparing the charts and typing.

[1] Poole and Lieberman, (1972).

FIGURE 1

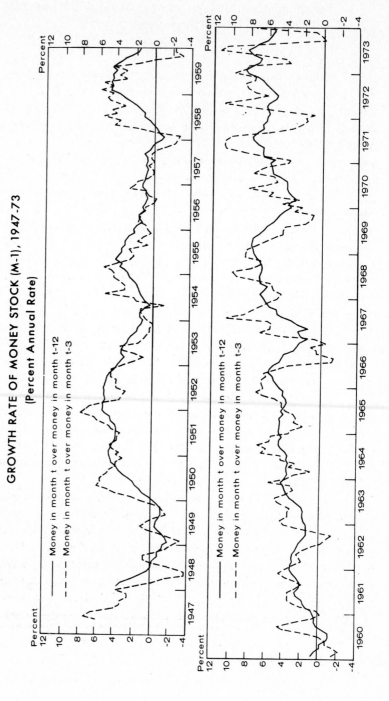

GROWTH RATE OF MONEY STOCK (M-1), 1947-73
(Percent Annual Rate)

16

FIGURE 2

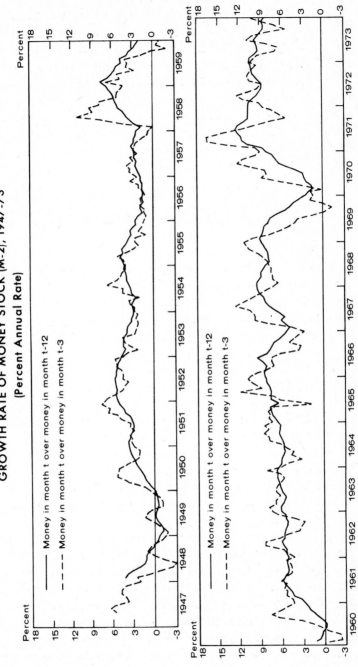

GROWTH RATE OF MONEY STOCK (M-2), 1947-73
(Percent Annual Rate)

Money in month t over money in month t-12
Money in month t over money in month t-3

Money in month t over money in month t-12
Money in month t over money in month t-3

from fluctuating money growth is not realized.

In the second major section of the paper the issue is the effects on GNP of short-run fluctuations in money growth. Here the findings are completely ambiguous. In fact, it is argued that there is no real possibility of discovering how quickly money affects GNP on the basis of post-war U.S. data. The reason is that to determine the pattern of the distributed lag effects of money on GNP it is necessary to first sort out seasonal influences. It· is an unfortunate fact of life that for post-war U.S. data the seasonal effects on GNP are so much larger than the monetary effects that there is no way of being confident that the method selected* for handling seasonals does not seriously distort the estimates of the distributed lags for money.

I. EFFECTS OF SHORT-RUN MONEY GROWTH ON INTEREST RATE STABILITY

One of the most frequently heard arguments for short-run fluctuations in the rate of growth of the money stock is that such fluctuations serve the useful function of smoothing money market interest rates. The structure of this argument is that the interest rate has an equilibrium component, which may change relatively slowly over time, and a random component caused by disturbances in the financial markets associated with new financings, destabilizing shifts in investor "psychology," and so forth. The central bank, it is argued, can improve the efficiency of the money markets by permitting the money stock to grow more or less rapidly as required to smooth short-run fluctuations in interest rates.

Many proponents of interest rate smoothing recognized that the efficiency gains from smoothing must be modest at best. Markets that are left alone do not "fall apart." Nevertheless, the argument continues, why not smooth interest rates? Abnormally high or low money growth only matters if it is continued over a span of many months. Nothing will be lost and something may be gained if money growth fluctuates up and down, averaging out to an appropriate rate, in the process of smoothing money market rates.

A final part of the argument concerns the central bank's traditional role as the lender of last resort. Surely, it is argued, the central bank must stand ready to intervene in panic, or potential panic, situations such as the Penn Central bankruptcy. Day-by-day smoothing of money market rates simply makes this function a continuous one applied to disturbances of all kinds and all sizes.

Previous criticisms of these arguments have suffered, I believe, from accepting the basic premises of the interest smoothing arguments. Only two counter-arguments have been offered. The first is that the proponents of interest rate smoothing underestimate the ability of financial markets to cope with interest rate stability. The second is that, in practice, the rate of growth of money has not averaged out to appropriate levels over periods of several quarters or more.

Far more compelling arguments against interest rate smoothing can be offered. These arguments are: (1) the basic model of interest rate fluctuations relied upon by proponents of smoothing is wrong: (2) attempts at short-run smoothing have in fact increased interest rate instability; and (3) more stable money growth would not in any way compromise the lender-of-last- resort function.

After discussion of each of these arguments, the question of the impact on interest rates of temporary disturbances in money supply and demand will be considered. It will be argued that the private market can smooth some disturbances and that there is no reason to expect that the remaining disturbances will be of much importance.

The Model of Interest Rate Fluctuations. The proponents of interest rate smoothing implicitly use a model of the following kind:

$$(1) \quad R_t = R^e_t + u_t,$$

where R_t is, say, the three-month Treasury bill rate, R^e_t is the relatively slowly changing equilibrium level of the bill rate, [2] and u_t is a random disturbance. The disturbance term may exhibit positive serial dependence, but it is assumed that disturbances due to "market psychology," or whatever, die out eventually. Also, to maintain a clear distinction between the equilibrium bill rate and the disturbances it must be assumed that the disturbance is statistically independent of the equilibrium rate.

With these assumptions, and assuming that the serial covariance of the changes in interest rates depends only on the lag between observations and not on time, the covariance between the change in the bill rate one period and the change m periods before is

$$(2) \quad \text{Cov} (\Delta R, \Delta R_{-m}) = \text{Cov} (\Delta R^e, \Delta R^e_{-m}) + 2 \text{ Cov} (u, u_{-m}) - \text{Cov} (u, u_{-m+1})$$

$$- \text{Cov} (u, u_{-m-1}).$$

For interest rate smoothing per se to be sensible, it must be assumed that Cov $(\Delta R^e, \Delta R^e_{-1})$ is small. Otherwise, the smoothing operation will prevent the interest rate from adjusting to changes in the equilibrium interest rate.

---

[2] The equilibrium rate may be thought of as the rate consistent with the expenditure sector of the economy moving along a target path chosen with regard to the general objectives of stabilization policy.

The behavior of the disturbance term, u, may be represented quite generally by assuming that

$$(3)\quad u_t = \sum_{k=0}^{\infty} Q_k e_{t-k}, \qquad\qquad \text{Cov}(e_i, e_j) = 0,\ i \neq j$$

$$= \sigma_e^2,\ i = j$$

Applying this expression to equation (2) yields

$$(4)\quad \text{Cov}(\Delta R, \Delta R_{-m}) = \text{Cov}(\Delta R^e, \Delta R^e_{-m})$$

$$- \sigma_e^2 \sum_{k=0}^{\infty} Q_k\ [(Q_{k+m-1} - Q_{k+m}) - (Q_{k+m} - Q_{k+m+1})].$$

If we assume that u_t is a stable stochastic process, then $Q_k e_{t-k}$ must be a convergent series. Since $|Q_k|$ must approach zero for large values of k, $|Q_k - Q_{k+1}|$ must also approach zero. If the Q_k are all positive, [3] then it is clear that for some m large enough, say m > m*, the term in square brackets in (4) is positive for all k, thereby making $\text{Cov}(\Delta R, \Delta R_{-m})$ negative if $\text{Cov}(\Delta R^e, \Delta R^e_{-m})$ is zero. If the Q_k are not all positive, then some of the covariances for m > m* may be positive but some must also be negative.

In this world, interest-rate smoothing may be viewed as reducing the variances of u. But if the policy is based only on observed fluctuations in the interest rate, then the variance of u cannot be reduced to zero short of outright pegging. Smoothing can be expected to damp changes in interest rates, but to leave the general pattern over time almost unchanged.

In fact, there is a substantial body of evidence that the covariances of changes in security prices are approximately zero. Since security yields are a function of security prices, the yield changes must also have near zero covariances. Evidence directly relevant to this paper is available in the careful study of the Treasury bill market by Richard Roll (1970).

Roll's evidence includes estimates of the covariances for weekly bill rate changes in successive weeks (m=1) for bills with maturities from one to twenty-six weeks. Roll's Table 6-16 suggests that the covariance in successive weeks for one- and two-week bills is very slightly negative while the covariances for bills with maturities from three to twenty-six weeks may be very slightly positive. However, hardly any of these covariances are statistically significant according to Roll's tests.

---

[3] If the Q_k are all negative we can factor out -1.

Roll also presents a table (Table 6-15) of serial correlations between one-week yield changes for bills of one-week maturity for lags of one to ten weeks. While seven of the ten correlations are negative, all are small (less than 0.1 in absolute value) and none is statistically significant.

The efficient markets theory and the available evidence both suggest that the model of equation (1) is fundamentally wrong. A much more accurate representation of the behavior of interest rates may be the random walk model.

$$(5) \ R_t - R_{t-1} = u_t, \ Cov(u_i, u_j) = 0, i \neq j$$

$$= \sigma_u^2, i = j.$$

With this model, systematic interest rate smoothing appears impossible. Suppose, for example, that money growth is permitted to rise to reduce the size of a particular u_t. If the money growth rate averaged over the two periods is to be held at a target level, then money growth in period $t + 1$ must be below target. With the random walk interest rate model, the lower money growth will be accompanied by a positive value of u_{t+1} half the time; in these cases the size of ΔR_{t+1} will be increased. The question is whether the increased variance in period $t+1$ necessarily offsets the reduced variance in period t.

To investigate this question, consider the following simple model. Suppose that the underlying disturbances causing changes in the interest rate are represented by the u's. Furthermore, suppose that the actual change in the interest rate is w_t, where w is determined by u and by the deviation of rate of change of money, ΔM, from its trend value according to

$$(6) \ w_t = -\lambda \Delta M_t + u_t, \lambda > 0.$$

With smoothing, M_t is dependent on w_t according to

$$(7) \ \Delta M_t = \beta w_t, \beta > 0.$$

Also, assume that the money stock is kept on a target path except for one-period deviations. Thus, if $\Delta M_{t-1} \neq 0$
(7) is replaced by

$$(7a) \ \Delta M_t = -\Delta M_{t-1} .$$

At the end of period 0 money is assumed to be on target. Thus, the policy over the next two periods is given by

21

(8) $\Delta M_1 = \beta w_1$.

(9) $\Delta M_2 = -\Delta M_1$.

Solving (6) and (8) simultaneously, we obtain

(10a) $w_1 = \dfrac{1}{1 + \lambda\beta} \; u_1$

(10b) $\Delta M_1 = \dfrac{\beta}{1 + \lambda\beta} \; u_1$.

From (6), (7a), and (10b),

(11) $w_2 = \left(\dfrac{\lambda\beta}{1 + \lambda\beta}\right) u_1 + u_2$.

   If we imagine this policy being followed faithfully over a long time, w_1 might represent the model of interest rate changes in the first and third quarters of every year and w_2 in the second and fourth quarters. Assuming that the u's have mean zero, the variance of the quarterly changes in the interest rate will be

(12) $\sigma_w^2 = 1/2 \, E\,[w_1^2] + 1/2 \, E\,[w_2^2]$

$$= \sigma_u^2 \left[1 - \frac{\lambda\beta}{(1 + \lambda\beta)^2} \right] .$$

It is easily shown that the variance is minimized when $\beta = \dfrac{1}{\lambda}$; at this minimum $\sigma_w^2 = 3/4 \, \sigma_u^2$.

   While this policy reduces the variance of quarterly changes, it leaves the variance of half-year changes unaffected. In the absence of smoothing, the variance of half-year changes is

(13) $VAR(u_1 + u_2) = 2\sigma_u^2$.

With the smoothing policy, the variance is

(14) $VAR(w_1 + w_2) = VAR(w_1) + VAR(w_2) + 2\,Cov(w_1, w_2)$

$$= \left(\frac{1}{1 + \lambda\beta}\right)\sigma_u^2 + \left[\left(\frac{\lambda\beta}{1 + \lambda\beta}\right)\sigma_u^2 + \sigma_u^2\right] + \left(\frac{2\lambda\beta}{(1 + \lambda\beta)}\right)\sigma_u^2$$

$$= 2\sigma_u^2.$$

This policy has the obvious problem that it increases the probability of large changes in interest rates every second period. On the other hand, it might be defended on the ground that it spreads the impact of a large u over two periods.

In any event, the important message from this argument is that the smoothing policy $\Delta M_t = \beta w_t$ must from time to time be replaced by $\Delta M_t = -\Delta M_{t-1}$ if money growth is to average out to its target rate. If the straight smoothing policy is maintained, then the level of the money stock becomes a random walk.

The policy of smoothing rates on one-period bills will also affect the behavior of rates on bills of longer maturity. Consider, for example, the behavior of the rate on two-period bills. Let $R_{1,t}$ and $R_{2,t}$, respectively, be the rates at time t on one- and two-period bills. The rates on the one-period bill for t=1, 2, will be

$$R_{1,1} = R_{1,0} + w_1,$$

$$R_{1,2} = R_{1,0} + w_1 + w_2.$$

At time 0, the expectation of the one-period yield for period 1 is

$$E_0[R_{1,1}] = R_{1,0}.$$

Thus, following the expectations theory of the term structure of interest rates,

$$R_{2,0} = 1/2R_{1,0} + 1/2E_0[R_{1,1}] = R_{1,0}.$$

At t=1, however, we have

$$E_1[R_{1,2}] = R_{1,1} + E[w_2]$$

$$= R_{1,0} + \left(\frac{1}{1 + \lambda\beta}\right)u_1 + \left(\frac{\lambda\beta}{1 + \lambda\beta}\right)u_1$$

$$= R_{1,0} + u_1.$$

Thus,

$$R_{2,1} = 1/2R_{1,1} + 1/2 E_1 [R_{1,2}]$$

$$= 1/2\left[R_{1,0} + \left(\frac{1}{1 + \lambda\beta}\right)u_1\right] + 1/2\left[R_{1,0} + u_1\right]$$

$$= R_{1,0} + 1/2\left(\frac{2 + \lambda\beta}{1 + \lambda\beta}\right)u_1.$$

Also, it is clear that

$$R_{2,2} = R_{1,0} + u_1 + u_2.$$

From these results we can calculate the changes in the rate on the two-period bill.

$$R_{2,1} - R_{2,0} = 1/2\left(\frac{2 + \lambda\beta}{1 + \lambda\beta}\right)u_1,$$

$$R_{2,2} - R_{2,1} = 1/2\left(\frac{\lambda\beta}{1 + \lambda\beta}\right)u_1 + u_2.$$

With the smoothing policy (i.e., $\beta > 0$), the impact of u_1 on $R_{2,1}$ is reduced, but to a smaller degree than is true for $R_{1,1}$. Thus, if $R_{1,0} = R_{2,0}$, a positive disturbance in period 1 ($u_1 > 0$) will raise both yields but the increase will be greater for R_2. This result raises additional questions.

A well-confirmed generalization about fluctuations in interest rates is that short rates fluctuate more than long rates. But if the pure random walk model were strictly correct, short and long rates should fluctuate the same amount in the absence of smoothing ($\beta=0$); with smoothing, changes in long rates should frequently be greater than changes in short rates. These results follow, of course, from the fact that if one-period rates followed a random walk, then the best forecast of all future one-period rates would be given by the current one-period rate.

Another observation is that if the random walk model (or the more general submartingale model) were strictly correct for one-period interest rates, then the probability of the one-period rate staying within the bounds of, say, 0 to 15 percent over the last fifty years would be extraordinarily low. This argument, along with term structure argument, suggests that changes in short-term interest rates must be subject to some sort of negative serial dependence at some lags.

These observations, plus the evidence accumulated by Roll and others, suggests that the best model of the short-term interest rate may be that given by equations (1) and (3) but with the assumption that the Q_k in equation (3) are nearly constant for a significant number of terms and then decline only slowly toward zero. If this representation is accepted, then the question is whether the Q_k decline within the span of time in which significant fluctuations in money growth have little or no impact on general economic activity.

Evidence on the Q_k over longer periods of time appears in Table 1 in the form of serial correlation coefficients for changes in the quarterly average of the 3-month Treasury bill rate and for changes in the quarterly average of the Aaa corporate bond rate. If the daily changes in each of these rates followed a random walk, then the serial correlation for lag 1 of quarterly average data should be about 0.25 as demonstrated in Holbrook Working (1960). For lags of 2 and greater, however, the serial correlations would be zero under the random walk hypothesis.

Table 1

Serial Correlation Coefficients for Interest
Rate Changes (Quarterly data, 1952-72)

Serial Correlation Coefficient

Lag	Change in 3 mo. Treas. bill rate	Change in Aaa Corp. bond yield
1	0.353	0.364
2	-0.221	-0.098
3	-0.102	-0.006
4	0.045	0.042
5	-0.118	-0.015
6	-0.240	0.038
7	-0.174	-0.005
8	-0.034	-0.065
9	-0.027	0.182
10	-0.079	0.159
11	-0.102	-0.162
12	-0.031	-0.154

Under the null hypothesis that the correlation is 0.25 at lag 1 and zero at lags 2 and above, a correlation coefficient in Table 1 for lag 1 is significant at the 5 percent level on a two-tail test if it falls outside the range from 0.023 to 0.477; for lags 2 through 12 a coefficient is significant if it exceeds 0.195 in absolute value. [4]

The correlation coefficients for the bill rate at the seasonal lags of 4, 8, and 12 quarters are all quite low in absolute value suggesting that enough of a seasonal has been introduced into the money stock to eliminate interest rate seasonals. The coefficient for lag 1 is above the value, 0.25, implied by the null hypothesis and, although not statistically significant, it is in the direction to be expected from interest rate smoothing. Ten of the eleven coefficients for lags 2 through 12 are negative, but only those for lags 2 and 6 are statistically significant suggesting that there is some tendency, but a weak and gradual one, for reversal of bill rate changes. None of the coefficients for the Aaa bond yield are significant.

These results are consistent with the view that negative serial dependence for interest rate changes is quite weak at any given lag. Furthermore, the negative dependence is probably stretched out over a very long period of time. For the purposes of short-run monetary management, therefore, the bill rate ought to be treated as if it followed a random walk. If the monetary growth rate is to be controlled over a span of, say, two quarters, short-run interest rate smoothing can be expected to simply stretch out interest rate changes, generating positive serial dependence in the short run, rather than to decrease the distance between peaks and troughs in the level of the rate.

Another method of obtaining evidence on the value of interest rate smoothing is to examine the actual record. It seems reasonable to assume that rate smoothing is being attempted whenever money growth accelerates (decelerates) at the same time interest rates are rising (falling). The question is then one of the frequency with which the interest rate falls (rises) in the period following a period of rate smoothing.

Table 2 provides some evidence on this question. The data underlying the table consist of monthly average series for the money stock (M-1) seasonally adjusted and the 3-month Treasury bill rate. Quarterly rates of change of money and interest were defined by $\Delta R_t = R_t - R_{t-3}$ and $\Delta M_t = \log M_t - \log M_{t-3}$, respectively. The acceleration of money growth was measured by $\Delta^2 M_t = \Delta \log M_t - \Delta \log M_{t-3}$. With monthly data, each year there are 12 overlapping obser-

---

[4] Based on the approximate test described in George E.B. Box and Gwilym M. Jenkins, (1970, 34-36).

vations for ΔR and $\Delta^2 M$, or three (not independent) sets of four non-overlapping quarterly observations.

As shown in the table, for the quarters ending in March, June, September, and December, in 41 of the 88 quarters in the 1952-73 period $\Delta^2 M$ had the same sign as ΔR. Of these 41, in 26 cases ΔR_{t+3} had the same sign as ΔR_t. Thus, the bill rate continued to move in the same direction more than half the time in the quarter following a change in the rate of growth of the money stock in the direction required for interest rate smoothing. [5]

The argument so far has been based on the assumption that changes in the rate of growth of money have an inverse effect on the nominal interest rate. However, the fact that in the long run the rate of money growth has a direct rather than inverse effect on the nominal interest rate has been neglected. If the policy represented by equation (7) were followed all the time, equations representing the impact of money growth on inflation and on the nominal interest rate would probably combine with (7) to produce an unstable system. If the

Table 2

Serial Dependence of Interest Rates
Following Interest Rate Smoothing, 1952-73

No. of Observations	Quarters Ending:			
	Mar., June. Sept., Dec.	Jan., April, July, Oct.	Feb., May, Aug., Nov.	Total
same sign for $\Delta^2 M$ and ΔR	41	43	39	129
same sign for $\Delta^2 M$, ΔR, and ΔR_{+1}	26	22	28	76
Row 2 ÷ Row 1	0.63	0.51	0.72	0.62

---

[5] If the daily observations on the 3-month bill rate were a random walk, non-overlapping quarterly first differences defined by $\Delta R_t = R_t - R_{t-3}$ would have a serial correlation of about 0.063. Note that while first differences of monthly average data three months apart produce much less serial correlation than first differences of quarterly averages, there is still some serial correlation and so the proportions in the bottom row of Table 2 should not be tested against the null hypothesis that the porportion is 0.5

ΔR's do exhibit a weak negative covariance it must be because bounds on the rate of growth of money stabilize the system.

The Effectiveness of Interest Rate Smoothing. If it is accepted that short-run interest rate changes are essentially serially uncorrelated, then it follows that only very limited rate smoothing is possible. In the smoothing model in the previous section a reduction in the variance of rate changes one quarter was accomplished at the expense of an increase in the variance of rate changes the following quarter. Furthermore, if money growth one quarter has any effect on GNP, and therefore on the demand for loanable funds and interest rates, the following quarter, then the subsequent increase in the variance of rate changes will be higher yet. In this case the net result of quarterly smoothing will be to make the variance of rate changes measured over half-years higher rather than lower.

The primary argument against interest rate variability per se seems to be that rate variability generates capricious capital gains and losses that are undesirable for the same sorts of reasons that unstable income is undesirable. If this argument is accepted, as seems reasonable, then the policy goal should be to reduce the distance between interest rate peaks and troughs rather than simply to reduce the variance of month-to-month and quarter-to-quarter changes. That these two objectives are not the same is demonstrated by the simple model of the previous section in which the variance of quarterly changes could be reduced without reducing the variance of half-year changes. On this view, the issue is not one of trading off stability in interest rates against stability in money growth, because short-run rate smoothing is in fact counter-productive.

There is reason to believe that the policy of interest rate smoothing has become increasingly counter-productive as participants in the financial markets have come to expect that the Federal Reserve System will react to marked deviations in money growth. Because an understanding of this argument requires an understanding of current monetary policy procedures, a brief description of these procedures seems appropriate.

The Federal Open Market Committee (FOMC) has regular meetings once a month in Washington. At each meeting the policy decisions are formalized in a Directive given to the Open Market Account Manager at the New York Federal Reserve Bank. Although the Directive, which is released to the public with a lag of approximately 90 days, [6] is framed in non-quantitative language, the Open Market Manager is also given carefully-specified quantitative instructions. [7]

---

[6] By August of 1975 this lag had been reduced to 45 days.

[7] Numerical ranges for the Federal funds rate have been reported in the FOMC's Policy Record since early 1974.

28

These instructions have two main features. First, the Manager is told to hold the weekly average Federal funds rate within a certain range. Second, the Manager is told to push the Federal funds rate toward the upper (lower) part of the range if the money stock and/or RPD's (member bank reserves held against private deposits) are coming out above (below) desired ranges. The FOMC sets the funds rate and the short-term money stock and RPD ranges according to its best estimates of the ranges required to reach a longer run money stock growth target.

If the funds rate and money stock ranges turn out to be inconsistent, the Manager holds the funds rate within its range while permitting money growth to run high or low. However, if the money stock appears to be running far off target the Manager may suggest to the Chairman of the Board of Governors that he call a special FOMC meeting to consider the advisability of changing the Directive. The Manager is especially likely to take this step if all the various money stock and reserves measures are running far off target.[8]

These policy procedures are well understood by the government securities dealers, large commercial banks, and probably many others. Participants in the financial markets quickly discover qualitative changes in the procedures through examination of Federal Reserve statements and publications, observation of Federal Reserve and financial market behavior, and discussions with Federal Reserve officials.[9] Moreover, a substantial amount of quantitative information such as the typical size of the Federal funds rate range in FOMC instructions is known because numerous past employees of the Federal Reserve System are now employed by financial institutions and, more recently, from the more detailed information now available in the Policy Record.

With knowledge of the basic structure of policy-making it is possible to make a rather accurate estimate of the current stance of monetary policy by observing the actions of the Open Market Desk. For example, it will be clear to the market that policy has shifted if the Open Market Desk has been seen to intervene a number of times to supply reserves at a funds rate of X percent and then following an FOMC meeting does not intervene until the funds rate reaches $Y > X$ percent.

Since the financial community knows how the Fed operates, it not only can interpret the significance of current open market operations but also can from

[8] For a more complete description of current policy procedures see "Open Market Operations and the Monetary and Credit Aggregates - - 1971," Federal Reserve Bank of New York Monthly Review 54 (April, 1972), 79-94.

[9] After attending a number of meetings and conferences that include both Fed and non-Fed participants, I have developed the personal feeling that Fed officials are basically quite open and candid in talking with non-Fed people about the qualitative features of Fed policies and operations. However, Fed officials are extremely careful not to disclose quantitative information or information directly related to current policy decisions.

time to time predict quite accurately the future direction of Federal Reserve policy. In particular, when the money stock is observed to grow at an abnormally high or low rate for some period of time, it is clear that the odds are high that the Fed will act to reverse the money growth trend by changing the Federal funds rate within the range given to the Open Market Manager, or by changing the midpoint of the range. Moreover, it is known that the Federal Reserve typically moves the funds somewhat slowly rather than in one jump to a new target range.

This situation is analogous to the one that developed under the Bretton Woods System of fixed exchange rates. Currency speculators knew that the authorities were watching trade and reserve figures, and they knew in which direction the exchange rate would move if the authorities altered the par value. And the behavior of the speculators obviously increased the pressure on the authorities to act.

Whenever it becomes clear in which direction the Federal funds rate will move if it moves, speculators in the money markets act in such a way as to increase the discrepancy between the actual and desired rates of money growth. To see why the discrepancy is increased it is necessary to consider the combined activities of the commercial banks, the government securities dealers and the non-bank public.

For the purposes of this discussion, the security dealers may be aggregated with the large banks. The dealers hold inventories of securities financed largely by short-term loans from large banks. If the dealers were consolidated with the banks, bank loans to the dealers and the dealers' demand deposits held with banks would disappear from the consolidated balance sheet; in this fashion it can be seen that the operations of the dealers and the operations of commercial bank securities departments have practically identical impacts on the reserve position of the commercial banking system. Because dealer demand deposits are relatively small, it is only changes in the consolidated total of bank plus dealer loans and investments that affect the money stock.

Large commercial banks and dealers are, on the average, heavy borrowers of very short-term funds. In fact, large banks not infrequently borrow in the Federal funds market more than their required reserves. For example, for the 46 large weekly reporting banks net borrowings of Federal funds supplied an average of 66 percent of required reserves in 1973, with a range on a weekly average basis from 40 percent to 96 percent. Large banks making continuous use of Federal funds will naturally be looking into the future to decide if there is a cheaper way of financing their requirements over the next, say, 30 days.

If the large banks expect the Federal Reserve to push up the Federal funds rate, then it may appear to them cheaper to switch some of their financing out of the funds market. The banks may sell treasury bills, or issue large CDs. In either case, upward pressure on bill and CD rates develops. Moreover, the banks' securities departments and the government securities dealers hold substantial inventories of government securities, and they will want to tighten up on these inventories for fear of capital losses from interest rate increases.

The importance of capital gains and losses on short-term money market instruments is frequently not fully appreciated by economists. To understand the magnitude of the effect involved, let $P_{n,t}$ be the price of a discount security with n days to maturity on day t, and let $R_{n,t}$ be the corresponding yield to maturity where the yield is based on continuous compounding and on a 365 day year. Expressing the yield to maturity in decimal form we have

$$(15) \quad P_{n,t} = 100^{\frac{n}{365} R_{n,t}}.$$

The holding period yield over a span of m days up to time t is

$$(16) \quad \Pi_{m,t} = \frac{365}{m} [\log P_{n,t} - \log P_{n+m, t-m}]$$

$$= R_{n+m, t-m} - \frac{n}{m} (R_{n,t} - R_{n+m, t-m}).$$

From this expression it is obvious that relatively small changes in the yield to maturity can wipe out the yield over short holding periods. Securities dealers and bank securities departments must take a view on very short-term interest rate movements. Their inventories of securities are largely financed by borrowing overnight money; and while they are unlikely to be put out of business overnight by a change in interest rates, it is clear that a series of bad guesses on the course of interest rates can produce a return too low to sustain the business.

While the money center financial institutions react sensitively to interest rates, non-financial firms react more slowly. The prime rate, and business loan rates scaled up from prime, tend to lag behind money market rates. This lag could not exist if business borrowers arbitraged quickly and massively between money market instruments and bank loans. Nevertheless, many firms do have a choice as to whether to use surplus funds temporarily to reduce bank loans or to invest in money market assets for a few days. Firms needing funds may draw on their bank lines or sell money market assets. Large firms may issue their own commercial paper. Although the prime rate is ordinarily above money market rates, the smaller the spread between the prime rate and money market rates, the greater will be the demand for bank credit. When the spread is relatively low, for example, a firm projecting cash needs for several weeks might resort to bank loans one week and rely on funds realized from maturing Treasury bills the next week;

conversely, when the spread is high it might be cheaper to absorb the transactions costs of selling bills one week, delaying the resort to bank credit to the next week. Interest rate expectations will also be important in the timing of resort to bank credit since some banks do not immediately apply a changed prime rate to outstanding loans.

The rise in bank credit in response to the narrowing of the spread between the prime rate and money market rates has an impact effect raising demand deposits and the money stock. Under the current system of lagged reserve requirements, these deposit increases generate an increased demand for reserves in two weeks; the resulting upward pressure on the Federal funds rate is then cushioned by injections of reserves by the Open Market Desk.

The longer the Fed permits relatively high (or low) money growth to continue, the more convinced market participants will be that interest rates will rise (fall) in the short run and the greater will be the tendency for the money stock to grow too fast (slow). Once on this track, the Fed must push rates high (low) enough that market participants become convinced that rates are unlikely to move very much further. When this change in anticipations will occur will depend on the level of rates and the observed rate of money growth.

It should be emphasized that market participants do not have to believe that reported changes in the money stock have any genuine economic importance. All they have to believe is that the Federal Reserve attaches some importance to the reported figures. Moreover, the market need only believe that the Fed will not push rates down when recent reported money growth is, say, at a 10 percent annual rate and that the Fed will not push rates up when recent money growth is, say, at a 2 percent annual rate. If the money growth trend does reverse without the Fed taking any action, banks and dealers always have time to alter their positions with little risk of loss, since it will be at least several weeks before the probability of the Fed pushing rates down equals that of the Fed pushing rates up.

It is the one-sided nature of possible Fed action, if any, on interest rates that makes it profitable to speculate on short-run interest rate movements. And while this speculation does not prevent the Open Market Desk from pegging the Federal funds rate within the range mandated by the FOMC, it does from time to time generate substantial changes in the rates on Treasury Bills, CDs, etc. The current Fed procedures may, therefore, generate greater short-run variability in money market rates, other than the Federal funds rate, then would prevail under a bank reserves target without smoothing of the Federal funds rate.

The most important effect of current Federal Reserve operating procedures is probably not that of smoothing money market interest rates but rather that of permitting banks to operate to a considerable extent as quantity-takers in the business loan market. Banks lend large sums on demand as a result of formal arrangements for lines of credit and informal customary practice. Banks know they can honor these commitments in the short run at a not unreasonable cost because they know that the Federal Reserve limits short-run fluctuations in the Federal funds rate. If the Federal Reserve did not control the funds rate so closely, banks would have to be more cautious in approving lines of credit, and business borrowers would have to be more cautious in their own cash management since they could not rely quite so extensively on guaranteed immediate access to bank credit.

The Lender of Last Resort Function. There is nothing in the above argument that is inconsistent with the central bank continuing to serve as the lender of last resort. It is clear that there are times when lenders suddenly refuse to extend further credit to basically sound firms as happened at the time of the Penn Central bankruptcy in June, 1970. In such situations the maintenance of a policy of holding the Federal funds rate within a target range does not automatically bring the Federal Reserve into the market as the lender of last resort.

For the Fed to serve as lender of last resort in times of financial panic it must do something more than maintain a policy-as-usual posture. It must act in a way appropriate to the particular disturbance that caused the panic. Since there is no evidence that financial panics happen all by themselves, there is no connection between interest rate smoothing per se and the lender of last resort function. With or without a smoothing policy, the Fed must stand ready to react to a spectacular bankruptcy, a war scare, or whatever. A policy-as-usual stance of closely controlling the money stock is not inconsistent with a policy-in-emergency stance of pumping in funds as required to prevent a growing financial panic.

Impact of Temporary Monetary Disturbances on Interest Rates. In recent years it has come to be widely accepted that in principle the impact on interest rates of purely monetary disturbances should be cushioned while the impact of aggregate demand disturbances should not be cushioned. [10] The issue that needs to be discussed with respect to this argument is whether the central bank must do the cushioning in the event of money demand disturbances, or whether the market can do the job.

When the market interprets either monetary or real disturbances to interest rates to be temporary, the result will be an adjustment in the term structure of interest rates with yields to maturity on short-term securities moving more than those on long-term securities. The rate on one-day loans will be most affected; the size of the effect on longer loans will reflect market expectations as to the duration of the disturbance.

There is in general no way for the market to smooth one-day interest

---

[10] Poole, (1970), 197-216.

rates through arbitrage operations of the type that smooth commodity prices. With storable commodities the difference between the price today and the expected price tomorrow is held to the cost of storage. But the use, or rental, of money for one day is not storable and so there is no way for arbitrage operations to smooth the one-day rental price of money. [11] It would never be profitable for someone to borrow one-day money when the rate is low in order to hold the funds idle; ignoring transactions costs, the owner of idle funds will always be better off if he invests them overnight at any interest rate above zero.

Since arbitrage over time will not smooth short-term rates, temporary disturbances in either the demand or supply of money may affect short rates substantially. In an environment of sharp fluctuations in short rates, firms will probably keep a somewhat greater margin of cash on hand than they otherwise would since the penalties are asymmetrical - - rates can fluctuate much farther above than below the median.

To understand the significance of fluctuations in short rates it is necessary to keep in mind that the annual rate of interest on, say, a one-week loan is obtained by taking the ratio of dollars of interest to dollars of loan and then multiplying by 52. Small changes in the dollars of interest translate into large changes in the annual rate of interest. Large changes in the interest rates on one-week loans are unimportant for the same reason large changes in the annual rate of growth of money over weekly periods are unimportant - - in both cases very few dollars are involved.

If the Federal Reserve were to pursue a money stock target month by month it is of course true that interest rates would be made more variable than desirable by virture of Fed efforts to hit a target subject to measurement and other errors. But what is the alternative? Participants in the financial markets are watching these same numbers and reacting to them. If the Fed were to react to the reported money figures by changing bank reserves instead of by changing the Federal funds rate, then the market would no longer have a one-way bet on interest rate movements. While data errors would generate some unnecessary Fed open market operations and therefore more Fed disturbances to interest rates than are desirable, it is not clear that the disturbances would actually be greater than now occur.

----

[11] This argument is not strictly correct since there are some cases in which the use of money is storable. The clearest example arises in connection with lending in the Federal funds market. Since reserve requirements for member banks are defined on an average basis over a statement week running from Thursday through the following Wednesday, the use of borrowed Federal funds to increase reserves held at the Fed on Thursday is completely substitutable for their use on the following day. However, ignoring the reserve excess and deficiency carryover provisions, Federal funds borrowed on Thursday cannot be substituted for those borrowed the previous day.

A qualitative feel for how interest rates might behave in the absence of a Fed smoothing policy may be obtained from examination of the 4-6 month commercial paper rates shown in Figure 3. The solid line is the commercial paper rate from 1890 to 1913 [12] while the dotted line is the commercial paper rate from 1950 to 1973. [13] Rates were obviously much more variable in the earlier than in the later period when each period is considered as a whole. However, the conclusion as to variability is not so clear if allowance is made for the occurrence of banking panics in the earlier period and attention is focused on the last six years of the later period.

Severe instability in money supply was clearly the cause of several of the sharp peaks in interest rates in the earlier period. There were banking difficulties in the second half of 1890, the summer of 1893, and the autumn of 1907. Monetary uncertainty connected with silver agitation reached a peak in 1896 with the nomination of William Jennings Bryan as the Democratic candidate for President. McKinley's victory over Bryan in November reduced but did not end the uncertainty. The interest rate peak in late 1899 was also associated with monetary uncertainty because the outbreak of the Boer War in October of that year threatened to curtail gold output.[14]

One other sharp interest rate rise in the earlier period is readily explainable. The sharp peak in early 1898 was caused by the outbreak of war with Spain in April. This is obviously the sort of event that may well call for special central bank intervention.

If the eye scanning Figure 3 can overlook the sharp interest rate moves associated with the events just described, interest rate fluctuations over the 1890-1913 period are somewhat less smooth than those recently, but the picture is certainly not one of extreme instability. What the pre-Federal Reserve period shows is the need to avoid sharp changes in the stock of money rather than the need for central bank intervention explicitly designed to smooth interest rates.

Finally, it is worth noting that there are many ways in which the Federal Reserve could reform the basic reserve requirements structure in order to

---

[12] Data from Table 10, column 3, in Frederick R. Macaulay, (1938).

[13] The data for 1950-63 are from Board of Governors of the Federal Reserve System, Supplement to Banking and Monetary Statistics, Section 12; data for 1964-1973 from Federal Reserve Bulletin, various issues.

[14] The source of the material in this paragraph is Milton Friedman and Anna J. Schwartz, (1963, Ch. 3, 4).

FIGURE 3

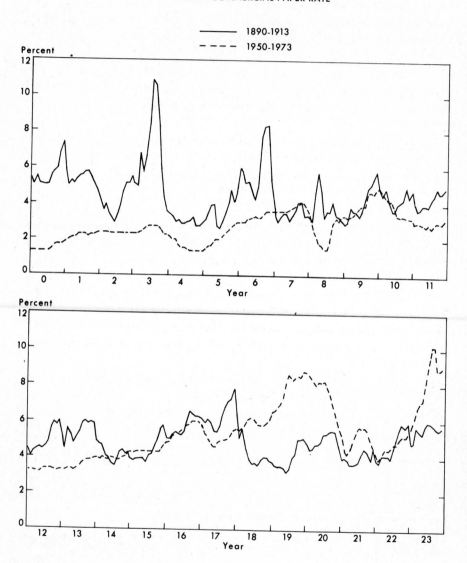

4-6 MONTH COMMERCIAL PAPER RATE

——— 1890-1913
– – – 1950-1973

minimize money supply disturbances. [15] And even without these reforms it would be a simple matter to build in an automatic device to limit week-by-week interest rate movements. For example, commercial banks could be permitted carryovers of unlimited reserve deficiencies or excesses with the provision that in the following statement week 110 percent of any deficiency would be added to required reserves and 90 percent of any excess added to available reserves. With this provision the Federal funds rate in a particular week could never differ from the rate expected the following week, r*, by more than $0.1r*$.

II. SHORT-RUN EFFECTS OF FLUCTUATIONS
IN MONEY GROWTH ON GNP

Monetarists, non-monetarists, and anti-monetarists all seem to agree that short-run fluctuations in money growth have little or no impact on economic activity. [16] The question to be asked is: how do we know that this "fact" is a "true fact" rather than the opposite, which is, presumably, a "false fact?"

My point in raising this issue is not primarily to argue against the conventional view of long lags. Rather, I want to argue that the evidence for this position is surprisingly weak, perhaps in part because the long lags argument seems so sensible on a priori grounds that few have closely examined its validity.

Theoretical argument. The theoretical argument for long lags seems to be based on the combination of an inventory theoretic view of the demand for money, which generates a delayed response of interest rates to changes in the stock of money, and the view that interest rate changes affect investment expenditures with a lag. [17] These two pieces of theoretical argument will now be examined in turn.

---

[15] For a substantial list of possible reforms see William Poole and Charles Lieberman (1972).

[16] A notable exception to this general view may be found in Arthur B. Laffer and R. David Ranson, (1971). Laffer and Ranson, using quarterly not seasonally adjusted data, argue that there is no evidence that changes in money growth have lagged effects.

[17] This argument is inadequate on a theoretical level as shown by Donald P. Tucker, (1966). However, the argument can be rescued, from Tucker's criticism by assuming that investment depends primarily on the long-term interest rate while money demand depends on the short-term interest rate. With the expectations model of the term structure, the demand for money may be cleared by temporary changes in the short rate that do not appreciably affect the long rate.

The demand for real money balances is ordinarily treated as a distributed lag function of interest rates and real income (or real wealth). It is assumed that individuals (and firms) adjust their holdings of real balances in response to changes in income and interest. Individuals do not adjust their balances to every wiggle in income and interest rates since they wait to see if the wiggles are "permanent" in some sense. But when the central bank changes the stock of money, there must be a large enough change in income and/or interest rates to pursuade individuals to hold the extra balances.

Under this view, changes in the stock of money produce larger short-run than long-run effects on income and/or interest rates. The accepted view puts the impact almost entirely on interest rates, generating the interest rate "spiking" phenomenon so familiar to users of large econometric models.

To the extent that changes in the stock of money are supply determined, the spiking phenomenon should show up in the form of negative serial correlations for changes in interest rates. An increase in the stock of money in a particular month should drive rates down, but rates should rise again in succeeding months. However, the serial correlation coefficients reported in Table 1 do not suggest that the spiking phenomenon exists. As was argued earlier, the pattern of the coefficients suggests a slight positive serial dependence at lag 1 and zero (or possibly weak negative) dependence at other lags.

This evidence against the existence of interest rate spiking is consistent with evidence from term structure studies. In the standard term structure equation the long rate is viewed as a distributed lag on the short rate. If the spiking phenomenon existed, the coefficient on the contemporaneous short rate should be small since sharp changes in the short rate would be viewed as transitory. In fact, estimated term structure equations usually find that the contemporaneous short rate carries the largest coefficient. [18]

An argument consistent with this evidence is that in the post-war period the Federal Reserve has cushioned interest rate movements so that the stock of money has been essentially demand determined. When the Fed moves the short rate the long rate follows, although it does not initially move as much, while the money stock is determined by the interaction of the commercial banking sector and the non-bank public. Under this view, if the Fed were to give up cushioning

---

[18] See, for example, Franco Modigliani and Richard Sutch, (1966). In a term structure equation making the long-term government bond rate dependent on the 3-month Treasury bill rate the authors estimated the coefficient on the contemporaneous bill rate to be 0.316 while none of the estimated coefficients on 16 lagged values of the bill rate exceeded 0.07.

interest rate movements and instead concentrate on controlling the money stock, then the spiking phenomenon would appear. [19]

The spiking phenomenon clearly does occur in the Federal funds rate. When, after an open market operation, banks find themselves with excess reserves at the end of a given statement week, they first repay funds borrowed at the discount window, and then bid the Federal funds rate down to near zero levels. Conversely, when borrowing is high and banks are under Fed administrative pressure not to borrow further, the funds rate can be bid to surprisingly high levels by banks with deficit reserve positions.

In the case of bank reserves, the reason for the spiking behavior is clear. On the last day of a statement week, there is no substitutability between reserves held that day and reserves held the next day. But in other financial markets many individuals and firms can be pursuaded by high rates to put off borrowing for a time; conversely, when rates fall some borrowing plans may be accelerated or lending plans delayed.

The subject at issue is the extent to which these changes in borrowing and lending plans affect economic activity. It seems likely that to a considerable extent these changes in plans take the form of individuals and firms temporarily drawing down or building up cash balances, delaying or speeding up scheduled payments, or other similar activities that do not affect real activity. But the changes in plans may also take the form of speeding up or delaying purchases of goods and services. The empirical question is the extent of these real effects in the short run.

Empirical Evidence. At the outset it should be emphasized that the empirical question at hand is a very difficult one. Changes in the level of the money stock over short periods of time have simply not been very large in the United States even though the fluctuations that have occurred appear large when measured at annual rates of growth. It is, therefore, very difficult to estimate the short-run effects of money on GNP given everything else that is going on. While it must be true that very short-run fluctuations in the annual rate of growth of money have little impact on the level of GNP, it is not clear that short-run fluctuations in money have little impact on the rate of change of GNP.

Previous efforts to obtain evidence on the lag in the real effects of changes in the money stock are unsatisfactory for two reasons. First, almost all

---

[19] There is evidence that in a business cycle context deceleration of money growth leads first to a rise and then to a fall in interest rates. The analysis of this paper, however, is concerned with interest rate behavior in response to changes in money growth over much shorter runs than those relevant to the general business cycle. For the business cycle evidence, see Phillip Cagan, (1972).

previous studies have relied on seasonally adjusted data. Second, most previous studies have used distributed lag functions that have been constrained to be smooth. [20]

The standard method of seasonally adjusting U.S. data is the Census X-11 seasonal adjustment program. This adjustment procedure substantially smooths the data. [21] The result is that a sharp change in any variable in a particular quarter is distributed in part into adjacent quarters. It seems highly likely that such an adjustment procedure will distort findings as to speeds of response.

The use of constrained lag distributions may also distort estimates of the speed of response. In many cases, of course, there is a valid reason for using constrained lag distributions in an effort to overcome other estimation problems. But when the speed and pattern of response is itself the issue, the use of constrained lag distributions seems inappropriate.

In regression of changes in GNP on changes in the money stock a common finding is that without constraints on the lag distributions the coefficients of the lagged changes in money alternate in sign. This phenomenon also appears when not seasonally adjusted data are used as can be seen from Table 3.

The regressions reported in Table 3 were run on not seasonally adjusted quarterly data transformed by taking first differences of natural logarithms multiplied by four to convert from quarterly to annual rates of change.' The sample period consists of the 84 observations from 1952:1 through 1972:4. The selection of 1952:1 as the first observation, although based on the notion that the world changed somewhat with the Treasury-Federal Reserve accord in March, 1951, was basically arbitrary.

The precise estimates obtained are substantially affected by the choice of sample period and so should not be taken too seriously. However, the tendency for alternating signs for the coefficients of lagged money does not seem to depend on the choice of the sample period. For the 1952-72 period this tendency shows up in a modified +, -, +, +, - pattern in the M1 regression. Can the alternating signs possibly make good economic sense?

---

[20] For example, see James L. Pierce and Thomas D. Thomson, (1972). Using the St. Louis model, a model estimated on seasonally adjusted data and with lags constrained to be smooth, Pierce and Thomson perform some simulation experiments of the effects of erratic money growth and find that large fluctuations in money growth of up to two quarters duration matter little if money growth over four quarters hits the desired long-run target rate.

[21] For an explanation of why this smoothing occurs and some estimates of the extent of smoothing of the money data, see Poole & Lieberman, (1972, 325-32).

Table 3

Regressions of GNP on Money, 1952-1972

(Data not seasonally adjusted measured as quarterly first differences at percentage annual rates)

Regression Coefficients (t-values)

Monetary Variable	Constant	Seasonal Dummy			Money Stock With Lag					R^2	SE	DW
		I	II	III	0	1	2	3	4			
M1	0.218 (8.568)	-0.538 (-19.960)	0.024 (0.762)	-0.237 (-10.230)	0.861 (4.451)					0.954	0.054	1.93
M1	0.223 (6.974)	-0.484 (-11.368)	-0.012 (-0.226)	-0.330 (-7.065)	1.063 (4.377)	-0.492 (-1.961)	0.194 (0.799)	0.383 (1.543)	-0.096 (-0.394)	0.956	0.053	1.94
M2	0.251 (12.278)	-0.598 (-31.325)	-0.045 (-2.189)	-0.277 (-14.849)	0.691 (4.038)					0.952	0.055	1.83
M2	0.221 (9.328)	-0.566 (-21.235)	-0.022 (-0.790)	-0.274 (-10.458)	0.663 (2.815)	-0.206 (-0.689)	0.020 (0.065)	0.146 (0.515)	0.373 (1.622)	0.954	0.054	1.85

Note: The R^2 is corrected for degrees of freedom.

41

There is certainly no reason in principle to rule out alternating signs. For example, if GNP depended on money and positively on the first difference of money, then the coefficient on money with lag 0 would be positive and the coefficient on money with lag 1 would be negative. In Table 3 the results of the M1 equation with lags are consistent with a model of the following type.

$$Y_t = a_0 t + b_0 M_t + b_1 M_{t-1} + b_2 \Delta M_t + b_3 \Delta M_{t-1} .$$

When this equation is differenced, we obtain

$$\Delta Y_t = a_0 + (b_0 + b_2) \Delta M_t + (b_1 - b_2 + b_3) \Delta M_{t-1} - b_3 \Delta M_{t-2} .$$

On the other hand, it might be observed that there is very little difference in the R^2 between the regression with and the regression without lagged values of money. The lagged values of money may be simply "stealing" some of the effect due to the contemporaneous value of money. Or is it the other way around with the lags actually being there but with the contemporaneous value of money picking up the lagged effects when lagged values of money are left out of the regression?

Ordinarily it would make sense to argue that if additional lags do not increase the R^2 then the additional lags do not belong in the regression. In this case, however, the argument is questionable and Table 4 shows why.

Table 4 gives the autocorrelations for $\Delta \ln \text{GNP}$, $\Delta \ln \text{M1}$, $\Delta \ln \text{M2}$, $\Delta \ln \text{V1} = \Delta \ln \frac{\text{GNP}}{\text{M1}}$, and $\Delta \ln \text{V2} = \Delta \ln \frac{\text{GNP}}{\text{M2}}$ for lags of from 1 to 12 quarters. This table has several surprising features.

Consider first the GNP autocorrelations. At lags 4, 8, and 12 the quarters being compared are the same quarters 1, 2, and 3 years apart. The seasonal pattern of GNP is so pronounced that the correlation between the change in GNP and the change three years earlier is 0.936. The seasonal regularities apparently have far more impact than three years worth of monetary and fiscal policy actions. Similar seasonal regularities may be observed by comparing the GNP autocorrelations at lags 1, 5, and 9, at 2, 6, and 10, and at 3, 7, and 11.

The autocorrelations for money tell a similar, though slightly less striking, story. The rate of change of M1 has, for example, high autocorrelations at lags 4, 8, and 12. With such high multi-collinearity it is clearly not possible to be confident about how a monetary impact should be apportioned among the various lagged values of money.

Examination of Table 4 also suggests a reason for the negative coefficient of $\Delta \ln M_{t-1}$ in the GNP regression. The autocorrelations of GNP at lag 1 and of money at lag 2 are both negative. Thus, in the GNP regression, $\Delta \ln M_{t-1}$ may be

Table 4

Autocorrelation Coefficients for GNP, Money, and Velocity
1952:1 - 1972:4

Lag	Δ lnGNP	ΔlnM1	ΔlnM2	ΔlnV1	ΔlnV2
1	-0.7105	0.0740	0.3971	-0.7281	-0.7165
2	0.4737	-0.5474	-0.0993	0.4954	0.4902
3	-0.7197	-0.0258	0.1373	-0.7379	-0.7357
4	0.9527	0.8369	0.5737	0.9544	0.9459
5	-0.7226	-0.0180	0.0992	-0.7335	-0.7280
6	0.4334	-0.5807	-0.2445	0.4645	0.4553
7	-0.6911	-0.0225	0.0693	-0.7072	-0.7083
8	0.9534	0.8340	0.5627	0.9516	0.9446
9	-0.6835	-0.0007	0.1499	-0.7053	-0.6955
10	0.4239	-0.5760	-0.2123	0.4542	0.4496
11	-0.6776	0.0162	0.1217	-0.6908	-0.6927
12	0.9360	0.8397	0.6294	0.9412	0.9317

serving in part as a seasonal proxy. Or perhaps there is an interaction between seasonality and the level of business activity. For example, when aggregate demand is strong, it would not be surprising to see production in seasonally slack quarters rise relative to production in seasonally strong quarters since output might be at capacity in the seasonally strong quarters.

Another feature of this data may be analyzed with aid of Table 5. The second column of the table gives autocovariances for $\Delta \ln V1$ for the lags listed in the first column. For lag 0 the entry gives the variance. The velocity autocovariance may be partitioned by virtue of the relationship,

$$E[(\Delta \ln V1_t) \, (\Delta \ln V1_{t-m})]$$

$$= E\,[(\Delta \ln GNP_t - \Delta \ln M1_t) \, (\Delta \ln GNP_{t-m} - \Delta \ln M1_{t-m})]$$

$$= E\,[(\Delta \ln GNP_t) \, (\Delta \ln GNP_{t-m})]$$

$$-E\,[(\Delta \ln GNP_t) \, (\Delta \ln M1_{t-m})]$$

$$-E\,[(\Delta \ln GNP_{t-m}) \, (\Delta \ln M1_t)]$$

$$+E\,[(\Delta \ln M1_t) \, (\Delta \ln M1_{t-m})].$$

At every lag, the velocity autocovariance is a bit smaller than the GNP autocovariance; the covariance between money and GNP does explain a little. However, the sizes, in absolute values, of the coefficients for $(\Delta \ln GNP_t)$ $(\Delta \ln M1_{t-m})$ and $(\Delta \ln GNP_{t-m})$ $(\Delta \ln M1_t)$ are not grossly different. There is about as much relationship between lagged GNP and money as between lagged money and GNP.

It is obvious from Table 5 that the seasonal covariances of GNP are far larger than those of money; at lag 0 the GNP variance is 15 times that of money. What this means is that unless the seasonals are handled perfectly, it will not be possible to obtain accurate estimates of the distributed lag effects of money, and perhaps of many other variables as well.

To obtain accurate estimates the experimental variables should have large variances relative to the uncontrolled variables. In this case, little is known about the seasonal variables except that their effects are large. For example, in Table 3 the seasonal dummy for the first quarter picks up a 50 percent annual rate of decline in GNP! The current state of seasonal adjustment technology places us in the awkward position of accounting for the single most important determinant of quarterly changes in GNP either by using a seasonal dummy variable or by pre-

Table 5

Decomposition of $\Delta \ln V1$ Autocovariances

m	$\dfrac{\Delta \ln V1_t}{\Delta \ln V1_{t-m}}$	$\dfrac{\Delta \ln GNP_t}{\Delta \ln GNP_{t-m}}$	$\dfrac{\Delta \ln GNP_t}{\Delta \ln M1_{t-m}}$	$\dfrac{\Delta \ln GNP_{t-m}}{\Delta \ln M1_t}$	$\dfrac{\Delta \ln M1_t}{\Delta \ln M1_{t-m}}$
0	0.05377	0.06339	0.006578	0.006578	9.003534
1	-0.03908	-0.04492	-0.008141	0.002569	0.0002619
2	0.02658	0.02997	0.0008508	0.0006043	-0.001934
3	-0.03952	-0.04532	0.002899	-0.008789	0.00009234
4	0.05101	0.05986	0.005988	0.005861	0.002992
5	-0.03929	-0.04556	-0.008579	0.002244	-0.00006463
6	0.02506	0.02758	0.0001046	0.0003250	-0.002088
7	-0.03812	-0.04381	0.002889	-0.008660	-0.00008101
8	0.05134	0.06053	0.005492	0.006713	0.003011
9	-0.03806	-0.04334	-0.008120	0.002844	-0.000002487
10	0.02450	0.02687	0.00009692	0.0002270	0.002049
11	-0.03711	-0.04280	0.003489	-0.009123·	0.00005876
12	0.05141	0.06039	0.005577	0.006477	0.003075

Table 6

Seasonal Factors for GNP, 1947-72

Year	I	II	III	IV
1947	95.5	97.4	100.3	106.8
1948	95.6	97.4	100.3	106.6
1949	95.8	97.4	100.3	106.3
1950	96.1	97.5	100.2	106.0
1951	96.3	97.8	99.9	105.8
1952	96.4	98.1	99.6	105.7
1953	96.4	98.5	99.3	105.8
1954	96.3	98.7	99.2	105.9
1955	96.1	98.9	99.2	106.0
1956	95.9	99.0	99.2	106.0
1957	95.7	99.1	99.2	106.0
1958	95.6	99.2	99.2	106.0
1959	95.5	99.5	99.0	105.9
1960	95.5	99.7	98.8	105.8
1961	95.6	99.9	98.6	105.8
1962	95.7	100.1	98.5	105.7
1963	95.8	100.2	98.4	105.5
1964	95.9	100.2	98.5	105.3
1965	95.9	100.3	98.6	105.0
1966	96.0	100.4	98.7	104.8
1967	95.9	100.6	98.9	104.5
1968	95.9	100.8	99.0	104.3
1969	95.8	101.0	99.0	104.2
1970	95.8	101.1	98.9	104.2
1971	95.8	101.1	98.9	104.2
1972	95.8	101.1	98.9	104.1
Average	95.9	99.4	99.2	105.6

46

adjusting the series through the use of seasonal dummies or ratio-to-moving-average methods.

The ratio-to-moving-average method of preadjustment has already been criticized on the ground that it smooths the data. Table 6 provides a view of what happens. The seasonal factors in the table were obtained by running the not seasonally adjusted GNP figures through the Census X-11 program. If factors for the same quarters in adjacent years are compared it is found that adjustments of 0.1 or 0.2 up and down are not uncommon. An adjustment of 0.1 affects the rate of growth of the seasonally adjusted GNP by about 0.1 percent, or 0.4 percent at an annual rate. If the seasonal factors for adjacent quarters are each adjusted by 0.1, but in opposite directions, the seasonally adjusted annual rate of growth is affected by about 0.8 percent. Such changes are of a comparable order of magnitude to the hypothesized distributed lag effects of changes in money growth we are trying to uncover.

The use of fixed seasonal factors, whether estimated by ratio-to-moving-average or regression methods, avoids the artificial smoothing problem but generates another problem. From Table 6 it appears that the seasonal factors for GNP for some quarters are drifting slowly over time, and fixed factors can make no allowance for such drift. Finally, no method of seasonal adjustment based only on calendar time can uncover interactions between seasonal and monetary effects.

My guess is that we will be unable to obtain good estimates of the distributed lag effects of money until we are lucky (or unlucky) enough to observe some large transitory changes in money growth relative to past seasonal patterns. If I am right, then no one will be able to make a convincing case that short-run instability of money growth of the sort experienced in the past does or does not produce substantial effects on GNP. The policy-makers will be able to vote their own prejudices on this matter; only if they go too far will they generate the evidence required to resolve the issue.

III. SUMMARY AND CONCLUSIONS

The purpose of this paper has been to analyze the importance of short-run fluctuations in money growth. It was found that there is no evidence to support the position that short-run fluctuations in money growth are valuable in smoothing short-run fluctuations in interest rates. It was also found that there is no evidence that short-run fluctuations in money growth either do or do not destabilize the general economy; this issue cannot be resolved on the basis of post-war U.S. experience. Short-run changes in the money stock have simply been

47

too small relative to other short-run disturbances - - especially seasonals - - for their effects to be accurately estimated.

Since there is no evidence that month-to-month and quarter-to-quarter fluctuations in the money stock within the range of post-war U.S. experience have much benefit or do much harm, the desirability of such fluctuations is basically a non-economic issue. As long as the FOMC recognizes that a series of individually-unimportant short-run deviations of money growth from target in the same direction is a long-run deviation, then there should be no problem. What must not be done is to regard short-run fluctuations in the money stock as bygones; there must be a conscious effort to reverse excessively high or low money growth. Given that money control errors have so often been positively correlated, and regretted after the fact, and that the benefits of money growth fluctuations seem so small, I would certainly opt for the simple-minded naive operating policy of keeping the level of the money stock as close to its target growth path as practicable.

REFERENCES

1. Box, George E.B. and Gwilym M. Jenkins. Time Series Analysis. San Francisco: Holden-Day, 1970.

2. Cagan, Phillip. The Channels of Monetary Effects on Interest Rates. New York: National Buruea of Economic Research, 1972.

3. Federal Reserve Bulletin, various issues.

4. Friedman, Milton and Anna J. Schwartz. A Monetary History of the United States. Princeton: Princeton University Press, 1963.

5. Laffer, Arthur B. and R. David Ranson, "A Formal Model of the Economy," Journal of Business 44 (July 1971), 247-70.

6. Macaulay, Frederick R. The Movements of Interest Rates, Bond Yields and Stock Prices in the United States Since 1856. New York: National Bureau of Economic Research, 1938.

7. Modigliani, Franco and Richard Sutch, "Innovations in Interest Rate Policy," American Economic Review 56 (May 1966), 178-97.

8. Pierce, James L. and Thomas D. Thomson, "Some Issues in Controlling the Stock of Money," in Controlling Monetary Aggregates IV: The Implementation, Federal Reserve Bank of Boston, 1972.

9. Poole, William, "Optimal Choice of Monetary Policy Instruments in a Simple Stochastic Macro Model," Quarterly Journal of Economics 84 (May 1970), 197-216.

10. Poole, William and Charles Lieberman, "Improving Monetary Control" in Arthur M. Okun and George L. Perry (eds.) Brookings Papers on Economic Activity 2 (1972), 293-335.

11. Roll, Richard. The Behavior of Interest Rates. New York: Basic Books, 1970.

12. Tucker, Donald P., "Dynamic Income Adjustment to Money Supply Changes," American Economic Review 56 (June 1966), 433-40.

13. Working, Holbrook, "Note on the Correlation of First Differences of Averages in a Random Chain," Econometrica 28 (October 1960), 916-18.

LESSONS OF FLOATING EXCHANGE RATES

Charles P. Kindleberger
Ford Professor of Economics
Massachusetts Institute of Technology

I. INTRODUCTION

There has been wide divergence of opinion about the recent state of the world economy, and about the contribution to that state of the existing system, if one can call it that, of floating exchange rates. In a paper written in the Spring of 1974, before the Herstatt bank failure in Cologne, Peter B. Clark suggested that all was serene: trade and investment have grown in the years since the Smithsonian agreement and since the dollar was floated in March, 1973. The supply of forward exchange has increased. Lagged adjustments show that the balance of payments and the domestic economy are isolated from short-run reversible movements. There is no direct evidence that floating has exacerbated inflation. While foreign trade of developing countries has experienced increased volatility, developed countries have been protected from exchange crisis. In particular, foreign-exchange markets have coped confidently with the 350 percent increase in the price of oil under flexible exchange rates, whereas there would have been a panic under fixed rates.

Congressman Henry L. Reuss, whose subcommittee on international economic questions of the Joint Economic Committee has embraced the system of floating rates as more than a stop-gap, claimed in a conference in Italy in September 1974 that the world economy was in good shape because of floating. Although there were particular economic problems in particular countries, he ascribed the resilience of the world economy to floating. A paper by David Meiselman reproduced in the New York Times went further and suggested that flexible exchange rates have been helpful in the control of inflation since they enabled individual countries to determine their own money supply. In a seminar at M.I.T. in May 1974, Walter Wriston admitted that The First National City Bank which he heads enjoyed and made money from floating exchange rates, and suggested that if changing rates were a headache for business, it was their number three headache, not the number one.

Opposed to these optimistic views is a variety of opinion. Leonard Silk wrote in the New York Times of July 28, 1974, of the "mess" in the world economy. Academic economists such as Robert Triffin talk of the danger of panic; Richard Cooper talks of the world finding itself on a precipice. Central and commercial bankers appear highly nervous after the difficulties in foreign-exchange speculation of the Franklin National Bank and the Herstatt, not to mention those of Lloyds Bank in Ticino, the Banque de Bruxelles, et al. The June 1974 report of the Bank for International Settlements expressed concern that the rate for the dollar had moved in three cycles. The New York, London, Tokyo and Frankfurt stock markets suggest a world of investors seeking to get liquid. Euro-currency banks have ceased to lend except to long-established and top credit-rating customers.

The issues in the divergence of view are factual, theoretical and interpretative and cover a variety of specific questions:

(1) What produced the failure of the Bretton Woods sytem? In particular, was the system faulty, could it have been managed satisfactorily, or is it impossible to separate the questions?

(2) How did exchange-rate changes affect balances of payments on current account? What does the experience teach us about elasticities of demand and supply in international trade?

(3) How did capital movements respond? In particular, were short-term capital movements stabilizing or destabilizing; and were long-term capital movements cut off by exchange risk?

(4) What does the experience of these years teach about the merits of rival economic models of payments adjustment under flexible exchange rates?

(5) Does floating achieve economic disintegration, and in particular does it provide for national monetary autonomy?

Analysis of these questions is difficult for a number of reasons. The foremost of these is the inability to control the experiment, or as modern economic historians would put it, to establish the relevant counter-factual. That is, how the position would be altered if only the exchange-rate system were altered and all else were confined within the cage of ceteris paribus. Secondly, the discussion tends to veer back and forth between the impact of floating on a single country whose viewpoint is adopted, and the impact on the world, that is, between floating as a national policy and floating as a payments sytem. Our interest is in the latter. A third difficulty is that economics is more effective in dealing with partial- than with general-equilibrium problems. Debate frequently defies consensus because the protagonists use different assumptions as to which is the most important market on which to focus and what are the appropriate assumptions as to how the rest of the general-equilibrium system behaves.

In what follows I give my own account of the failure of the Bretton Woods system (in Section II); sketch how the depreciations and floating of

1971-73 affected balances of payments (in Section III); deal with the theory of adjustment (in Section IV); and address the issue of monetary autonomy (in Section V). A brief conclusion seeks to bring the threads of the analysis together and to offer both policy prescriptions and a forecast of the evolution of the floating system. In summary, the paper holds:

(1) The dollar exchange system was mismanaged and could have worked satisfactorily.

(2) Floating has not produced the sought-for changes in current accounts because of low elasticities.

(3) Short-term capital movements were largely destabilizing and required central-bank intervention.

(4) The absorption model of adjustment is superior to the elasticity and the monetary approaches.

(5) If capital movements continue under floating, as has been the case, monetary autonomy cannot be achieved for a single country.

II. <u>THE BACKGROUND OF FLOATING</u>

To judge the success or failure of the world system of exchange-rate flexibility it is important to summarize the circumstances of world trade and payments in 1971 when the system came into operation. Two views of the breakdown are widely held. One is that of Triffin and Rueff - - that the exchange standard is inherently unstable because the reserve-currency country is ineluctably led to overissue international money as it seeks to acquire goods and investments. The other is that of students like Samuelson who hold that the dollar has long been overvalued because of the asymmetry between the dollar as a reserve currency which could not be adjusted, and every other currency which could be depreciated against the dollar, as happened in 1949, 1958, 1967, etc. (ignoring the upward revaluation of the DM and the guilder in 1961). There are difficulties with each view. The fundamental weakness in the exchange standard in my judgment is not the spineless characters of authorities of the reserve currency, or their greediness, so much as the instability owing to Gresham's law of a system with two reserve assets, and the inability of the reserve currency to maintain its reserve position as it issues liquid assets to the rest of the world on demand - - so-called international financial intermediation. I doubt the overvaluation of the dollar until 1970 or so, when in some sudden and not clearly understood fashion, the old regressions using prices and incomes suddenly showed a sharp break. The only hypothesis which goes any distance to explaining why the United States lost exports and increased imports so abruptly is that its exchange rate had been adjusted to a dynamic comparative advantage, under which old exports losing out to imitation and United States direct investment abroad were replaced by new products, innovated in the United States, and that this innovative process had precipitously halted. The speed of the changes is against such a theory, but there is no alternative explanation for a swing of almost $5 billion in the trade balance between 1970 and 1971, with exports rising less than a billion dollars when imports rose by almost six. [1]

In the early 1930s, the world suffered from the accumulation of a large body of foreign short-term claims - - of Frenchmen on London, of the world on New York, and of New York on Central Europe, especially Germany. These short-term balances were, to use a phrase of Herbert Hoover's, one he liked so much he used it twice in his _Memoirs_, "like a cannon ball loose on deck in a storm." At the present time, accumulation of nervous short-term dollars abroad is largely the result of failure to understand the exchange-standard system. In 1970 the Treasury-bill rate came down in the United States while the call-money rate rose in Germany. A flood of funds from New York to the Euro-dollar market and another from the Euro-dollar centers to Germany brought the German rate down. Foreign-exchange holdings of the Bundesbank rose from under $3 billion at the end of 1969 to $8.5 billion in 1970 and $12.5 billion in 1971. In one market there can only be one price. When New York and Frankfurt money markets were joined through the Euro-currency market, any attempt to achieve independent interest rates was doomed to failure and could only result in issuing too many dollars in New York and acquiring too many in the Federal Republic. Government debt in the hands of the Federal Reserve System went up $16 billion or 25 percent in two years, but government debt in the hands of foreigners rose by 200 percent from $11 to $33 billion. The Exter model in which a dollar created is a dollar exported turned out to be more than half right.

Capital outflows did not move President Nixon and Secretary Connally as much as the sudden and unexplained deterioration of the current-account balance, and one can give credit (or blame) for the Nixon-Connally shock of the import surtax and the arm-twisting which led to the Smithsonian devaluation to the trade account not to finance. But accumulation of large amounts of dollars abroad through failure to separate money markets joined through the Euro-currency nexus, or to understand their integration, had important effects

---

[1] See, for example, Stephen Magee, "United States Merchandise Trade in 1970 and 1971," unpublished paper, prepared for the council of Economic Advisers, Summer 1972. For an alternative view which maintains that price competitiveness explains United States exports of manufacturers as well, see United States Department of Commerce, International Economic Policy and Research, "Changes in U.S. Foreign Trade: The Post-1971 Experience in Perspective," (October 1974, Preliminary Draft) esp. p. 44, "Economic theory- - i.e., what _should_ have been happening- -appears to describe what actually has been happening extremely well."

on what followed. Had the dollars returned to New York, and German borrowers replaced dollar credits with DM loans, both resuming their "habitat," to use the term employed by monetary theory with respect to normal maturities, the market might have stabilized. It did not. The overhang remained over the market, and exchange rates responded to capital movements which responded to sentiment in a fashion reminiscent of Albert Aftalion's "psychological theory of the foreign exchanges," - - a theory developed to account for the variations of the French franc in the mid-1920s when the market was at the mercy of the whims of asset holders because they held short-term treasury bills which could not be converted into long-term debt to lock them in.

Another controversial matter must be raised: the capacity of the Euro-dollar market to create money and add to the supply of liquidity in the world. The issue turns on whether the Euro-currency market is like a commercial banking system which can create money, by a sizeable multiple of an increment of reserves, or whether it is like an S and L, which cannot, because such a small proportion of the funds it lends out are redeposited with it by the borrowers or by those who received funds in successive rounds of expenditure. Samuel Katz, for example, believed that the Euro-dollar market could not create money; Milton Friedman, that it could. The question, of course, is an empirical one, turning on what proportion of Euro-dollar borrowings were deposited in the Euro-dollar market. To the extent that they were spent for U.S. goods, for example, or remitted home as anticipated dividends, Katz was right. But to the extent that foreigners borrowed them for use abroad, and the central bank receiving them in exchange for domestic currency redeposited them in London, Friedman was right. If the two markets are fully joined, of course, it makes no difference where the funds are initially put, since a large volume of funds deposited in the United States from, say, the Bundesbank will lower interest rates in New York and stimulate a new outflow to the Euro-dollar market. Friedman would then be right on this score. This is the case today after the removal of all restrictions on capital outflows from the U.S.

The June 1971 decision of the large central banks to cycle dollars bought from the market in Europe back to New York rather than redeposit them carries the implication that at this time the Friedman thesis was correct.

The large dollar overhang from the 1970-71 outflow and from Euro-dollar multiple expansion as well or the market's continued uncertainty after the Smithsonian devaluation led to destabilizing speculation. This is another controversial question in which I part company with Milton Friedman who is unable to find a single empirical case of destabilizing speculation in history and has a priori reasons for believing it cannot occur. Speculation against sterling drove that currency off its Smithsonian level in July 1972. In December 1972 the Bundesbank defended the dollar, though the United States authorities did not, continuing the benign neglect begun vis-a-vis capital movements in 1970 and 1971. In February 1973 the Smithsonian parity of the dollar collapsed when the Bundesbank chose to support it no longer, and the dollar was floated, or rather permitted to sink. Secretary Shultz who had succeeded Connally, stated, in the Summer of 1973, with the agreement of much of the market, that the dollar was undervalued. But speculation did not turn around until the Federal Reserve system began to defend the currency in July 1973, albeit to the extent of only a few hundred million dollars. The Italian lira had floated out of the "snake" and into a relationship with the dollar in October 1973. The French franc followed it four months later. In the Fall of 1973, as the dollar strengthened under the impact of the high price of oil (oil was being sold for dollars, and it was expected that unspent foreign exchange accumulated by the oil producers would be held largely in dollars) the U.S. Treasury removed the last controls on capital outflows, presumably to hold down the rise of the dollar.

Since that time we have had managed floating, with management more evident in European than in the United States market intervention. Italian balance-of-payments deficits which did not respond to depreciation led to import restrictions, but the countries participating in the General Agreement on Tariffs and Trade undertook to resort to such measures only in extremis, and not to retaliate when a country which ran out of reserves was forced to impose them. The possibility of competitive exchange depreciation was limited both by an awareness of its dangers, and by the position of a number of countries - - Germany, Switzerland, the Netherlands, Australia and New Zealand - - that they had more to fear from inflation than from balance of payments deficits. The result was that they did not resist appreciation resulting from depreciation abroad. Australia and New Zealand, it should be noted, reversed that view in September 1974.

A last point which should be made in this historical account concerns the ambiguities surrounding international reserves in a world of managed floating and a two-tier system with the open-market price of gold a considerable multiple of the official price. In normal banking systems, reserves consist of high-powered money. Under floating, foreign exchange is not money or even near-money, if one defines money as something which has a fixed number of units of purchasing power, and near-money as capable of being converted into money at a virtually fixed price. The same is true of SDRs. Gold in central banks in particular is not money if these banks refuse to sell at $42.00 an ounce to other central banks, and any sizeable amount sold in the private market would drive the price down. The ambiguity relative to gold was resolved to some degree in early September 1974, when the Bundesbank agreed to lend $2 billion to the Banca d'Italia at 80 percent of the average private-market price of the previous three months. But the nature of the problem is well illustrated by the fact that a private banker, in conversation a few days before the announcement of the Bundesbank loan, stated that the G-10 agreement to lend on the basis of gold collateral seemed to him a limited step, and that his bank would lend on the basis of gold collateral only at $75.00 an ounce. Where a foreign-exchange rate or gold price may change, reserves of foreign exchange and gold no longer constitute money in the usual definition.

III. EXPERIENCE UNDER FLOATING

In this setting, the question arises whether floating exchange rates stabilized balances of payments and provided autonomy for domestic monetary policies, as predicted by the proponents of flexible exchange rates. The short answer, in my judgment, is that they did not. The reasons are basically two. First, the elasticity optimism of the late 1950s and 1960s which replaced the pessimism of the immediate post-war period, has given way again to pessimism; secondly, initiation of flexible exchange rates was not succeeded by a drying-up of capital movements, or by capital movements only in a stabilizing direction.

Depreciation of the dollar has been accompanied by a considerable improvement of the current account of the United States balance of payments, at least until the Organization of Petroleum Exporting Countries levied its $50/60 million annual tax on the world. The improvement was partly fortuitous, partly a result of the lower dollar rate. And in other countries, balances of payments did not respond to exchange-rate changes as called for by doctrine. The German balance of payments recorded its all time current-account surplus in the first quarter of 1974 despite a close to 40 percent appreciation of the DM against the dollar, and roughly 20 percent overall on a weighted basis. Appreciation for some time failed to produce a deficit in the Australian balance of payments. And no one suggested even for a minute that Saudi Arabia and Kuwait could eliminate their current-account surpluses, had they wanted to, by appreciation of the riyal and dinar. No feasible exchange rate would so restrict exports, given the inelasticity of foreign demand for petroleum, or so stimulate the expansion of imports, given the inelasticity on this front, to close the gap.

In the United States, strength in merchandise exports lay in foodstuffs and raw materials, stemming from the rise in the prices of wheat, cotton, soybeans, timber, not to mention steel scrap, etc. Where world demand was buoyant, in fact, the United States felt obliged to institute export controls on a number of items in shortest supply. Steel imports were not limited by depreciation, but imports of automobiles were. And machinery exports were stimulated.[2]

International-trade economists are busy exploring the issues raised by this failure of trade in goods and services to respond to exchange-rate changes as contemplated by the normal theory plus elasticity optimism. The first explanation was the so-called J-curve. In the short run, things get worse before they get better. Imports measured in domestic currency increased more than exports, as the terms of trade turned against the country before the changes in quantities which would ultimately make up for the failure of export prices to rise by as much as import prices did. This explanation had a high rate of obsolesence and had to be abandoned.

The so-called "pass-through" problem took its place. Some companies failed to pass through the changes in prices implied by exchange-rate changes - -

---

[2] The Department of Commerce study cited takes a much more favorable view of the effect of dollar depreciation on the U.S. balance of payments on current account, and brushes aside the fortuitous elements such as the increase in exports of non-manufactured goods in 1973 of 75 percent by value.

at least in the short run. Where a sizeable portion of foreign trade - - as much as 40 percent - - was conducted inside multinational companies, one would expect changes in sourcing of inputs and marketing of outputs to be altered only slowly. The first reaction would be to continue to serve existing plants and markets as before, and to alter the source of materials and components, as well as to change the direction of sales of output, only as profit calculations dictated in the longer run. For many purposes, quantity is more important than price: a chemical company wants to be certain of access to feedstocks, and regards price as a secondary matter. Or in some commodities such as pharmaceuticals, overhead costs are high, and marginal costs low as a percentage of selling price, so that there is still much profit left in serving old markets and maintaining old sources of supply, despite changes in exchange rates.

On these scores, current payments did not respond to changes in exchange rates, as called for by economic theory as set out by the proponents of flexible exchange rates. But the opponents were wrong too, because world trade continued to grow in real terms in 1972 and 1973, despite the increase in exchange risk. The world boom of 1972 and 1973 contributed to expansion. Fear of inflation may have led to some flight into commodities for import, but these of course had to be exported and commodity hoarding would work in the opposite direction on this front. Continued expansion may be attributable to inertia, or hysteresis. It is remarkable that the short-run contracts made at one set of exchange rates were adjusted when exchange rates changed, often to split the difference between, for example, the shipyard and the company placing an order for a new tanker. In sellers' markets, as in oil, each depreciation of the dollar was taken as a sign for raising the price of oil in dollars in which contracts had been made, although when the dollar appreciated there was no downward adjustment. It is nonetheless remarkable that world trade was not more affected, or perhaps even not affected at all, by the disorder and lack of calculability in foreign-exchange rates, as the theory would imply.

For a time, it seemed that the same result had followed in capital movements. In the short run, devaluation of the dollar in 1971 led to a decline in Euro-dollar bond lending, and a move into DM, Swiss franc and unit-of-account loans. But lending is a field in which, par excellence, quantity is more important than price. In 1972 Euro-dollar lending rose sharply to new heights, justifying Clark's remark quoted at the outset of this paper that investment had been impervious to the uncertainties generated by a world of flexible exchange rates. Since 1972, however, the position has changed again, and Euro-bond lending has declined continuously. Euro-bond issues fell from $6.3 billion in 1972 and $4.2 billion in 1973, and the first eight months of 1974 have witnessed a further decline of more than 50 percent from 1973 levels. Demand is strong, especially from companies in Europe with squeezed profits and large investment programs that increasingly depend on outside funds. It is not clear whether the response to exchange risk is asymmetric, with borrowers willing to incur, say, debts in dollars, but few foreign investors willing to go long. This possibility seems excluded, however, because all currency denominations behaved in much the same way on an annual basis between 1971 and 1974, and the decline between 1973 and 1974 (eight months) was 90 percent in DM as compared with little more than half in U.S. dollar Euro-bonds.

The sharp contraction of the Euro-bond market was accompanied by sizeable expansion in Euro-currency long-term loans with interest rates adjusted each six months to the London Inter Bank Offer Rate (LIBOR) - - another classic example of quantity coming to dominate price. Governmental and parastatal units in especially France, Britain and Italy borrowed billions of dollars in this way from Euro-currency banks at rates up to 15 years until in the Summer of 1974, following the failures of the Franklin National and Herstatt Banks from speculation in foreign exchange, the Euro-currency banks began to hold back from such loans. Euro-banks started off blithely enough, lending long for 15 years against liabilities of typically five days, in the belief that any withdrawal of dollars by depositors would be controlled by recycling. In the Summer of 1974, concern was less for the nervousness of depositors than for the credit worthiness of borrowers. Euro-dollar depositors were locked in so long as any central bank which purchased the dollars to make its local currency available to parties withdrawing from the Euro-dollar market would in turn redeposit the dollars in Euro-currency centers. Fear of default by some large borrower, which was first felt in the Summer of 1974, created a new and much more dangerous risk.

Outside the Euro-currency market, floating does not appear to have discouraged international investment. Portfolio movements both in and out of the United States rose prior to the decline in stock-exchange averages in the Summer of 1974. United States direct investment outward declined slightly in 1972 from the high level of 1971 and much more sharply in 1973, to levels of 1967, which were, however, still substantial. Foreign investment in the United States, on the other hand, rose considerably, suggesting the possibility, currently under investigation, that direct investment is responsive to over- and undervaluation of exchange rates.

In short-term markets, however, capital movements neither dried up nor turned tamely stabilizing. Leads and lags operated against the dollar as multinational corporations, many of which protested that they never sold dollars, at least postponed buying them with foreign profits. Inside the United States the demand for loans was substantial and some considerable part of it appears to have been for selling dollars short. How much of the short-term capital outflow in 1972 and 1973 was speculative, leaning on the dollar to drive it still further down, and how much was a continued response to differential interest rates lower in the United States than in Europe cannot readily be determined. Exchange speculation seems, however, to have spread widely.

The initial view of the banks was that they enjoyed flexible exchange rates. They widened margins, and increased turnover. Walter Wriston's statement, noted above, that the system was good for banks, and that if industrial companies regarded it as a headache, it was the number three headache, not the number one, was made before the failure from excessive speculation of the Franklin National Bank and the Herstatt. Banks have learned that their foreign-exchange departments can run exchange risks during the day, within which foreign currencies may fluctuate by as much as 3 or 4 percent, even when they close out net positions at the end of the day. And all banks have become more alert to the credit worthiness of the names whose paper they buy. In the early stages, foreign-exchange departments spent time calculating spreads and gave little thought to credit worthiness, an issue handled in another department of the bank. The troubles of the Spring of 1974 changed this.

Within industry, the problems of large and small firms differed. Large multinational corporations with sophisticated analysts in their treasurers' offices had little difficulty adjusting to floating. They were used to forecasting price levels, interest rates, exchange rates, and deviations of exchange rates from interest and purchasing power parities. Staffs may have been expanded, and the financial vice-president, treasurer or comptroller gained a wider access to the top management of the firm. James Burtle remarked in a conference on floating exchange rates held at M.I.T. in the Fall of 1973 that floating exchange rates in Latin America over the last twenty years had brought financial men to the top of companies, over personnel specialized in production, marketing, research, and the like. When the "public good," international money, is not available, companies have to provide it for themselves. Many small companies probably withdrew from international trade, despite evident proliferation of services of banks and consultants in offering advice on foreign-exchange questions. Tourists were particularly affected. I received one letter from a college friend asking when was the best time to take a once-in-a-lifetime trip to Europe for which he had been saving for 20 years; and in Scotland last January I picked up a young hitchhiking Canadian couple who were shortening their world tour by 25 percent because they had held on to dollars doggedly until July 1973 and then moved into DM at the top of the market.

Was private speculation stabilizing or destabilizing? This thorny question turns on unresolved issues of definition, but I would judge it to have been both destabilizing and profitable. The criterion I use to judge whether speculation is stabilizing or destabilizing is whether it narrows or widens the variance in the movement of price (in this instance, the exchange rate) over time. This criterion is not unambiguous when there is a trend. If the equilibrium rate at period t+1 differs from that at period t, it is not self-evident that the variance in the rate is higher or lower if the new rate of t+1 is achieved instantly at period t or gradually over time. Much, doubtless, depends on the rate of change of other variables in the system. Since the dollar moved through three cycles, however, first one side and then the other side of trend, it is evident that the variance has been widened, and speculation has been destabilizing. I find unacceptable the criterion that speculation is stabilizing so long as the speculators at time t make a reasonable judgment of what the rate will be at time t+1, based on the knowledge they have at time t. The issue whether speculation is useful or disturbing turns on the clarity of knowledge the speculators bring to their work, and particularly whether they have an accurate long-run view of what the rate should be, and government does not. Criteria must be applied ex post, and not ex ante.

I further find unpersuasive the Friedman a priori contention that speculation is always stabilizing, since for speculators to continue in business - - as most of them do, leaving aside the clearly destabilizing efforts of the Franklin National, Lloyds, Banque de Bruxelles, etc. - - they must buy low and sell high. In the first place, all speculators can lose under conditions of destabilizing speculation, with inside professionals driving the rate up and selling out at the top (or down and covering short positions at the bottom) to amateurs, who lose more than the professionals gain, and turn to other pursuits to recoup before they or a new group engage in the next bout of speculation. The outside amateurs are the sheep who get fleeced in the stock market and in the exchange market. Moreover central banks and other official operators do not have profits, but rather the public good of stability, in their objective functions. The Bank of Japan lost large amounts of its operations in dollars, as Ryutaro Komiya's paper for the Williamsburg Conference in May 1974 indicates, and the Bundesbank is reported to have lost an amount in excess of its capital. Both felt it necessary to intervene to prevent speculation from increasing the variance of foreign exchange movements beyond the wide limits experienced. Such speculation is surely destabilizing when it moves economic variables such as price levels and money incomes in ways which prove irresistible when the exchange rate returns to its former level, an outcome the central banks sought to avoid. The Friedman a priori criterion presupposes a zero trend and a full cycle out of home into foreign currency and home again. When there are stocks and a trend, depreciation of the currency in which reserves are denominated produces losses without regard to stabilizing or destabilizing action on the part of the authorities. The profits criterion I regard as useless and inferior to a very short-run stabilizing standard of moving against the market, buying when it falls, selling when it rises. On this basis, private speculators destabilized, the Japanese and German authorities stabilized.

I may say, however, that I regard the performance of the United States monetary authorities as sub-optimal, to put it mildly. Under the exchange standard, it makes sense for the reserve currency to give up control of its exchange rate in return for its role as determiner of world monetary policy (given joined capital markets). When the fixed-rate standard is changed, the benign neglect of the earlier period is what young people today call a "cop-out." The United States has a share in the responsibility of managing the world economy. Part of that responsibility is to provide, with managed floating, a coherent system of managing exchange rates. For the world's largest economy to ignore the day-to-day movements of the dollar, but to seek from time to time in staccato efforts to depress it and later to raise it, is highly irresponsible. In December 1972 and January, February 1973 this country left the entire burden of managing the dollar to the Germans and the Japanese, and helped in fact to talk the currency down when these countries were trying to hold it up. When the currency started to recover in the Fall of 1973, our authorities removed the rather ineffective controls on the outflow of capital in order to encourage bear speculation. Even when it was trying to go in the other direction, in July 1973, the operations of the Federal Reserve Bank of New York were minimal compared with those of the Bundesbank. Part of the difficulty, I believe, is the two-headed nature of our Federal Reserve System, with direction in Washington and operations in New York.

The fact is that floating exchange rates did not effectively separate capital markets, and hence did not provide monetary autonomy to the several countries in the system. The point was made clear in May 1974 when Chairman of the Board of Governors of the Federal Reserve System, Arthur Burns, stated somewhat petulantly that United States monetary policy was made in Washington and not in Paris or Frankfurt. If the statement had been true, it would have been unnecessary. What it marked was a change in the relationship between United States and European monetary policy. Prior to 1972, United States monetary policy had dominated, and when the two markets pulled in different directions, American policy had come out on top. In 1973 Europe won. The Federal Reserve System found that it could not hold down the rate of interest and reversed its policy. The position was later dominated by petrodollars, and the market therefore afforded no test of Mundell's position that monetary policy is effective with fluctuating exchange rates not because of failure of capital to move, but because it continues to respond to interest rates. The generalization was based on Canadian experience. When Canada wanted to contract, it could raise interest rates. This would attract capital, appreciate the exchange rate and apply deflationary pressure more by depressing foreign trade prices, cutting exports and increasing imports than by reducing domestic investment. When Mundell indicated this relationship, I thought it unique to Canada, based on inelastic expectations of the market that, in the long run, a dollar would be close to a dollar, whether Canadian or United States, and that a one percent difference in long-term interest rates dominated a possible swing in exchange rates within a range of five percent either side of par, amortized over fifteen or twenty years. The failure of flexible exchange rates to halt capital movements to and from the United States throws doubt on the view that the Canadian experience is exceptional. It is true that exchange-rate instability in Britain dried up capital movements inward to that country (though not necessarily outward or short-selling movements which were inhibited by exchange controls). It is not clear today what one can say about the impact of flexible exchange rates on capital movements beyond that they do not seem to have reduced them seriously.

IV. LESSONS FOR THEORY

What lessons does the experience of recent years have for us in the realm of the theory of devaluation? Here is perhaps where we can achieve the greatest gains. We have three models of balance-of-payments adjustment, all partial-equilibrium insofar as they assume that other markets than the one being concentrated on clear easily and readily without feedback on the market initially clearing. Each is related to a different system of accounting: the elasticities approach to the input-output table; the absorption approach to the national-income accounts; the monetarist approach to the statement of sources and uses of funds. Only the monetarist approach potentially allows for complete treatment of capital flows, but its practitioners for the most part abstract from these and assume that changes in real balances affect changes in expenditure rather than those in assets or liabilities, i.e., result from changing consumption and/or investment and not wealth or the composition of wealth. And none of them makes much allowance for the possibility that exchange-rate changes can affect the course of inflation and deflation, apart from the direct effects of exchange-rates on (usually) exports and imports.

All three models can be viewed as a variant of the balance-of-payments accounting identity:

$$B \equiv X - M - LTC - STC - G,$$

64

where B is the balance of payment on current account, X is exports of goods and services, M is imports of goods and services, LTC is long-term capital exports (imports bearing an implicit minus sign), STC is short-term capital exports (imports bearing an implicit minus sign), and G gold imports (exports bearing an implicit minus sign).

If current-account is in balance,

$$B = X - M = 0 = LTC + STC + G,$$

while the basic balance

$$B = X - M - LTC = 0 = STC + G.$$

The elasticities approach emphasizes the market for foreign exchange

(1) $B = X - M.$

The absorption approach can be dealt with gross or net. In gross form

(2a) $B = Y - (C + I_d + G),$

where C is consumption, I_d is domestic investment and G is government expenditure. $C + I_d + G$ can be summed into "absorption" (A) and then

(2a') $B = Y - A.$

On a net basis, the approach can be given aggregated or disaggregated. Aggregated

(2b) $B = S - I_d,$

where S is saving. Disaggregated, saving is broken down by sectors among households, government and corporations, and

(2b') $B = S_p + S_g + (S_c - I_d).$

This indicates that the balance of payment on current account is the counterpart of the net surpluses or deficits of households (S_p), government (S_g) or corporations ($S_c - I_d$). If one shifts to basic balance, the net deficits or surpluses have to be adjusted for long-term foreign borrowing or lending. In either case, the approach assumes that the foreign-exchange market adjusts to

65

the leading changes in surpluses and deficits, and ignores the market for money. On the monetarist approach,

(3) $B = dMn - Cr$,

where dMn is the change in the money supply and Cr is credit creation. This assumes that the primary market in which changes occur is the market for money holdings, and that incomes and foreign exchange fall smoothly into place.

Analysis of exchange-rate changes proceeds somewhat differently under each separate approach. In the elasticities model, for example, X disaggregates into PxQx (value representing price x quantity). The analysis can be undertaken in foreign exchange or local currency. Depreciation, for example, lowers Px in foreign exchange or leaves it unchanged, and in the former case this may increase PxQx, leave it unchanged, or reduce it, depending upon whether the elasticity of demand abroad is greater than, equal to or less than one. And so on in the familiar Marshall-Lerner analysis. Nothing is said about capital movements, although in a highly risk-averse world, they might be assumed to dry up. Some go so far as to say that with flexible exchange rates, the balance of payments always balances. This can mean either that private capital movements are zero, X identically equal to M, with no need to move gold or official capital or that any divergence between X and M is intentional, based on autonomous capital movements, i.e., to LTC. Recent experience has shown both views to be wrong.

In the absorption model, depreciation may produce an initial change in X - M, the so-called "impact effect," but clearing the market for domestic income needs to be worked out. With idle resources - - the Keynesian assumption - - and a positive marginal propensity to save, Y rises more than A and improves the balance of payments on current account. With full employment this cannot occur. (In what follows it is necessary to abstract from the index-number problem of defining income when the prices of foreign-trade goods change relative to home goods.) As Alexander put it, the question is how the change in exchange rate affects A (or $(C + I_d + G)$). Alexander posed and rejected three possibilities: money illusion, income redistribution and the real-balances effect. Tsiang added a monetary effect through a rise in interest rates as money income rose but nominal money supply remained unchanged. Recently Hinshaw has emphasized that the rise in the prices of foreign-trade goods- not merely Px and Pm but the prices of close substitutes which are produced and consumed domestically- - affects spending directly, resulting in a rise in S_p.

Most economic theorists reject reliance on money illusion, although it surely plays a part for S_g in the disaggregated model where there is a progressive income tax, and the government holds G constant. Corden insists that it is possible to reduce real wages through exchange depreciation when this is impossible to do through lowering nominal wages or through fiscal policy. This view was attacked as money illusion. Cooper defended it, denying that it was money illusion. The passage in European Monetary Integration, (edited by Krause and Salant) is not crystal clear, but Cooper has explained privately that he has in mind an institutional response. Labor is prepared to resist measures which attack wages or incomes directly on the ground that these disturb traditional spreads and differentials. Roundabout and broadly macro-economic measures such as exchange depreciation or inflation--if I express his thought accurately--will meet less resistance than direct measures. Real-balance theorists emphasize that any help for the balance of payments from depreciation is transitory. Balance holders have to restore their real balances which have been reduced by the rise in foreign-trade prices. Once these have been built back up, they resume old spending ways; and the balance of payments returns to the status quo ante.

The monetarist model assumes that the most important market in the system is that for money, and that households and corporations, in the disaggregated form, and perhaps government, are prepared to adjust spending so as to maintain real balances. In contrast to the absorption model, where money illusion may exist, in the monetarist view, depreciation has its effect through raising foreign-trade prices and reducing the real value of the money supply, and the entire economy is acutely conscious of the fact. Households and business cut spending to restore the level of real balances. This liberates goods which are sold as exports (or not bought as imports) to (from) foreign countries and improves the current account.

It is widely maintained that the absorption and monetarist approaches are identical, and this identity can in fact easily be achieved by a few key assumptions. [3] But the spirit of the two models is different. The absorption model focuses on the relationship between income and expenditure; the monetarist approach concentrates on expenditure changes brought about by changes in real balances. The absorption approach anticipates that the effects of an exchange rate change will be sustained; the monetarist approach believes that they will be ephemeral and disappear when real balances have been restored.

A major advantage of the monetarist approach is that it permits adjustment through capital movements. It seems unrealistic to me to contemplate

---

[3] See, for example, Joanne Salop, "A Note on the Monetary Approach to the Balance of Payments," paper presented to the Conference on the Effects of Exchange Rate Adjustments, U.S. Treasury Department, Washington, D.C., April 4-5, 1974.

that the major effect of a 10 percent depreciation in circumstances where foreign trade prices are, say, 20 percent of total income will take place through the 2 percent reduction in real balances, rather than through a foreign-trade change impinging on income and absorption; but assume that it does. Real balances can be restored not by changes in expenditure, as the absorption approach calls for, but by reductions in wealth, i.e., restoring real balances through a portfolio adjustment, by selling off foreign assets or incurring liabilities to foreigners. This has been the initial response of markets to the rise in the price of oil, and similar recycling was the first step in the adjustment process in, say, the transfer of the Franco-Prussian indemnity. If the monetarist approach proceeds through changes in wealth, and absorption operates through changes in the relation of expenditure to income, the two are not identical.

In the three approaches, the change in prices of foreign-trade goods which are not exported or imported but are produced and consumed domestically usually has no direct effect on income. (An exception is the redistribution version of the absorption model, dismissed by Alexander, but found by Diaz-Alejandro to be important in Argentina, and I believe, of critical importance in producing the success of the French 1958 devaluation.) Normally, it is thought that changes in domestic prices affect the incomes of producers and consumers in the economy in opposite directions and by offsetting amounts. Thus if export-type but not exported goods rise in price, the gain in income to producers is offset by the loss to consumers, and the two effects are assumed to cancel out.

In The World in Depression, 1929-1939, I argued that this offset does not hold. Appreciation of the dollar, the French franc, and the mark from 1929 to 1932 lowered prices of export goods and reduced especially farm income and farm spending. Gains in real income to urban dwellers from 50-cent wheat and five-cent cotton in the United States, however, did not produce offsetting increases in non-farm spending from declines in domestic sales because of: (1) lags; (2) money illusion; and (3) dynamic contraction, largely through bank failures in farm areas. Appreciation was deflationary through its effect on incomes and spending, quite apart from the impact effect on the balance of trade and the foreign-trade multiplier. I first noted this effect in The Dollar Shortage (1950, 105ff) and called it the Hansen effect after a 1948 contribution of Alvin Hansen.

In today's world of inflation, depreciation is likely to raise prices in the depreciating country and leave them unchanged in the appreciating country, in contrast to the early 1930s when it lowered prices in the appreciating country and left them unchanged in the depreciating country. (This position altered in 1933 when the United States depreciated and its prices rose, for reasons which are not entirely clear.) Depreciation and appreciation of the dollar in three cycles since 1971, according to the BIS 1974 report, will thus raise world prices on balance in ratchet style, and generate dynamic inflationary forces inside separate countries. The calculation of Nordhaus and Shoven in Challenge (May-June 1974, 18) that devaluation (by 10 percent from November 1972 to August 1973) was responsible probably for one-fifth to one-sixth of the wholesale inflation of 18.2 percent of the period takes inadequate account, in my judgment, of the dynamic effects of earlier depreciation and the "structural" inflationary impact. In recent years, structural inflation with exchange depreciation has been a phenomenon limited to Latin America and its existence there hotly debated. I believe that the world experienced structural deflation in 1929-32 and is experiencing structural inflation now. Floating exchange rates which fluctuate on one side and the other of equilibrium (stable) rates will add to world inflation in a sellers' market and to deflation in a buyers' market. One has only to note that petroleum prices were adjusted upward each time the dollar was devalued, but not downward when it recovered.

In the New York Times of September 20, 1974, a letter of Bent Hansen urges the United States to attack inflation by appreciation of the dollar. This again assumes the applicability of a partial-equilibrium model in which world prices are fixed, and United States prices of foreign trade goods can be adjusted to them by varying the exchange rate. In the ratchet model with continuing shortages, the outcome contemplated by Hansen would not be realized. Instead, world prices would rise (just as world prices fell in 1931 when Britain devalued). If the United States balance of payments deteriorated with appreciation, as the elasticities model forecast but with limited certainty in the light of recent German experience, and the dollar were subsequently depreciated, U.S. prices would now rise as the ratchet took over.

Monetarists in this debate strenuously object to the elasticities, absorption and price-ratchet types of analysis. They note, properly, that in the long-run, the market for money has to clear, and that if the monetary authorities insist on letting it clear without an increase in supply, or with supply increases limited to some long-run normal rate, disequilibria in the foreign-trade and domestic-output markets cannot be sustained, or that, in the long-run, the gains of one group in the society must be offset by losses in another. If the monetary authorities would resolutely resist expansion of the money supply, for example, deflation would balance trade following depreciation.

This takes a view of the proceedings which is politically pure or innocent. Adjustment in the balance of payments is a political exercise. There is a burden, which must be borne by one or more groups. Depreciation rewards some groups and penalizes others. If the monetary authorities add further penalties for the same or other groups - - for example, unemployment to the real-income losses of consumers of foreign-trade goods, they may exceed their capacity to run the system. The easiest way to clear the market for money is to expand the money supply. To resist such expansion may lead to financial, economic or political breakdown, as the present (Summer 1974) period of high interest rates is beginning to demonstrate in more than one country. [4]

In addition, as already noted, the monetarists have not sorted out the various circumstances in which real wealth will be maintained, and within wealth, real balances, at the cost of real consumption, and those circumstances when real consumption will be maintained at the expense of real wealth. The readiness of most countries to incur liabilities to the members of the Organization of Petroleum Exporting Countries while maintaining consumption suggests the possibility that the initial reaction is to protect consumption at the expense of wealth, as the Duesenberry consumption function suggests for a household.

On this showing, our theories of exchange-rate adjustment are deficient to the extent they are partial-equilibrium in character. It is not scientifically warranted, in my judgment, to choose one market as dominant and to assume that all other markets will clear as a trivial exercise once the chosen market has been cleared. Exchange depreciation is an important and essentially unpredictable exercise in general-equilibrium theory. Even two markets are insufficient as most politically-sensitive economists felt in 1947 when Henry Hazlitt suggested in Will Dollars Save the World? that the European balance-of-payments deficit could readily be handled by a policy of balancing budgets and depreciating exchange rates to the purchasing-power parity.

Of the several partial theories, I conclude on the basis of perhaps insufficient study, that the absorption approach is the most effective. The German balance-of-payments surplus after a 17 percent overall appreciation, 40 percent at the peak against the dollar, and the British deficit exclusive of oil, suggest that domestic spending and saving dominate exchange-rate

---

[4] Some years ago, Fritz Machlup wrote a paper entitled "Equilibrium and Disequilibrium: Misplaced Concreteness and Disguised Politics" in which he attacked Nurkse, among others, for including an unemployment constraint in his definition of equilibrium. Currently he characterizes deflation at a time of serious unemployment as "politically impractical" and advisers who recommend it as failing to understand some of the unalterable facts of life. See his "Exchange-Rate Flexibility" in Banca Nazionale del Lavoro Quarterly Review, No. 106, September 1973, p. 9. Advocates of flexible exchange rates continue to cast aspersions on the character and intelligence of those who believe in fixed. See for example, Harry G. Johnson, "The Problems of Central Bankers," Economic Notes, Monte dei Paschi di Siena, Vol. II, No. 3 (September-December 1973), p. 8: "The world may eventually become used to floating exchange rates, the system that the majority of academics of scientific integrity have always recommended." For an early example, see Milton Friedman's footnote attack on those who quote Nurkse in "The Case for Flexible Exchange Rates," Essays in Positive Economics, in American Economic Association Readings in International Economics (Homewood, Ill.: Irwin, 1968), p. 427.

adjustments and I should think, real-balance effects. And structural inflation and deflation are side effects of exchange-rate changes which we have totally ignored, when the concept has not been dismissed with contempt by monetary economists.

V. CAPITAL MOVEMENTS AND FLOATING

The other principal weakness in our theoretical understanding of the world monetary economy is in the behavior of capital movements under floating exchange rates. When economists thought about the subject at all, they either thought capital movements would dry up because of exchange risk, or they believed that they might continue. Furthermore, economists divided between those who thought they would be stabilizing and those who were prepared to allow for instability. Almost none contemplated the messy world in which capital would sometimes dry up, sometimes behave in a stabilizing fashion and sometimes be destabilizing, or in which private capital would move out of a country but not in, and if controls were avoided, require funding by official reserves.

Note first that the existence of capital movements upsets many of the cliches about the effects of flexible exchange rates. Take for example Henry Wallich's aphorism, not cliche, that one can have any two of fixed exchange rates, joined capital markets or independent monetary policies, but not all three. If capital chooses to move under flexible exchange rates one can only have one. With flexible exchange rates and capital movements, independent monetary policies are compromised. It is still necessary to manage the money stock and interest rates with an eye to the rest of the world, or in the case of small countries, to yield monetary policy to world forces. Large countries like the United States have to concern themselves with the large dollar overhang, so long as it remains unresolved, and all countries must be wary of how the large and growing volume of liquid funds belonging to OPEC is managed. The liquidity issue remains for the world, despite the view that floating exchange rates make liquidity issues disappear. The issue, however, is one of excess liquidity, not of a potential deficiency, as many believed from 1958 on, an excess developed after 1968 by failure to understand how a reserve standard should be run. Floating not only does not eliminate problems of monetary dependence and volumes of liquidity, it may, as noted, add an inflationary (or in other circumstances deflationary) fillip from the price side.

Two issues deserve mention. If monetary policy cannot be independent with capital movements, it may become necessary to devise machinery to get Euro-currency markets under some sort of control lest world money supplies be built up or run down in perverse ways in that setting. Institutional and political difficulties abound. Institutionally, steps to regulate Euro-currency markets in a given territory will merely drive them elsewhere, to the Cayman Islands or Singapore, or new atolls as yet undeveloped. Politically, moreover, an OECD effort to regulate the Euro-currency markets might be interpreted as a move to control OPEC receipts from oil, and thus spread confusion from financial to commodity markets. It might also be viewed as a power play on the part of the United States to retake for New York the leadership in world capital markets lost in 1963 when the Interest Equalization Tax was levied.

The second question goes to the heart of the fixed-vs-floating exchange-rate issue. A number of economists from different ranks--Johnson and Friedman from the flexible, for example, and Mundell from the fixed--have suggested that a compromise be devised between fixed and flexible, under which rates would be fixed within regions, and flexible between blocs. Johnson has asserted that banana republics should not have independent exchange rates because they know that the price of bananas that counts is the one in foreign exchange (absence of money illusion in bananas). Friedman and Meltzer believe that small countries should not have independent monetary policies, but tie to a larger unit and take their money supply and interest rates from it. Rates for the dollar, European Monetary Unit, yen, etc., would move freely against one another. All other countries would fix their exchange rates and monetary policies in terms of one of the few floating currencies.

This system appeals to me neither on economic nor political grounds. I would invert the scheme to fix the structure of the main currencies, and let the smaller countries use fixed or flexible rates as they chose. Coherence and unity for the world economy require that key currencies be fixed in relation to one another, to use John Williams' expression which he first employed, to my knowledge, in the Preparatory Commission for the World Economic Conference at its meeting in 1932--another time when coherence in the structure of world exchange rates was needed. It is unimportant to the "public good" of world economic stability what the Canadian dollar/U.S. dollar rate may be, or the Danish krone/pound sterling rate. What matters is the relationship among the dollar, yen, Deutschemark, pound sterling, French franc et al. The ingenious suggestion has been made, that what is now needed is another Tripartite Monetary Pact along the lines of that of September 26, 1936, but this time among the United States, Japan and Germany.[5] They would settle on exchange rates, but not necessarily immediately, and agree not to sterilize capital movements among themselves. They would necessarily have to agree on a common

---

[5] See Ronald I. McKinnon, "A New Tripartite Monetary Agreement or a Limping Dollar Standard?" Essays in International Finance (Princeton: Princeton University Press, International Finance Section, No. 106, October 1974).

monetary policy. Such a framework would constitute a basis on which the rest of the world could adjust, once and for all, or continuously, as separate countries chose. The proposal has the damaging political drawback that it would be interpreted as an attack on the European Monetary Union and especially the French franc. It could not be undertaken except with the enthusiastic support of the French. To wait for some stability in the system for the European Monetary Union to take shape and acquire strength, would be to delay matters too long. But such a scheme is the only possible basis for establishing a pivot to replace the dollar which has lost its legitimacy as international money in the brutal events since August 1971.

VI. CONCLUSION

In conclusion, I side with the group which finds the present leaderless and rudderless system of floating full of dangers. It is not disasterous as some feared. Expansion of trade and failure of investment to decline faster have been impressive. The experiment has been favored by the concern of Germany, the Netherlands, Australia (until lately), etc., more with inflation than the balance of payments, and by widespread restraint in avoiding beggar-thy-neighbor action. It has handled well--in the early stages--the disruptive impact of the multiple increase in the price of oil. There are, however, signs of tension and stress, in bank failures, in the loss of credit standing of some countries which still face continued deficits, in the difficulties of arranging contracts continuously--though the first adjustments were made smoothly--without an international money. The world has avoided a contest for international economic dominance. The danger is that it may face a vacuum in the area, with the United States yielding its leadership which was regarded as illegitimate both abroad and at home, and no country or group of countries taking its place. There is no evident lender of last resort, and if there were, its position would be unenviable: in a world where quantity is everything and price is unimportant, the penalty rate at which Walter Bagehot insisted the lender of last resort should discount freely, no longer holds much terror for the discounter. In these circumstances, last becomes first or at least early resort.

The dollar is technically strong with many speculators short of it, but psychologically weak. Its recent recovery has been owing to oil. The Swiss franc on the other hand is technically weak, with too many long of it, and a weak current account, but psychologically, and hence in market position, strong. In these circumstances, economists have difficulty forecasting.

There is no likely agreement on SDRs, the link, convertibility, the price of gold, rules for management of flexible rates, including agreement not to manage. The prospect is that the world will muddle along without clear direction, until little by little, assuming that a liquidity crisis is avoided, the market settles gradually on a system of fixed rates, or rates held steady within narrow margins, which governments ultimately find it easy and convenient to support. As one who believes in international money, I hope so. The difficulties of harmonizing policies and Phillips curves sufficiently to sustain such a system are recognized. I nonetheless insist that a system of permanently fixed rates, adjusted only when policies go wrong and not from time to time as a regular device, plus the adoption of monetary and fiscal policies to make them work, is a first-best solution, attainable perhaps only in the very long-run, but superior for world economic unity and coherence to floating rates, the movable peg, crawling peg and the like. I believe in money in the international economy as in the domestic, and in the Darwinian uneven social process which will, in the end, produce an international money.

REFERENCES

1. Alexander, Sidney, "The Effects of a Devaluation on a Trade Balance," I.M.F. Staff Papers, Vol. II (April, 1952), 263-78.

2. Bank for International Settlements, Forty-Fourth Annual Report, 1st April 1973 to 31st March 1974, Basle, June 10, 1974.

3. Cooper, Richard N. Discussion of Corden's paper in L.B. Krause and W.S. Salant,(eds.,)European Monetary Unification and Its Meaning for the United States. Washington, D.C.: Brookings, 1973, p. 200.

4. Corden, Max W.,"The Adjustment Problem," in L.B. Krause and W.S. Salant,(eds.,)European Monetary Unification and Its Meaning for the United States, Washington, D.C.: The Brookings Institution, 1973, 159-84.

5. Diaz-Alejandro, Carlos F. Exchange-Rate Devaluation in a Semi-Industrialized Country, The Experience of Argentina, 1955-1961, Cambridge Mass.: The M.I.T. Press, 1965.

6. Exter, John, "The Gold Losses," speech before the Economic Club of Detroit, May 7, 1962, published by the First National City Bank of New York.

7. Friedman, Milton, Hearings before the Joint Economic Committee, Congress of the United States, June 26, 1973.

8. _____, "The Case for Flexible Exchange Rates," in American Economic Association, Readings in International Economics, Homewood, Ill.: Irwin, 1968.

9. Hansen, Bent, New York Times, September 20, 1974.

10. Hazlitt, Henry. Will Dollars Save the World? New York: D. Appleton - Century Co. , 1947.

11. Hinshaw, Randall, "Elasticity Pessimism, Absorption and Flexible Exchange Rates," in Willy Sellekaerts, (eds.,) International Trade and Finance: Essays in Honour of Jan Tinbergen, London: MacMillan, 1973.

12. Johnson, Harry G., "The Problems of Central Bankers," Economic Notes Monte dei Paschi di Siena, Vol. II. No. 3 (September-December 1973).

13. Kindleberger, Charles P. The Dollar Shortage. New York: Wiley, 1950.

14. _____. The World in Depression, 1929-1939. London: Allen Lane, 1973.

15. Machlup, Fritz, "Equilibrium and Disequilibrium: Misplaced Concreteness and Disguised Politics," The Economic Journal LXVIII (March 1958), pp. 1-24.

16. _____, "Exchange-Rate Flexibility," in Banca Nazionale del Lavoro Quarterly Review, No. 106, (September 1973).

17. Magee, Stephen, "United States Merchandise Trade in 1970 and 1971," Unpublished paper, prepared for the Council of Economic Advisers, Summer, 1972.

18. McKinnon, Ronald, "A New Tripartite Agreement or a Limping Dollar Standard? "Essays in International Finance, Princeton University: International Finance Section, No. 106, (October 1974).

19. Meltzer, Allan, Hearings before the Joint Economic Committee, Congress of the United States, June 21, 1973.

20. Nordhaus, William and John Shoven, "Inflation 1973, The Year of Infamy," Challenge, Vol. 17, No. 2. (June 1974)14-22.

21. Salop, Joanne, "A Note on the Monetary Approach to the Balance of Payment," paper presented to the Conference on the Effects of Exchange Rate Adjustments, U.S. Treasury Department, Washington, D.C., April 4-5, 1974.

22. Silk, Leonard, New York Times, July 28, 1974.

23. Tsiang, S.C., "The Role of Money in Trade-Balance Stability - Synthesis of the Elasticity and Absorption Approaches," American Economic Review, Vol. LI, No. 5 (December 1961), 912-36.

24.   United States Department of Commerce, International Economic Policy
        Research, "Changes in U.S. Foreign Trade: The Past - 1971 Exper-
        ience in Perspective," (October 1974, Preliminary Draft).

25.   Wallich, Henry, "The Monetary Crisis of 1971 - Lessons to be Learned,"
        Jacobsson Memorial Lecture, delivered September 24, 1972 at the
        Great Hall, International Monetary Fund, Washington, D.C.

FLOATING FOREIGN EXCHANGE RATES 1973-74:

THE EMPEROR'S NEW CLOTHES*

Ronald I. McKinnon

Stanford University

The relative merits of fixed versus floating exchange rates can be seriously debated only if both are feasible as alternative economic policies. During most
of the postwar period, for example, both options have been open bilaterally to
Canada and the United States. However, major industrial countries are now experiencing markedly differential rates of price inflation that generate expectations
of incipient price and cost disalignments in the future. Hence, the clearing of
foreign exchange transactions apparently requires continuous changes in relative
currency values to avoid exorbitant losses in currency convertibility and in the
freedom of international trade in goods and services. Return to a parity system of
fixed rates is out of the question, unless it were preceded by domestic monetary
reforms and international monetary cooperation of a far-reaching kind beyond the
purview of the present paper[1] -- and probably beyond that of most monetary
authorities as well.

Though economists recognize the imperial necessity of floating rates at
the present time, our experiences in 1973-74 have been surprising. The models of
international trade and monetary adjustment developed in the 1950s and 1960s
to portray continuous flexibility on the one hand, and the impact of major appreciations and depreciations on the balance of trade on the other, seem seriously
deficient. In discharging my obligation to do "An Assessment of Recent Experience Concerning Floating Exchange Rates," I shall concentrate on the unexpect-
edly large daily, monthly, and quarterly fluctuations in exchange rates among major

* I would like to thank Sven Grassman and Allan Meltzer for helpful comments.

[1] The monetary conditions for reestablishment of a successful parity system have been explored by the present author in (1974 and (1975).

currencies that continue to the present writing. Their consequences for the "dis-alignment" of international price levels, in the sense of purchasing-power parity, and for the allocative efficiency of commodity trade are then explored.

However, the macroeconomic repercussions of exchange-rate fluctua-tions on domestic price inflation, on real output and employment, or on each country's trade balance are omitted. Hence no attempt is made to review the efficacy of the elasticities approach versus the absorption approach versus the monetary (asset-adjustment) approach to the balance of payments. Instead, I concentrate more on the direct microeconomic causes and consequences of insta-bility in the foreign exchanges.

Foreign exchange transactions are analyzed in Part I from the point of view of the direct participants: banks, multinational corporations, and individuals, whether they be hedgers, commercial traders, or speculators. In Part II, the impact of floating exchange rates on the alignment of national price levels is investigated.

I. TRANSACTING WITHOUT SPECULATORS

Writers in the 1950s and 1960s who espoused freely floating exchange rates[2] did not foresee certain peculiar characteristics of the present (1974) system of floating rates:

(1) Current movements in spot exchange rates of 20 percent quarter-to-quarter, 5 percent week-to-week, or even 1 percent on an hour-to-hour basis are now not unusual; although they are very large by historical standards.[3]

(2) Concomitantly, bid-ask spreads in the spot market have widened significantly from the 1960s.[4]

(3) Bid-ask spreads in forward markets have risen relatively more sharp-ly - - particularly in longer-term contracts where trade has tended to diminish. Interbank forward trading - - although not necessarily bank-customer forward trading - - may have declined.[4] Floating rates have not induced any noticeable expansion in the facilities for forward trading across pairs of currencies, or in longer-term contracts.

---

[2] Without attempting to cover the extensive literature on the subject, Friedman (1953), Sohmen (1961), Johnson (1972),, Machlup (1972) are taken to be representative authors for this purpose.

[3] For a more detailed statistical analysis of short-term movements in spot exchange rates, see Hirsch and Higham (June 1974).

[4] Appendix A contains a description of representative changes in bid-ask spreads in both spot and forward interbank markets from the 1960s through 1973-74.

(4) Forward rates have been poor predictors of future spot rates.[5]

(5) Some commercial banks have suffered severe foreign exchange losses, and a few have gone bankrupt.

(6) Official intervention has continued at a level as high or higher than under the old fixed rate system.[6]

These points more or less describe the state of the foreign exchanges during 1973 and 1974, after the breakdown of the Smithsonian Agreements. (The continuing high volume of foreign commodity trade, despite exchange instability, is analyzed below in Part II.) While volatile hourly and daily changes in exchange rates are difficult to portray graphically, weekly quotations from February 1973 for the German mark in U.S. dollars are provided by Chicago's International Monetary Market (Figure One below). Not only are the weekly and quarterly movements large for this particular exchange rate, they seem cyclical without a pronounced trend.

One might contrast this volatility and the high cost of foreign-exchange transactions in 1973-74 with a statement made by Machlup (1972, p. 70) that is indicative of his feeling about the smoothness of adjustment in a flexible rate system:

> Under a system of greater flexibility such serious disalign-
> ments of exchange rates would never, or hardly ever, arise,
> and expectations of change would be confined to minuscule
> adjustments. Profits from small changes can be only small,
> inviting only moderate speculation, which can be easily
> discouraged, if this is wanted, by relatively minor differ-
> entials in interest rates.

Machlup was not alone. Other notable writers such as Friedman, Johnson, and Sohmen have maintained similar views on the gradualness of adjustment under floating rates, which they contrasted favorably with the sharp discrete changes and one-way speculative frenzies of the old pegged-rate system. Under floating rates, it was imagined that forward markets and hedging facilities would expand to offset future uncertainty; private speculation would stabilize the spot and forward markets. In contrast, the fragmentary evidence from the 1973-74 period points in the opposite direction.

---

[5] For example, none of the principal turning points in the wide movements in the dollar-mark exchange rate in February 1973, in July 1973, in January 1974, or in May 1974 could be predicted from looking at forward rates. See Appendix A for a discussion of this point.

[6] See John Williamson (1974) for statistics on the turnover of official reserve holdings.

FIGURE 1

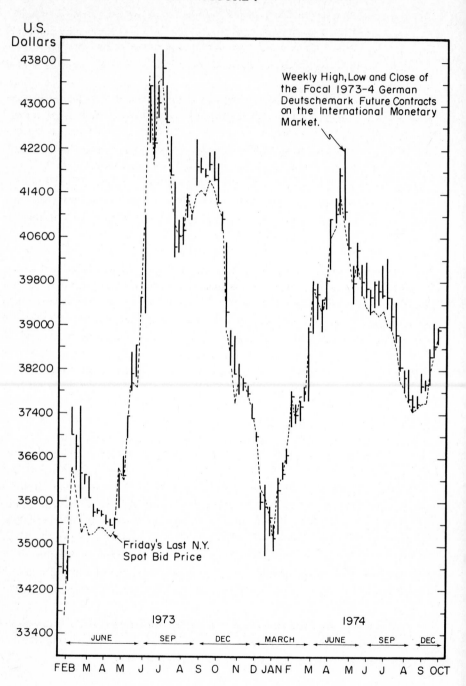

Though floating exchange rates are recognized as a necessity at the present time, why has past theorizing failed to comprehend the present "disordered" and high-cost state of the markets for foreign exchange as described by points (1) through (6) above? The easiest explanation is that the world has been subject to a number of unpredictable shocks -- general inflation emanating from the United States, delayed dollar devaluation, a grain crisis, an oil crisis, and so on. Such successive shocks, and the consequent difficulty in making a full evaluation of their economic consequences, have made smoother, lower-cost operation of the foreign exchanges impossible.

Alternatively, if he takes official reserve turnover as a significant indicator of intervention (Williamson, 1974), a purist might suggest that the no-par system has not settled down because governments continue to intervene. The coalescence of private expectations regarding correctly aligned exchange rates is interrupted because official intervention is so unpredictable. Thus the current system of dirty floating hardly constitutes a pure test of how freely flexible exchange rates might behave.

Both the "exogenous-shock" and the "purist" explanations are consistent with the a priori reasoning that Machlup, Friedman, and others have used to justify a system of uninhibited floating. Indeed, both explanations likely have some validity. I would submit, however, that an important institutional element was lacking from the earlier defenses of floating rates, the importance of which has only now become apparent. The questions of who was to be a stabilizing speculator, and what would be the source of private capital for such speculations, were never directly addressed. Rather, this particular issue was superseded by a rough-and-tumble debate over whether private speculation would be stabilizing or destabilizing. An implicit consensus had been reached that there would be no restraints on the availability of private speculative capital on the huge scale needed.

The contrary hypothesis, advanced here, is that the supply of private capital for taking net positions in either the forward or spot markets is currently inadequate. Exchange rates then move sharply in response to random variations in the day-to-day excess demand by merchants for foreign exchange. Once a rate starts to move because of some temporary perturbation, no prospective speculator is willing to hold an open position for a significant time interval in order to bet on a reversal -- whence the large daily and monthly movements in the foreign exchanges and high bid-ask spreads. Bandwagon psychologies result from the general unwillingness of participants to take net positions against near-term market movements.

Thus, the problem seems not to be one of excessive destabilizing speculation, but rather one of the absence of speculation over time horizons longer than a day or two.

83

Banking Risk versus Currency Risk

Perhaps implicit in the traditional theory of flexible rates, the commercial banks were the natural candidates for the role of stabilizing speculators. After all, the principal spot and forward markets for foreign exchange are interbank markets. Expertise in the foreign exchanges is largely confined to employees of the large banks and, to a lesser extent, multinational corporations.[7] Whatever tentative speculative efforts were made, however, seem to have been cut short by a rash of bank failures for those on the losing end. Governments and central banks have now pressed commercial banks to balance more strictly their net position in foreign exchange. Hence, commercial banks are restricted - - and perhaps correctly so - - from taking speculative positions.

Official restraints on net foreign-exchange positions of commercial banks parallel similar restraints on their domestic loan portfolios and liquidity reserves that have long been regulated. Most banking textbooks emphasize the uneasy trade off between the unique role of the commercial banks to provide a secure means of payment against their more general role as financial intermediaries between savers and investors -- a role that ordinarily demands aggressive investment and money-market behavior. The commercial banks can attract capital easily by issuing money -- legal tender often guaranteed by the state . In return, the government sees fit to limit their aggressiveness in the capital market -- possibly reducing immediate real yields in the economy -- by safety-first regulations designed to secure money as a means of payment. In addition, reserve requirements permit control over the nominal money base and, ultimately, official control over the nominal price level.

In the international sphere, excessive speculative risk in the foreign exchanges might also impair the security of deposits in purely domestic currency. Hence central banks may well limit the net foreign-exchange exposure of their commercial banks to, say, 20 percent of their owners' equity. This and similar constraining regulations are designed to reduce "banking risk"-- the possibility of insolvency on the part of the custodians of the domestic money supply.

However, banking risk pervades international as well as domestic trade. Central banks have largely withdrawn from trading one currency for another at a known parity. But responsibility to clear foreign currencies remains with the commercial banks-- who provide currencies on demand to depositors or honor forward commitments requiring the trade of domestic for foreign money. Large shifts in relative currency values, or the imposition of unexpected foreign exchange controls, militate toward a risk-avoidance view of securing interbank payments in

---

[7] The relative wages of experienced foreign-exchange traders have been bid up sharply under the floating-rate regime.

84

international monies against default. It is one thing for a nonbank individual or firm to risk holding a foreign currency unhedged against exchange-rate changes: this "currency risk" was indeed envisaged by proponents of flexible exchange rates as a real social cost of doing international business. It is quite another matter however, for the nonbank firm to be continually worried about the insolvency of the bank on which it has a foreign-currency claim. The currency risk was foreseen by the old literature but the banking risk was not. Hence a fairly strong case can be made for banks that specialize in foreign-currency transactions to maintain balanced positions that limit their speculative activities and so reduce the banking risk to other firms and individuals.

This point has been recognized by the managements of major commercial banks, and, with a slightly longer lag, by central banks. Large American banks rather quickly responded to the currency fluctuations beginning in 1973 by requiring that their foreign-exchange dealers more strictly limit their net open position in any one foreign currency at the end of each trading day. In addition to this general stricture, balance requirements have been imposed at every maturity in spot and forward trading; a short forward position can no longer be balanced by a long spot position in the same currency. However, the Federal Reserve Bank has not yet tried to formally regulate the foreign-exchange positions of American commercial banks.

On the other hand, European commercial banks have, traditionally, been more willing to take net positions in foreign exchange if only to serve their relatively greater volume of foreign-exchange transactions. Foreign-exchange dealings have been thought by some to be an "art" in which European financial institutions have particularly great expertise. However, in response to a few commercial-bank failures and other large foreign-exchange losses, European central banks have now promulgated a series of directives that formally limit the net foreign-exchange positions of their commercial banks. Instead of learning how to speculate successfully in a floating rate system as time passes, commercial banks are becoming more conservative nonspeculators: negative learning by doing. Thus it is not surprising that central banks have been partially drawn back into the market to take balancing positions in foreign exchange although they no longer have parity obligations.

From this angle, one sees a bit better the social advantages of a central bank's "speculating" to maintain an official parity, as was done under the Bretton Woods system. Even when a central bank was eventually forced to adjust discretely its pegged rate, and so take large bookkeeping losses, commercial banks could bail themselves out and get what foreign exchange they needed to cover their commitments at a known price. Similarly, multinational corporations could also easily take defensive positions against discrete appreciations or depreciations.Thus private positions in foreign exchange had not to be balanced so closely on a continuous basis. The willingness of governments to take large losses under Bretton Woods did secure the safety of the payments mechanism to a degree greater than was recognized by academic economists. In effect, some of the losses that used to be borne by central banks have now been shifted to commercial banks and firms. The resulting fear of bankruptcy has impaired confidence in interbank clearing domestically and internationally.

In summary, the withdrawal of central banks from their parity commitments has shifted the currency risk of exchange-rate changes to private speculators as expected, but brought also an increase in banking risk (insolvency) that was not anticipated. This increase in banking risk has reduced the supply of capital available for currency speculation.

Forward Trading and the Capital Constraint

Banking risk is related to another common thene in the literature on floating exchange rates: private trading in the forward markets for foreign exchange would expand once central banks withdrew from their parity commitments. However, a good part of the increase in demand for forward cover that floating rates might have portended seems to have been shifted to the spot market. Firms wishing to hedge simply buy (or sell) foreign currencies ahead of their needs and hold them spot in the form of interest-bearing assets in the Eurocurrency market (Krul, 1974). Facilities for forward trading per se do not seem to have expanded as predicted. [8]

Many academic treatises have stressed the irrelevance of forward markets for hedging commodity trade because a trader could always purchase foreign currency spot and hold it until needed. However, in times of payments uncertainty and fear of default by firms or banks with forward contracts, a substantial asymmetry arises. The implicit or explicit margin required by banks of their customers in order to make a forward commitment would normally rise with the fear of unexpected oscillations in exchange rates - - currency risk. Since the cost of the margin requirement is likely to be substantial (unless covered by implicit seigniorage from non-interest-bearing demand deposits), the firm wishing to hedge may find it more advantageous to hold foreign currency spot where, implicitly, the margin requirement is 100 percent but full interest compensation is paid. While the standard textbook analysis gives no reason to believe that holding spot is preferable to buy-

---

[8] Since writing the above, an important caveat should be added. Sven Grassman has direct information that forward contracting by Swedish banks with their nonbank retail customers approximately doubled (measured as a proportion of spot trade) from 1972 to 1974. This is not inconsistent, however, with a drying up of interbank forward trading as per Nicholas Krul's analysis.

ing forward, currency risk raises the margin costs of forward contracting and shifts nonbank firms to holding spot. In addition, the desire of each commercial bank to maintain balance in foreign currency at every forward maturity makes organization of forward trading more awkward.

On the other side of the coin, firms may doubt the ability of banks to meet forward payments; hence banking risk leads them to prefer to hold foreign currencies spot -- aside from the higher costs of forward contracting. There is always a good chance that current deposits in foreign currency can be quickly withdrawn if the solvency of the bank providing the deposits comes into question; whereas a company holding forward contracts, which mature in several months, is helpless if the delivering bank appears on the brink of insolvency.

In summary, the threat of default from either currency risk or banking risk effectively shortens the term structure of forward financing in the foreign exchanges. This shortening manifests itself in higher bid-ask spreads in forward quotations (Appendix A), but perhaps more importantly in a shift by firms to hedging by holding spot foreign exchange -- largely in Eurocurrency markets.

Well, what difference does it all make? The standard textbook analysis would suggest none: forward contracting and holding foreign exchange spot were thought to be exactly equivalent. However, there is a capital constraint that has been made rather more acute by the current turn of events. Companies who want foreign currency in the future must find 100 percent of the capital in the present and convert spot. Forward contracting might in the old days have required only a 5 percent to 10 percent margin. Either more of a company's equity or more of its borrowing capacity now has to be utilized in hedging spot. A company's ability to be venturesome and exploit other profitable investment opportunities is thereby reduced.

How does this shortening of term influence the capital constraint facing commercial banks overall? Instead of a series of relatively longer-term forward commitments, the meeting of which can be planned with due deliberation the banking system now finds itself extending very short-term credit and issuing current deposits (withdrawable virtually on demand) in foreign currencies to those customers who otherwise might have taken less liquid forward positions. Thus pressure on the "owned" capital of the banks magnifies their liquidity problems; the volume of business which they are able to conduct on attractive terms declines. In short, the heightened uncertainty has increased the capital requirements of both banks and their customers and restricted the scope of their operations. The social costs of shifting from forward to spot are of some consequence, contrary to what past literature on forward markets in foreign exchange might have suggested.

This capital constraint on the ability of banks to meet demands on them has, of course, been further exacerbated by the need to recycle "hot" oil money in huge quantities with an unduly short term structure. Hence the oil crisis further reduces the capability of the commercial banks to act as stabilizing speculators. This unfortunate complication, which greatly increases the uncertainty already plaguing financial markets and threatens the structure of international commodity trade, could hardly have been foreseen in the past literature on flexible exchange rates and forward trading. Thus the oil problem is exogenous to my main theme and will not be analyzed further.

Multinational Corporations and Other Nonspeculators

What ever happened to the multinational corporations, those ogres of speculative runs under the old fixed-rate regime? Surely these giants of unlimited international wealth and power need not hesitate to take a net position in this or that currency if it appears to be seriously "disaligned" (Machlup's terminology). However, the division of labor seems important to them: they prefer to be merchants and manufacturers rather than foreign-exchange speculators. Many companies have clearly defined policies against speculation in the foreign exchanges.

More strongly perhaps, evidence exists of excessive hedging of items on the multinationals' balance sheets. The current profusion of literature on the translation problem across a firm's balance sheets denominated in several currencies seems aimed at complete risk avoidance. Yet rigid adherence to either of the two main accounting rules for translation -- the monetary-nonmonetary method or the current-noncurrent method -- coupled with a desire to hedge against foreign-exchange losses in a formal accounting sense, can inadvertently aggravate foreign-exchange risk in the true economic sense and reduce profits.

Insofar as multinationals are now reluctant to take net positions in foreign exchange for reasons adumbrated above, hedging future imports or exports of goods and services requires that they hold spot positions in foreign exchange that must be fully financed -- and so impinge seriously on the multinationals' capital constraint. Given the current state of the stock market and the financing needs of ordinary business, the freeing of capital for speculative purposes in the foreign exchanges can hardly be given a high priority by big companies whose existence in the long run depends on their expertise in manufacturing or commerce.

With both commercial banks and multinationals minimizing their net foreign-exchange exposure, it is not evident that private individuals have sufficient capital, knowledge, or ease of access to the market to take up the slack. Commercial banks have never made it easy for individuals who were not major depositors to take speculative positions. The International Monetary Market of the Chicago Mercantile Exchange does cater to individuals, but it is not booming. The contractual obligations for actual delivery of foreign exchange are complex, and trading in foreign currencies is not a game that nonspecialists can easily play.

Speculating Without International Money

Beyond these institutional restraints on banks, multinational corporations, and individuals, there may be a somewhat deeper explanation of the inadequate availability of private speculative capital in the current environment. I refer to the problem of the "riskless asset" alias the "home currency" alias "international money."

Let us first distinguish arbitrage from speculation since the former seems not to present difficulties under floating rates. Define arbitrage to take place at a single point in time, where traders (mainly banks) simply buy and sell foreign exchange to make cross rates among n-1 currencies consistent with the n-1 bilateral exchange rates of each with an nth currency. The nth currency can be chosen arbitrarily without having the properties of international money. As is well known, the total number of exchange rates to be arbitraged in an n-country world is $1/2\, n(n-1)$. Accurate multilateral arbitrage across currencies is, of course, a necessary condition for efficient multilateral trade in goods and services. However, it is not sufficient once intertemporal international resource allocation is considered.

Arbitrageurs seem to operate reasonably efficiently under the present system of symmetrically floating exchange rates. An increase in the bid-ask spread in foreign currencies from 1972 to 1974 (Appendix A) suggests slightly greater costs - - salaries of foreign-exchange traders, bank capital, and so forth - - from floating in comparison to the old pegged-rate system. However, serious multilateral inconsistencies in spot-exchange rates are not evident. Continued intervention by various governments in the foreign exchanges has not seemingly provoked any obvious conflict in international economic policies. [9] Of course massive failures by commercial banks in any one country, or official restraints on free convertibility in making payments, could hinder arbitrage - - but this has yet to happen.

Let us define "speculation" to be the purchase of one currency for another (forward or spot) in order to hold an open position through time in anticipation of a favorable change in relative currency prices. In arbitrage, the emphasis is on multilateral currency trading at one point in time,[10] whereas the risk

---

[9] Somewhat to my surprise, as in an earlier paper (McKinnon 1969) I had suggested that official interventions at cross purposes would be likely in the absence of a parity system.

[10] However, a finite time interval is required to conduct any arbitrage transaction.

and gain in speculating comes primarily from the way exchange rates move through time - - perhaps over extended periods. A peculiar combination of expertise in the foreign exchanges, knowledge of economic policies in particular countries, and access to finance is required for speculation to be privately profitable and socially stabilizing.

The recent sharp but largely reversed movements in exchange rates seem to be prima facie evidence of the absence of stabilizing speculation.[11] If so, what in the current system of generally floating rates and differing national price inflations militates against successful speculation, although not against successful arbitrage? Official restraint on the net foreign-exchange positions of commercial banks is one obvious candidate; private uncertainty about the future of national monetary policies is another. In the latter category, private speculation is rendered more difficult in the absence of any recognized international money that could otherwise act as a stable and liquid international store of value. Speculators need a haven, a relatively riskless asset, from which they can operate.

To tackle this last point analytically, the concept of international money is divided into an unrestricted and into a somewhat more limited meaning. The free international circulation of gold coins, whose value in exchange depends simply on their weight and fineness, is an example of unrestricted international money. If, in addition, one places strict limits on fiduciary national monies issued at par with international money, the exchange-rate problem simply disappears. Relative national monetary values become unalterably fixed. Hence, the concept of unrestricted international money is not analytically useful for analyzing the present system of floating exchange rates. One can imagine (with some difficulty) the European Monetary Union recalling all national currencies of member countries, and issuing its own notes and deposits that were recognized as the sole legal tender in Europe: international money in an unrestricted form over a limited number of countries.

The existence of international money since World War II, however, has taken a more limited form. The United States dollar was not legal tender or a medium of exchange for purely domestic transactions in most important countries. Indeed, in countries with freely convertible currencies, the domestic currency itself serves as international money in the sense that nonbank firms and individuals can write cheques on demand deposits in domestic currency in order to meet international payments. By and large, individuals and firms that are domestic residents need not hold chequing accounts abroad in foreign currencies, and generally find such overseas accounts to be inconvenient as long as the dom-

---

[11]A "perfect markets" theorist might object on the ground that the exchange markets were efficiently absorbing significant but contradictory bits of relevant information.

estic currency remains freely convertible into foreign exchange. Exporters typically invoice their overseas sales in terms of the domestic currency as long as it is convertible.[12]

However, the position of banks is quite different. They are responsible for converting domestic into various possible foreign currencies as intermediaries for their nonbank customers. To facilitate currency conversions, a typical commercial bank will hold a fairly wide portfolio of chequing accounts abroad in foreign currencies with correspondent banks. In order to limit the number of separate accounts and the diversity of foreign-exchange commitments that can be easily "covered," the commercial banks in, say, Sweden may well concentrate their overseas chequing accounts in recognized international currencies - - such as the U.S. dollar - - in which a high proportion of interbank trading is organized. Thus, instead of holding chequing accounts in Australian dollars to service customers dealing with Australia, a Swedish commercial bank may use U.S. dollar deposits as an intermediary claim on Australian dollars. In this sense, U.S. dollars (as well as British sterling balances) have served as "bank money" in the postwar period even though they may not be held by nonbank firms and individuals.

In forward trading, the use of an intermediary currency such as U.S. dollars is even more pronounced. Indeed a forward market between Swedish kronor and Australian dollars is unlikely to exist - - even at short maturities - - because of an insufficient volume of transactions. Hence, if a Swedish importer wants to buy Australian dollars forward with kronor, he first sells forward the kronor for U.S. dollars, and then sells U.S. dollars forward for Australian dollars through contracts that mature at the same point in time. Quite possibly, the Swedish importer will not undertake this dual transaction directly: his agent - - a Swedish commercial bank - - purchases forward Australian dollars against U.S. dollars while selling kronor against U.S. dollars. Thus the commercial bank may be left with the dual commitment in the interbank market in forward foreign exchange, whereas the Swedish importer simply has the forward obligation to sell Swedish kronor for Australian dollars to his banking agent.

We see, therefore, the importance of having a relatively riskless asset like U.S. dollars that can be used as "bank" money or more generally. Indeed, with $1/2\ n\ (n-1)$ exchange rates in a system of n convertible currencies, it is unlikely that well-developed spot markets will exist for each cross rate - - let along that there will be forward trading between each pair of currencies at several different maturities. How well has the U.S. dollar served in this intermediary role as a relatively riskless bank asset? From 1950 to 1966 its real value, measured in terms of internationally tradable goods and services, was well maintained

---

[12] See Sven Grassman (1973, ch. 2) for empirical verification that exporters from convertible-currency countries typically invoice in their own currencies.

(McKinnon 1971); the dollar was an attractive store of value and numeraire for longer-term international transactions. Moreover, the dollar was virtually fully liquid in facilitating private international transactions on current or capital account, and dollar assets bore an attractive interest yield. For official interventions to peg exchange rates and to acquire reserves, the U.S. dollar was the most convenient vehicle currency because official par values were established in U.S. dollars. Since the late 1960s however, high and variable American price inflation has made the U.S. dollar less useful as a "riskless" interbank foreign-exchange asset, but not so much as to supplant its intermediary role in the interbank market with some other currency.

Temporarily putting aside the important empirical question of the stability of the U.S. dollar, consider how private speculation would be conducted if a stable international money - - defined in our limited sense - - existed. Although one might still live in a world of n fluctuating currencies, speculators - - whether banks or nonbanks - - are now free to specialize in particular bilateral relationships between each of the other currencies and the international money in question. The breadth of market information required of any one trader is thereby reduced; the international money serves as a convenient repository (riskless asset) for defining the speculator's equity and his profits.

Let us illustrate with two commonly cited historical examples of smoothly floating exchange rates: the Austro-Hungarian gulden from 1879 to 1892, and the Canadian dollar from 1950 to 1962. In the first case, [13] British sterling served as international money, allowing free access to the London capital markets; in the latter case, the U.S. dollar served as the home currency, and the New York capital market was a source of finance to the Canadian economy.

If an individual speculator wanted to be short in gulden, he could do so conveniently by going long in sterling with funds raised or normally held in London. Of course, the speculator would have to follow weather reports on Austrian crops, chart the Austrian money supply, understand Austrian tariff policy, and follow Austria's numerous military imbroglios with diplomatic and strategic insight. Having mastered that, he could safely take his profits in sterling and not worry about being long in sterling half the time. He did not need to be directly concerned with the n-2 exchange rates between gulden and currencies other than sterling. The presence of secure international money, therefore, allowed the speculator to specialize in knowing Austria - - a reasonably big job in itself. The consequent reduction in informational uncertainty increased the availability of capital for taking open positions in 1879-92 gulden. Similarly, in

---

[13] Described in interesting detail by Leland Yeager (1969).

92

1950-62, speculators could conveniently use the U.S. dollar to take open positions against the Canadian dollar.

Hence, the correct analytical interpretation of the satisfactory Austrian and Canadian experiences with speculation is not quite the obvious one that they were alone in floating while the rest of the world was mainly on fixed rates. Even if most countries had been floating their exchange rates in the 1879-92 or 1950-62 periods, the presence of secure international money - - sterling or U.S. dollars - - would economize on information (provide a riskless asset) and allow speculators to specialize in one currency by always taking their positions in that currency against international money.

Put differently, in a regime of several floating currencies - - say, lire, marks, and dollars - - would a speculator always go short in that currency that was judged to be the "weakest" while simultaneously going long in that judged to be "strongest"? No, because of the fundamental problem of timing based on rapidly changing market information. Having studied the Italian situation with decentralized care, he may find a particular point in time opportune to take a short forward position in lire against U.S. dollars - - which is the one currency in which complete forward markets exist against all others. A while later (perhaps never), the German situation may develop favorably enough (according to our speculator's research) to warrant taking a long forward position in marks against U.S. dollars. His net dollar position is now zero. However, he did hold an open long position in dollars for a significant time period whose exact duration was uncertain after his lire transaction. Put more extremely, in the day-to-day or even the hour-to-hour smoothing of random exchange fluctuations, a speculator with highly specialized information on particular countries would prefer to deal only with the intermediary currency if he knew it to be safe.

From the above reasoning, the potential supply of speculative capital for the smoothing of foreign-exchange markets in 1973-74 is much reduced by the decline in the United States dollar as stable international money. For example, to go short in French francs for a year hence, in which currency should one be long at the end of that period? American monetary policy could go awry in the interim and greatly depreciate the U.S. dollar vis-a-vis some average basket of currencies or some representative bundle of tradable goods. Our potential foreign-currency speculator now needs expertise in several currencies in order to find a proper offset for his potential short position in francs. The increased uncertainty reduces his willingness to commit his own equity, and limits his capacity to borrow for speculative purposes.

In short, the markets for foreign exchange can tolerate diversity in $n-1$ national monetary policies without drying up the supply of speculative capital if and only if the nth currency is known to be stable. (Of course, the more erratic and uncertain the monetary policy in any of the n-1 countries, the more binding becomes the capital constraint on speculators in that particular currency.) On the other hand, if no consensus is reached on what is stable international money, there may be endless surges from one currency to another to find a home. Hot money flows - - whether by multinationals or Arabs - - are essentially defensive rather than speculative; they serve to widen rather than dampen fluctuations in relative currency values.

The Role of Central Banks in a No-Parity System

In summary, we have a dual explanation of why "stabilizing" private speculation has not developed in the way the old literature on flexible foreign exchange rates seemed to portend - - even on an hour-to-hour basis, let alone quarter-to-quarter. In the very short run, commercial banks are the only private institutions with convenient access to the foreign-exchange markets for taking transitory open positions as dealers. However, they are now unwilling to incur banking risk that jeopardizes their positions as custodians of the payments mechanism - - and are increasingly inhibited by central banks from taking such risks. This basic monetary function of the banks prevents high potential profits, from short-run smoothing of foreign exchange transactions, to attract them into making a stable market as dealers on a daily or hourly basis. However, do we want anything other than fairly conservative financial institutions to be responsible for clearing international payments - - or domestic payments for all that?

But nonbanks would have access to the spot and forward exchange market (using the banks as intermediaries) to hold open positions for longer-run speculations - - say weekly, monthly, or yearly. Aside from the capital constraint on all risky enterprise, these longer-run speculations are inhibited by uncertainty (as distinct from actuarial risk) on how individual national central banks might conduct their monetary policies. In particular, the absence of a generally accepted riskless asset (international money in a limited form) makes decentralized speculation in any particular currency very difficult, and greatly increases the implicit price demand for such risk-taking.

Hence central banks have been attracted back into the foreign-exchange markets in a big way because:

(1) They have a potential comparative advantage in long-run speculations through their control of national monetary policy.

(2) They can enter the interbank market for foreign exchange in the short run without being hampered by capital constraints and default risk.

94

II. THE EFFECTS OF EXCHANGE-RATE CHANGES
ON PRICES AND TRADE

Having explored several explanations for the continuing instability in foreign-exchange rates, can we say much about the real economic consequences of such fluctuations? Clearly, in the short run, costs of transacting in the foreign exchanges have risen sharply. For example, on September 29, 1972, the bid-ask spread in the interbank market to buy German marks (in terms of dollars) was only .016 percent of the spot rate, in a period where governments were still intervening to maintain a par-value system under the Smithsonian agreement, whereas, on October 1, 1974, when official exchange-rate obligations had been forcibly suspended with the great rate fluctuations described above, the bid-ask had widened to .106 percent of the spot rate - - almost a sevenfold increase! However, these costs may still seem "small" relative to the value of goods traded - - and indeed, as shown below, there is no evidence that trade flows have actually been dampened as exchange rates fluctuate more wildly.

Putting aside these increased short-run costs of making international payments in convertible currencies, can one say anything about the longer-run efficiency of international monies as a unit of account? Clearly, domestic-currency prices at given exchange rates should accurately reflect real costs of production across national boundaries if international commodity trade is to be efficient. How well such prices are aligned internationally over months or years - - the necessary planning horizon of most trading firms - - is explored below.

Alignments and Disalignments in National Price Levels

I have made some crude purchasing-power-parity calculations that can be related to this price-alignment approach. The wholesale price index in each country seems to approximate most closely a general index of tradable goods. [14] For each country, the year 1953 is chosen as being one where no obvious disalignments in exchange rates existed. Hence all domestic-currency indices for wholesale prices take 1953 to be 100, as shown in Table One. Exchange-rate adjustments since 1953 are reflected in the conversion of these domestic indices into U.S. dollars at several points in time from 1953 to June 1974. In short, the relative version of purchasing-power-parity theory, with 1953 as the base, is being applied across major convertible currencies.

---

[14] Moreover, prices of nontradable goods and services can be expected to diverge secularly across countries according to differential productivity growth, apart from foreign-exchange policy (McKinnon 1971).

Table One
Wholesale Price Indices for Industrial
Economies: 1953-74*
(1953 = 100)

	1960 Domestic Currency	1960 U.S. Dollars	1965 Domestic Currency	1965 U.S. Dollars	1970 Domestic Currency	1970 U.S. Dollars	1971 Domestic Currency	1971 U.S. Dollars
AUSTRIA	111	111	133.33	133.33	147.91	147.91	154.72	169.66
BELGIUM	102	102	114.29	114.29	125.19	125.19	124.44	139.01
CANADA	104	114.86	115.46	118.15	128.71	140.14	133.92	146.99
DENMARK	105	105	121.05	121.05	143.82	132.65	148.31	145.06
FRANCE	132	94.23	146.99	104.95	163.84	103.88	169.93	113.85
GERMANY	108	108	111.34	116.73	116.19	133.77	120.02	154.25
ITALY	99	99	114.14	114.14	129.94	129.94	133.37	140.33
JAPAN	102	102	102.94	102.94	113.56	113.56	112.25	128.37
NETHERLANDS	104	104	118.95	124.73	132.98	140.48	135.11	157.78
NORWAY	112	112	125.56	125.56	147.67	147.67	152.33	162.16
SWEDEN	112	112	131.18	131.18	152.38	152.38	158.33	168.36
U.K.	114	114	131.11	131.11	159.13	136.04	168.63	153.72
U.S.	109	109	113.04	113.04	127.16	127.16	132.14	132.14

Table One (continued)

	Dec.,1972		June , 1973		Dec., 1973		June, 1974	
	Domestic Currency	U.S. Dollars	Domestic Currency	U.S. Dollars	Domestic Currency	U.S. Dollars	Domestic Currency	U.S. Dollars
AUSTRIA	164.52	184.38	162.49	229.48	171.92	224.62	186.29	264.69
BELGIUM	134.81	152.98	144.55	200.49	154.81	187.33	170.32	224.05
CANADA	148.78	164.38	166.30	183.22	187.14	206.72	204.99	231.94
DENMARK	160.67	162.08	183.15	222.17	193.26	212.09	215.12	247.90
FRANCE	184.77	126.18	198.01	168.83	224.77	167.10	265.98	193.02
GERMANY	125.24	164.27	130.78	226.51	136.00	211.32	148.59	224.26
ITALY	143.24	153.69	159.66	170.84	181.44	186.54	226.41	217.92
JAPAN	118.72	141.52	128.14	173.88	152.94	196.64	173.53	219.89
NETHERLANDS	144.68	170.42	157.45	228.36	164.89	221.88	180.59	256.71
NORWAY	159.30	171.11	165.12	218.82	176.74	219.94	192.85	253.94
SWEDEN	166.67	181.60	179.76	226.26	195.24	220.05	225.05	266.34
U.K.	179.93	150.89	186.18	171.68	200.60	166.44	228.85	195.38
U.S.	140.80	140.80	156.60	156.60	166.45	166.45	178.23	178.23

*All indices are taken from various issues of the IMF "International Financial Statistics." For the years 1960, 1965, 1971 and 1972, the month of December is the point in time that price indices and exchange-rates are calculated.

To interpret the data presented in Table One, focus first on the bottom line - - the wholesale price index of the United States and the dollar standard of reference. By definition, all the dollar wholesale price indices line up to be 100 for 1953. After that, countries do experience different rates of inflation, some of which are offset by exchange-rate changes. For example, by June 1974 several depreciations by France had allowed her franc price index to rise above her dollar one - - 266 versus 193 respectively. Yet 193 for the French dollar index appears only modestly above the American index of 178 for the same month. The more general questions then to be posed are:

A. Are there fairly strong forces operating to align price indices
   in dollars across countries?

B. Insofar as disalignments occur under pegged exchange rates,
   can such disparities be used to predict how exchange rates
   will move in the future?

The answer to both questions seems to be a qualified "yes" for the old regime of quasi-fixed rates lasting to December 1970. Given the considerable diversity in constructing national wholesale price indices (some exclude agricultural products, others double-count them), the indices line up fairly consistently for the years 1960, 1965, and 1970. In December 1970, Sweden's index seems a little highly priced, whereas those of Japan and France seem low. The last might be explained by the propensity of the French to overdevalue, perhaps for mercantilistic reasons, as they did in 1969. The low index for Japan vis-à-vis the United States - - 113.6 versus 127.16 in 1970 - - did in fact presage the Japanese appreciation of 1971. On the other hand, one could look at the German index of 133.77 for 1970 and feel that the mark was more or less correctly aligned at that time. Apparently, the German appreciations in the 1960s had nicely balanced the slower increase in mark prices in Germany in comparison with dollar prices in the United States.

Given this view of price alignment, the sharp appreciations of European currencies against the dollar in 1971 seem mildly surprising. And their further relative appreciations in 1973 seem completely inexplicable to a theorist relying on some notion of purchasing-power parity. Indeed, by June 1973, the German dollar index was about 42 percent greater than American wholesale prices; even by June 1974 this discrepancy had only narrowed to 37 percent.[15] Changes in exchange rates in 1973 and 1974 cannot be interpreted as better aligning national price levels.

---

[15] Perhaps the difficulty is a statistical one revolving around the questionable choice of the 1953 base. Better data on a strictly comparable bundle of tradable goods between Germany and the United States would allow a more precise calculation of purchasing-power parity in an absolute sense.

Further, the very instability of exchange rates in the 1973-74 period militates against a pure price-alignment view. Wholesale prices in domestic currencies have not varied as much as foreign-exchange rates during those two years. Hence if one could identify price alignment across countries in any one month, disalignment would occur the next. In short, the sharp fluctuations in exchange rates in 1973-74 continually disaligned real cost structures. Whether commodity X should be produced in Country A or in Country B was not easy to calculate during 1973-74.

This hypothesis of continual disalignment in international prices need not conflict directly with the view that domestic prices have become more sensitive to changes in exchange rates. Both could reflect increasing international instability. Because international prices do not line up in intuitively plausible and stable ways, however, assigning to exchange-rate policy the main burden of maintaining domestic price stability [16] might be going too far: an overreaction to the older theories of the balance of payments and to the power of internal monetary policy. Nevertheless, the exchange rate is an important ingredient in determining the domestic price level, even in a large economy like the United States that is relatively closed to foreign trade.

False Trading: A Remote Possibility?

The sharp increase in international trade during the past three or four years, despite the turmoil in the foreign exchanges, is hard to interpret but difficult to controvert. Even the flow of trade in real terms among industrial countries has risen remarkably in the 1970's as Table Two (culled from the IMF's 1974 report) makes abundantly clear. This growth in trade significantly exceeded growth in real GNPs as portrayed in Table Three. Taking the sharp rise in the prices of tradable goods into account, the importance of foreign trade for gross national products has been further accentuated. For example, the nominal value of American exports relative to nominal American GNP rose from 4.5 percent in the first half of 1970 to 7.2 percent in the first half of 1974. [17]

---

[16] More implausible, in a world where money illusion is evaporating, is the second half of the "new" Cambridge view that the exchange rate be assigned to stimulate industrial growth in tradable goods through continuous undervaluation.

[17] IMF International Financial Statistics, line 70x over line 99a suitably averaged.

Table Two*

World Trade Summary, 1960-73 [1]

(Percentage changes in volume, in U.S. dollar value, and in unit value of foreign trade)

	Annual Average 1960-70 [2]	Change from Preceding Year			
		1970	1971	1972	1973
World Trade [3]					
Volume					
U.S. dollar value	9	9	6	9	12 1/2
Unit value [4]	10	14 1/2	12	18	37
	1	5	5 1/2	8	22
Imports					
Volume					
Industrial countries	10	9	6	11 1/2	11 1/2
Other developed countries	9	13	3 1/2	1	17
Less developed countries					
Major oil exporters	4 1/2	6 1/2	12	12	20
Other developing countries	6	8 1/2	6 1/2	11 1/2	9 1/2
Unit value [4]					
Industrial countries	1	5 1/2	5 1/2	7 1/2	22 1/2
Other developed countries	1 1/2	5 1/2	6 1/2	8 1/2	20
Less developed countries					
Major oil exporters	1	4	5	8	18 1/2
Other developing countries	1	4	6	8	19 1/2
Exports					
Volume					
Industrial countries	9 1/2	9 1/2	6 1/2	9 1/2	13 1/2
Other developed countries	7 1/2	8	5 1/2	11	16

Table Two* (continued)

	Annual Average 1960-70 [2]	Change from Preceding Year			
		1970	1971	1972	1973
Less developed countries					
Major oil exporters	9	11	8	7	12 1/2
Other developing countries	6	6 1/2	5 1/2	9 1/2	7
Unit value [4]					
Industrial countries	1 1/2	6	5	8	19 1/2
Other developed countries	2	4	4	13	25
Less developed countries					
Major oil exporters	-1	2	22 1/2	11	39
Other developing countries	1 1/2	5	-1	8 1/2	27 1/2

Sources: National economic reports, IMF Data Fund, and Fund staff estimates.

[1] For classification of countries in groupings shown here, see Annual Report 1974, IMF, Table 1 (and especially footnotes 2-4).

[2] Compound annual rates of change.

[3] Fund member countries (listed in Annual Report 1974, IMF, Appendix Table 1.1) plus Switzerland. Based on approximate averages of growth rates for world exports and world imports.

[4] Based on indices in U.S. dollar terms.

*Annual Report 1974, International Monetary Fund, page 13.

101

Table Three*

GROWTH OF WORLD OUTPUT, 1960-73
(Percentage changes in real GNP)

	Annual Average[1]			Change from Preceding Year				
	1960-70	1960-65	1965-70	1969	1970	1971	1972	1973
Industrial countries	4.8	5.1	4.5	4.8	2.6	3.7	5.6	6.4
Canada	5.2	5.6	4.8	5.3	2.5	5.6	5.8	6.8
United States	4.0	4.9	3.2	2.7	-0.4	3.3	6.2	5.9
Japan	11.1	10.1	12.1	12.1	10.3	6.8	8.9	10.5
France	5.9	5.8	5.9	7.7	6.0	5.5	5.4	6.1
Germany, Fed. Rep. of	4.9	5.0	4.8	8.2	5.8	2.7	3.0	5.3
Italy	5.6	5.3	5.9	5.7	4.9	1.6	3.1	5.9
United Kingdom	2.7	3.3	2.1	1.6	1.8	2.3	2.3	6.0
Other industrial countries[2]	4.9	5.0	4.7	6.1	5.6	3.2	4.6	4.2
Primary producing countries	5.6	5.3	5.8	7.0	6.4	5.6	5.7	7.1
More developed areas[3]	5.8	5.9	5.8	7.3	6.0	5.7	5.6	6.3
Less developed areas[4]	5.5	5.1	5.8	6.9	6.6	5.6	5.7	7.5
World[5]	5.0	5.1	4.8	5.2	3.4	4.1	5.6	6.5

Sources: National economic reports, secretariat of the Organization for Economic Cooperation and Development, secretariat of the United Nations, U.S. Agency for International Development, International Bank for Reconstruction and Develop-

Table Three (continued)

ment and Fund staff estimates.

[1]Compound annual rates of change.

[2]Austria, Belgium, Denmark, Luxembourg, the Netherlands, Norway, Sweden, and Switzerland.

[3]Comprise Australia, Finland, Greece,Iceland, Ireland, Malta, New Zealand, Portugal, South Africa, Spain, Turkey, and Yugoslavia.

[4]Comprise Fund member countries not listed above as "Industrial countries," or as being in "More developed areas" (footnote 3, above). In some of the other tables in this chapter, the less developed countries are subdivided to distinguish the "major oil exporters" (Algeria, Indonesia, Iran, Iraq, Kuwait, the Libyan Arab Republic, Nigeria, Saudi Arabia, and Venezuela) and "other developing countries."

[5]Fund member countries (listed in Annual Report 1974, IMF, Appendix Table I.1) plus Switzerland.

*Annual Report 1974, International Monetary Fund, page 4.

Given the unpredictable oscillations in foreign-exchange rates, and the high direct costs of buying and selling foreign exchange through widened bid-ask spreads, this high growth in world trade seems surprising. Should economists feel pleased that the international monetary chaos has not dampened real trade flows? Free traders might well associate the increased international commerce of recent years with rising welfare gains from foreign trade. And they are probably right.

Yet there is a potentially important qualification to the welfare gains from trade when exchange rates move rather wildly and differential price inflation is rampant. I refer to "false" trading: goods move according to transitory price-cost relationships that do not accurately reflect long-run comparative advantage. Remembering the rather rapid alignments and disalignments of national price levels on a month-to-month or quarter-to-quarter basis analyzed above, let us illustrate the possibility of false trading heuristically.

Trade takes place when the money costs of producing in Country A for shipment to Country B at the prevailing exchange rate are low enough to be privately profitable - - and vice versa. Suppose the domestic money costs of producing most manufactured goods are fairly stable (or slowly rising or falling) over periods of weeks or months. Let us also suppose the exchange rate begins to vary randomly up and down, or vary cyclically so as to show no trend. Due to the stickiness of domestic money costs, the exchange rate varies more than the domestic currency prices of manufactured goods.[18] When Country B's currency is abnormally appreciated, the pressure of manufactured exports will flow from A to B. When B's currency is abnormally depreciated, the flow will be from B to A. At least some such contractual commitments (possibly successfully hedged against foreign-exchange risk) will be honored by business firms in countries A and B, resulting in virtually the same manufactured good being shipped first in one direction, and then in another. Excess transport costs are incurred, and true comparative advantage (which country has the lowest real costs of production) becomes blurred.

With more than two countries, the possibility of false movements is greater: goods could move first from A to B and then from B to C, rather than directly from A to C. A sufficiently sharp change in exchange rates might even move the same goods from C back to A. Speculation in traded manufactured goods could reduce the incidence of such false trading, although the presence of stabilizing speculation in commodity markets is hardly consistent with the absence of stabilizing speculation in the foreign-exchange markets themselves.

---

[18] The prices of certain homogeneous primary commodities may be virtually instantaneously arbitraged across national boundaries so that their prices fluctuate with the exchange rate. However, at least some goods - - particularly manufactures - - are not in this category.

Is "false" trade due to exchange-rate disequilibria likely to increase the measured volume of world trade? One can't easily tell a priori. If country A's currency is unduly depreciated vis-à-vis country B's, exports from A to B are artificially stimulated but imports from B are curtailed. The resulting financial gap may be covered by a capital flow, or simply by a temporary change in the terms of trade in B's favor since its currency has appreciated and export prices may well be sticky in the home currency. In the multilateral case, exchange-rate instability may accentuate "false" transshipments of goods, but are these likely to be greater than the socially efficient multilateral trade that is inhibited?

At the present time, therefore, the welfare implications of the striking rise in the volumes of international trade are difficult to interpret. Who is to say a priori, or even econometrically, whether or not the current rise in international trade is a response to true comparative advantage - - itself difficult to define - - or reflects a churning of commodity and service transactions that reflects reduced efficiency in the world economy? But this uncertainty is insufficient reason for public intervention to block this or that trade flow. Chaotic as they are, the foreign-exchange markets still contain valuable information on relative costs - - information on which public authorities are unlikely to improve. However, the unit-of-account or standard-of-value role of international money - - in the broad sense of the convertible-currency system - - has been impaired.

Concluding Note

A clear consensus on our experience with floating exchange rates is impossible, yet a theme exists.

The same monetary instability that makes floating necessary is responsible for the absence of stabilizing speculation on the one hand, and for shifting cost-price disalignments on the other. Just as conventional macroeconomic theory - - whether Keynesian or monetarist - - has not captured the financial disorganization and welfare costs of unanticipated price inflation, [19] neither do conventional models of the balance of payments capture the potential efficiency losses in international trade from unknown differentials in national inflation rates. Indeed, national autonomy in macroeconomic policy has been a cornerstone of Keynesian and monetarist theorizing; but in practice unrestricted autonomy generates great

---

[19] Quixotically, formal Keynesian and monetarist theories both treat unanticipated inflation as being less harmful than inflation that is fully discounted. In the Keynesian view, unanticipated inflation might reduce the expected real wage and so increase employment and real GNP as conventionally measured. In the monetarist view, if people do not anticipate inflation, they might hold higher real cash balances. In neither approach is the welfare cost to ordinary people of future uncertainty given significant weight. At least in policy recommendations, although not in theory, monetarists have recognized the importance of being honest with the populace about the future value of money.

uncertainty. Whatever its failings, the old Bretton Woods parity system did provide information on foreign-exchange policies, and - - to a lesser extent - - on domestic monetary policies.

Both domestically and internationally, therefore, more complete information on national monetary regimes should be made available to private banks, manufacturers, and merchants. Indeed, the great value of any new international monetary agreement might be to force national monetary and fiscal authorities to reveal more precisely what their future obligations are to each other, and to everyone else.

APPENDIX A: FOREIGN-EXCHANGE QUOTATIONS

The following pages provide quotations on interbank bid-ask spreads, kindly provided on an informal basis by the Bank of America's foreign-exchange division in San Francisco. The quotations do not necessarily represent the exchange rates at which trade actually took place among banks - - in fact, the stated spreads may underestimate the spreads in actual trading. Moreover, customers of the banks involved might face wider bid-ask spreads - - although direct data on this seems unavailable. There is reason to believe, however, that these last two factors are fairly constant, and do not distort the significant changes in interbank quotations that have occurred from the 1960s or from a fixed-rate year like 1972, to floating rates in 1973-74.

Rather than a formal statistical analysis of changes in bid-ask spreads, I shall simply present "raw" data on the dollar prices of major foreign currencies available to a foreign-exchange trader for four representative points in time: September 29, 1972; June 18, 1973; January 31, 1974; and October 1, 1974. Further information going back to the 1960s is hard to get on a strictly comparable basis. However, fragmentary information for some countries from the 1960s can be informally compared to the data presented in the tables for 1972, 1973, and 1974.

In each of the four tables, bid-ask spreads in distant futures are greater than for spot quotations or near futures. As we pass from 1972 to 1974, bid-ask spreads widen substantially at every maturity - - particularly for those currencies that had been pegged under the old Smithsonian system. However, measured as a percent of the spot exchange rate itself, the bid-ask spread in distant futures has widened much more with the advent of floating rates. For German marks for example, the bid-ask spread in 1972 for 6-month futures was 2 basis points (.006 percent), whereas by January 1974 this spread had risen 14 basis points (.04 percent). Back in December of 1971 (not shown in tables), the spread was only about 5/8 of a basis point.

Looking at the percentage forward premia and discounts (from the figures in parentheses), major turning points in spot exchange rates - - as portrayed in Figure I above - - were not predicted accurately at all. The high premium on the Japanese yen in September 1972 is about the only accurate indication of changes in exchange rates to come in 1973. On the other hand, on June 18, 1973, almost all forward quotations showed (incorrectly) premia against the dollar just two or three months before the dollar rose sharply.

INTERBANK FOREIGN EXCHANGE QUOTATIONS:* September 29, 1972

(dollars per unit of foreign currency)

	Spot U.S. Terms		1 month		3 months		6 months		12 months	
	Bid	Offer	Bid	Offer	Bid	Offer	Bid	Offer	Bid	Offer
STERLING Floating	2.4205	2.4210	2.4148 (2.83D)	2.4159	2.4040 (2.73D)	2.4050	2.3879 (2.69D)	2.3892	2.3625 (2.40D)	2.3
CANADIAN DOLLAR Floating	1.0164 1/2	1.0167	1.0165 1/2 (.12P)	1.0170	1.0167 1/2 (.12P)	1.0172	1.0168 (.07P)	1.0172 1/2	1.0158 1/2 (.06D)	1.0166
BELGAIN FRANC C=.022314 **	.022625	.022635	.022658 (1.75P)	.022679	.022735 (1.94P)	.022765	.022835 (1.86P)	.022865	.022970 (1.48P)	.03
FRENCH FRANC C=.1955	.1994 7/8	.1995 1/2	.1995 3/8 (.30P)	.1996 5/8	.1998 1/8 (.65P)	.1999 1/2	.2000 5/8 (.58P)	.2002 1/4	.2004 3/8 (.48P)	.20
GERMAN MARK C=.3103	.3121 5/8	.3122 1/8	.3130 7/8 (3.56P)	.3132 3/8	.3149 3/8 (3.56P)	.3150 5/8	.3174 1/8 (3.36P)	.3176 1/8	.3215 1/8 (2.99P)	.3218
DUTCH GUILDER C=.3082	.3088 1/2	.3089 1/8	.3098 1/4 (3.79P)	.3099 7/8	.3117 3/4 (3.79P)	.3119 3/8	.3139 1/4 (3.29P)	.3141 7/8	.3170 (2.65P)	.3174
ITALIAN LIRE C=.001720	.001718 1/8	.001718 3/4	.001714 5/8 (2.44D)	.001717 1/4	.001709 1/8 (2.09D)	.001711 3/4	.001701 1/8 (1.98D)	.001703 3/4	.001685 1/8 (1.92D)	.001788
SWISS FRANCS C=.2604	.2630	.2630 5/8	.2638 1/2 (3.88P)	.2639 7/8	.2655 (3.80P)	.2656 1/8	.2676 1/2 (3.54P)	.2648 1/8	.2712 (3.12P)	.2714

108

INTERBANK FOREIGN EXCHANGE QUOTATIONS: * September 29, 1972 (continued)

	Bid	Offer	Bid	Offer	Bid	Offer	Bid	Offer	Bid	Offer
JAPANESE YEN	.003321 3/8		.003378 3/8		.003381 1/8		.003473 3/8			
C = .003247		.003322 1/2		.003344 1/2		.003393 1/2		.003491 1/2		
			(5.78P)		(7.33P)		(9.15P)			

* Figures in parentheses are percent per annum discount or premium over spot offer rate
**C indicates central rate under the short-lived Smithsonian System

INTERBANK FOREIGN EXCHANGE QUOTATIONS:* June 18, 1973

(dollars per unit of foreign currency)

	Spot U.S. Terms		1 month		3 months		6 months		12 months	
	Bid	Offer	Bid	Offer	Bid	Offer	Bid	Offer	Bid	Offer
STERLING	2.5840	2.5845	.25818	.25827 (0.84D)	2.5745	2.5755 (1.39D)	2.5643	2.5653 (1.49D)	2.5432	2.5445 (1.55D)
CANADIAN DOLLAR	1.0001	1.0004	1.0017	1.0022 (2.22P)	1.0038	1.0043 (1.56P)	1.0054	1.0060 (1.12P)	1.0056	1.0063 (0.59P)
BELGIAN FRANC	.026705	.026725	.026805	.026855 (5.84P)	.026935	.026985 (3.89P)	.027080	.027150 (3.18P)	.027440	.0225 (3.09P)
FRENCH FRANC	C.2360 / F.2365	.2362 / .2370	.2362	.2365 (1.65P)	.2365	.2368 (1.04P)	.2370	.2374 (1.06P)	.2380	.238 (0.75P)
DEUTSCHE MARK	.3909	.3912	.3911	.3916 (1.38P)	.3928	.3934 (2.25P)	.3955	.3962 (2.56P)	.4011	.401 (2.74P)
DUTCH GUILDER	.3686	.3690	.3696	.3703 (4.23P)	.3718	.3725 (3.79P)	.3739	.3747 (3.09P)	.3786	.379 (2.93P)
ITALIAN LIRE	C.001650 / F.001615	.00155 / .00125	.001654	.00163 (5.07P)	.001662	.001670 (3.63P)	.001667	.001678 (2.78P)	.001675	.001 (2.11P)
SWISS FRANC	.3289	.3292	.3303	.3308 (5.83P)	.3329	.3334 (5.10P)	.3358	.3363 (4.34P)	.3412	.332 (3.95P)
JAPANESE YEN	.003779	.0037782	.003792	.003800 (5.71P)	.003849	.003862 (8.46P)	.003919	.003937 (8.20P)	Not Available	

*Figures in parentheses are percent per annum discount or premium over spot offer rate

110

INTERBANK FOREIGN EXCHANGE QUOTATIONS:* January 31, 1974

(dollars per unit of foreign currency)

	Spot U.S. Terms		1 month		3 months		6 months		12 months	
	Bid	Offer	Bid	Offer	Bid	Offer	Bid	Offer	Bid	Offer
STERLING	2.2690	2.2710	2.2390	2.2422 (15.22D)	2.2070	2.2110 (10.57D)	2.1710	2.1750 (8.45D)	2.1115	2.115 (6.85D)
CANADIAN DOLLAR	1.0113	1.0116	1.0113	1.0118 (.24P)	1.0110	1.0115 (.04D)	1.0105	1.0110 (.1D)	1.0095	1.010 (.09D)
BELGIAN FRANC	.023545	.023575	.023485	.023560 (.8D)	.023380	.023425 (2.5D)	.023275	.023360 (1.8D)	Not Available	
FRENCH FRANC	C.1963 F.1925	.1966 .1930	.1946	.1953 (7.9D)	.1922	.1929 (7.5D)	.1904	.1911 (5.6D)	.1867	.189 (3.8D)
DEUTSCHE MARK	.3590	.3600	.3583	.3596 (1.3D)	.3575	.3590 (1.1D)	.3570	.3584 (0.8D)	.3568	.358 (0.5D)
DUTCH GUILDER	.3452	.3457	.3442	.3449 (2.8D)	.3423	.3432 (2.9D)	.3403	.3412 (2.6D)	.3382	.339 (1.7D)
ITALIAN LIRE	.001511	.001514	.001502	.001509 (4.0D)	.001490	.001497 (4.5D)	.001475	.001484 (4.0D)	Not Available	
SWISS FRANC	.3045	.3050	.3040	.3049 (.4D)	.3034	.3043 (.9D)	.3034	.3045 (.3D)	.3034	.304 (.2D)
JAPANESE YEN	.003347	.003348	.003306	.003315 (11.8D)	.003223	.003235 (13.5D)	.003172	.003188 (9.6D)	Not Available	

*Figures in parentheses are percent per annum discount or premium over spot offer rate

111

INTERBANK FOREIGN EXCHANGE QUOTATIONS:* October 1, 1974

(dollars per unit of foreign currency)

	Spot U.S. Terms		1 month		3 months		6 months		12 months	
	Bid	Offer	Bid	Offer	Bid	Offer	Bid	Offer	Bid	Offer
STERLING	2.3360	2.3368	2.3320	2.3332 (1.85D)	2.3194	2.3207 (2.76D)	2.2983	2.2996 (3.18D)	1.1590	1.160 (3.25D)
CANADIAN DOLLAR	1.0151	1.0154	1.0152	1.0159 (0.65P)	1.0162	1.0168 (0.55P)	1.0165	1.0171 (0.33P)	1.0169	1.017 (0.25P)
BELGIAN FRANC	.025500	.025530	- - - - - - - - - NOT - - - - - - - - AVAILABLE - - - - - - - - -							
FRENCH FRANC	.2113	.2114	.2103	.2105 (5.10D)	.2085	.2088 (4.92D)	.2053	.2057 (5.39D)	.2003	.201 (4.82D)
DEUTSCHE MARK	.3774	.3778	.3779	.3785 (2.22P)	.3796	.3803 (2.65P)	.3808	.3816 (2.01P)	.3838	.384 (1.88P)
DUTCH GUILDER	.37045	.37075	.37085	.37135 (1.94P)	.37245	.37295 (2.37P)	.37365	.37415 (1.83P)	.37355	.374 (0.97P)
ITALIAN LIRE	.001514	.001515	.001506	.001509 (4.75D)	.001486	.001489 (6.86D)	.001450	.001455 (7.92D)	.001389	.001 (6.93D)
SWISS FRANC	.3395	.3398	.34015	.3406 (2.83P)	.3406	.3410 (1.47P)	.3416	.3423 (1.50P)	.3439	.344 (1.46P)
JAPANESE YEN	.003352	.003355	.003350	.003357 (0.45P)	.003337	.003346 (1.18D)	.003335	.003344 (0.66D)	.003324	.003 (0.35D)

*Figures in parentheses are percent per annum discount or premium over spot offer rate

REFERENCES

1. Friedman, Milton. "The Case for Flexible Exchange Rates," pp. 157-203, in M. Friedman, Essays in Positive Economics. Chicago: University of Chicago Press, 1953.

2. Grassman, Sven. Exchange Reserves and The Financial Structure of Foreign Trade. Stockholm: Saxon House, 1973.

3. Hirsch, Fred and David Highman. "Floating Rates- -Expectations and Experience," Three Banks Review, June 1974.

4. International Monetary Fund. International Financial Statistics (various issues).

5. _____ Annual Report, 1974.

6. Johnson, Harry. "The Case for Flexible Exchange, 1969" pp. 198-228, in H. Johnson, Further Essays in Monetary Economics. Allan and Unwin, 1972.

7. Kasper, Wolfgang. "The Effects of Exchange-Rate Changes: Recent International Currency Experience," Canberra. August, 1974 (Processed).

8. Kouri, Pentti and Michael Porter. "International Capital Flows and Portfolio Equilibrium," Journal of Political Economy, May/June, 1974.

9. Krul, Nicholas. "Floating Exchange Rates and Euromarkets," prepared for a conference, What Have We Learned From a Year of Greater Flexibility of Exchange Rates? Williamsburg, Virginia, May 1974.

10. Machlup, Fritz. The Alignment of Foreign Exchange Rates. New York: Praeger, 1972.

11. McKinnon, Ronald I. "A New Tripartite Agreement or a Limping Dollar Standard?" Essays in International Finance, No. 106, Princeton University, October 1974.

113

12. _____ . "Beyond Fixed Parities: The Analytics of International Monetary Agreements" in Robert Z. Aliber(ed.) , The Political
Economy of International Economic Reform, (forthcoming).

13. _____ , "Monetary Theory and Controlled Flexibility in the
Foreign Exchanges," Essays in International Finance , No. 84, Princeton University, April 1971.

14. ___·_____,"Private and Official International Money," Essays in International Finance , No. 74, Princeton University, April 1969.

15. Sohmen, Egon. Flexible Exchange Rates. Chicago: University of Chicago
Press, 1961.

16. Williamson, John. "Exchange-Rate Flexibility and Reserve Use," Depart-
mental Memorandum, IMF (Processed), August 29, 1974.

17. Yeager, Leland. "Fluctuating Exchange Rates in the Nineteenth Century:
The Experiences of Austria and Russia," pp. 61-90, in R. Mundell and
A. Swoboda, Monetary Problems of the International Economy.
Chicago: University of Chicago Press, 1969.

ASSESSING EXPERIENCE WITH FLOATING EXCHANGE RATES:
A COMMENT

Peter B. Kenen

Princeton University

To judge the performance of floating exchange rates in 1973-74, one has first to answer explicitly these three questions: (1) What sort of float have we had? (2) What have we asked it to accomplish? (3) What standard of comparison can we use to judge it? My own answers to these questions will lead me to conclude that floating rates have served us fairly well, but to warn that this two-year experience does not supply an adequate rationale for a more permanent commitment to this or any similar exchange-rate regime.

What sort of float have we had? Let us agree immediately that it bears little resemblance to the textbooks' description of general and free flexibility, even as the pegged-rate regime that preceded it bore little resemblance to the textbooks' gold standard or, for that matter, to the Bretton Woods Agreement that spawned it. Many countries continue to peg their currencies to one of the key currencies (or to an average of currency values, including the market-basket SDR), and even those that disavow a parity or central rate have intervened frequently and massively to influence or stabilize exchange rates.

Anyone familiar with the theory of optimum currency areas, including McKinnon's contribution, ought not to be surprised by the continued prevalence of pegging. Small open economies - - the majority of countries - - are not optimum currency areas. Some of the smallest, economically or geographically, do not even constitute feasible areas. The reasons and consequences differ, however, with country size and degree of development, and are also different from some of those set forth in the earlier literature.

The smallest, least-developed countries are usually linked commercially to one major country or one international commodity market with a single currency of contract. For them, formal flexibility does not imply much variability. Their governments give other reasons for pegging the exchange rate. Third-world rhetoric stresses youth rather than dependence, and governments explain that they must peg exchange rates because domestic financial institutions are insufficiently experienced to conduct a well-functioning foreign-exchange market. But even if those governments could (or can) opt for floating, traders and bankers whose business is denominated in one foreign currency would act in ways that work to peg the rate.[1]

The larger, more-developed countries, including nations like Austria and the Netherlands, have found that flexibility vis à vis the currencies of countries with which they trade heavily (or those with which they must compete in third markets) can destabilize output and employment in their large traded-goods sectors. Furthermore, because they are developed financially as well as industrially, the exchange rate responds in the short run to differences in interest rates, not to trends or fluctuations in the prices of traded goods. In consequence, domestic and foreign monetary policies can have unwanted or excessive effects on the domestic economy. Countries of this type, then, have chosen to peg their currencies to those of their partners or competitors, or, what comes to much the same thing from the standpoint of domestic stabilization, have chosen to emulate the monetary policy of the country with which they have the closest financial relations. At the start of the current float, Austria pegged the schilling to a composite of foreign currencies, but has deleted one currency after another from that composite until, for all practical purposes, it has pegged the schilling to the mark. Switzerland has not pegged the franc, but the Swiss National Bank looks more and more like a branch of the Bundesbank; Swiss monetary policy has followed German, to avoid changes in the franc-mark rate harmful to Swiss industry in foreign and domestic markets.

Kindleberger is quite right. Canadian experience is not unique, and floating exchange rates do not confer autonomy in monetary policy. But this is because Mundell was right, not wrong, in his assertion that floating rates enhance the effects of monetary policy on domestic activity. The much-discussed stability of the Canadian exchange rate, currently and earlier, is due in part to firmly held (inelastic) expectations - - the dollar-is-a-dollar view to which Kindleberger says he used to adhere. But it is also due to what one might call the bill-rate-is-a-bill-rate view taken by the Canadian authorities, who rarely allowed their monetary policies to diverge substantially from those of the United States.

Switzerland and other countries have adopted this same dictum; they have geared their monetary policies to the requirements of exchange-rate sta-

---

[1] There is perhaps another way to make this point. In countries of this type, costs and prices in the traded-goods sector are determined in large measure by world prices and the exchange rate. There is little import-competing production, and domestic markets for exportables are quite small (as are those for the factors of production employed by the traded-goods sector). Costs and prices are not heavily influenced by domestic macroeconomic policies. Therefore, there is no fundamental reason for the exchange rate to change (or to expect that it will do so), and the convenience of traders and bankers is well-served by keeping it stable - - a motive sufficient to cause them to act in ways that tend to keep it stable. In more-developed economies, by contrast, domestic markets and policies impart more rigidity to home-currency costs and prices in the traded-goods sector , and changes in exchange rates are not redundant. In these countries, moreover, autonomous financial transactions bulk larger in the balance of payments - - capital mobility dominates the day-to-day determination of the exchange rate - - so that changes in rates may not be consonant with stable output and employment in the traded-goods sector.

bility. Under pegged exchange rates, small and medium-sized countries could not conduct independent monetary policies; movements of reserves determined the supply of high-powered money. Under flexible exchange rates, they are capable of independence; the central banks determine the supply of high-powered money. But they do not dare to exercise their independence.[2]

The most important point for present purposes, however, is that the relationships between major currencies have not been determined entirely by the market. There have been large movements of reserves, testifying to official intervention in the foreign-exchange markets, and there has been an unprecedented volume of official and quasi-official borrowing that has served the same purpose as outright intervention. Britain, France, and Italy borrowed billions of Eurodollars in the early months of 1974, and Japan borrowed heavily in the United States following the end of U.S. controls over bank lending to foreigners. When one adds the large usage of reserves to this huge borrowing, one has surely to conclude that official support of exchange rates was larger in 1974 than in any year before 1970, when the Bretton Woods system began to break down. [3]

Doctrinaire advocates of flexible rates seize upon this fact to explain away imperfections of the current float, especially the short-run instability of rates. If only the authorities would stay out of the market, they tell us, rates would behave in textbook fashion. Speculators would no longer have to anticipate the central banks' behavior - - they could concentrate on underlying economic trends - - and they would act to stabilize exchange rates. I share McKinnon's skepticism. In light of what we know about the difficulties of predicting prices, production, trade, and capital flows during these turbulent years, and in light of what McKinnon tells us about the risks of being wrong, I doubt that speculators would have been more venturesome or more stabilizing in the absence of official intervention.

Yet I cannot agree entirely with McKinnon's explanation for the deficiency of speculation. He is quite right to emphasize the lessons of Herrstatt - - that losses can be large relative to capital and that a long position in foreign currency can be frozen suddenly by someone else's error. These are good reasons for being risk averse. But he attaches too much importance to the decline in the international moneyness of the dollar. There has, of course, been a

---

[2] The assertion that flexible exchange rates confer monetary autonomy can have at least three meanings, and Kindleberger tends to elide them. It can mean that the authorities are able to control the stock of high-powered money. It can mean that they are able to control the interest rate. It can mean that they are able to pursue domestic objectives free of any balance-of-payments constraint. The first assertion is more or less accurate. The second has been contradicted by experience. The third is true but is not very meaningful when international capital mobility forges strong connections between national interest rates.

[3] See also John Williamson (1974).

117

significant decline. It started long before the float, when we ceased to believe that the dollar could not depreciate, and it has made speculation somewhat more difficult. When one expects the pound to depreciate, it is no longer sufficient to sell pounds for dollars; one has then to sell dollars for marks. There are two new costs to speculating - - the costs of choosing one's final destination and the costs of getting there. But neither of these costs is very large, nor are they uniquely connected to floating.

More important in my view is the fact which McKinnon dismisses because it seems too simple to explain so much. Speculators have been reluctant to take large positions because it has been extraordinarily hard to form firm opinions about trends in rates. The two years of floating have been uniquely complicated. They have been years of rapid inflation, of huge oil-related shocks to trade and payment flows, and of unusual political uncertainty in many major industrial countries, especially in the United States. It has been difficult to make short-term forecasts and correspondingly painful to act decisively on the basis of one's forecasts.

Textbook descriptions of flexible exchange rates tell us this sort of story. There is, they say, a system in equilibrium. It is disturbed by some small shock - - a change in relative rates of inflation, relative interest rates, or some such thing. The spot exchange rate moves immediately to or toward a new equilibrium, helped along by well-informed speculation. The float of 1973-74 resembles this description not at all. The system did not start out in equilibrium. It was not subject to a single, small shock, but to a series of large ones. And the economic implications of the shocks were not always readily discernible.

What have we asked the float to accomplish? I have already given part of my answer, but let me enlarge it. Remember, first of all, that the float began as a ragged retreat. There was no single decision to install a new exchange-rate regime. Nor was there any effort to clear away the wreckage of the old. The attitudes and circumstances that led individual governments to back away from pegged rates were the same ones that led them collectively to suspend the work of the Committee of Twenty and to set aside the timetable for European monetary integration. [4] Remember, too, that world payments were in flow disequilibrium - - there was a gaping deficit in the U.S. balance of payments - - and, as Kindleberger reminds us, in stock disequilibrium as well. To make matters worse, inflation rates were rising everywhere, and national financial markets were in disarray. There followed in short order the oil embargo, the increase in

---

[4] On the attitudes and circumstances that led to suspension of negotiations in the Committee of Twenty, see Peter B. Kenen (1974).

oil prices, the first signs of a worldwide recession, and a constitutional crisis in the United States.

Recall the situation in May or June of 1974. What was the long-term prospect for the dollar? Would Mr. Nixon refuse to resign and go to trial before the Senate? What would happen to U.S. foreign and economic policy during that ordeal? Was the U.S. economy already starting into a recession, and what would be done to combat it? Would interest rates decline? Would stock prices revive? Would the United States adopt a tough energy policy or would its oil bill rise rapidly? And where would the OPEC countries put their money? Would the overall effects of the increase in oil prices strengthen or weaken the dollar? There are times, and this was one, when it is hard to form a comprehensive view and harder still to hold it with conviction.

It is perhaps fair to say that, had the float not started in March 1973, it would have started in a more disorderly way during the weeks following the Yom Kippur War. The uncertainties unleashed by that episode and the sauve qui peut attitudes it spawned would have undermined any remaining commitment to the Bretton Woods sytem. But before we say what has been said too often and carelessly - - that floating rates have met the tests posed by the high oil price and petrodollar flows - - note one vital fact: the foreign-exchange markets have not yet been forced to deal with the massive financial flows associated with the oil situation. Oil payments and OPEC capital flows have not begun to cross those markets. Payments for oil have been made almost entirely in dollars and sterling, and most of the OPEC surplus has been lodged, at least temporarily, in those same two currencies. We do not yet know how well foreign-exchange markets will cope with a large shift in the destination or denomination of oil-related flows.

What standard of comparison should we use to judge the float? I have already given one reply to this question. It should not be compared to the textbook description of flexibility. But this answer is incomplete. The more important caveat, relevant especially to Kindleberger's paper, is a warning against any comparison with a well-functioning fixed-rate regime. The current float began because governments and central banks were unwilling or unable to obey the rules of the fixed-rate game and could not attach any operational meaning to the famous goal of "stable but adjustable" exchange rates.

What, then, is left as the standard of comparison? It is, I submit, our best guess about the way in which central banks and governments would have muddled through the flow and stock disequilibria of 1970-73, the inflation of 1973-74, and our other afflictions, had they been obliged to peg exchange rates from day to day, making only the infrequent parity changes allowed by the Bretton Woods rules.

119

Would they have done so badly? The British and Italians might have had to borrow more to cope with speculative capital outflows. The Germans would have complained bitterly about imported inflation, but would probably have found new ways to repel or sterilize capital inflows. The effective exchange rate for the dollar would not be far from what it is now - - some fifteen percentage points below what it was before August 15, 1971. The distribution of speculators' profits and losses would be a bit different, but no one (apart from the speculators) would care very much.

I do not disagree with McKinnon's assertion. Return to a system of fixed rates is out of the question. But I do disagree with his inference - - that there is an "imperial need for floating rates at the present time." The float was not inevitable. It was not and is not necessary, save to disguise the timidity of central banks and governments. And I doubt that floating rates will last very long. With Kindleberger, I believe that "the world will muddle along without clear direction until . . . the market settles gradually on a system of fixed rates, or rates held steady within narrow margins, which governments ultimately find it easy and convenient to support." I look indeed to the early emergence of something like a gliding-parity regime without announced parities, beginning with a gradual enlargement of existing currency areas - - the snake swallowing the French franc and some smaller morsels - - and the eventual stabilization of rates between those currency areas.

Change in exchange rates will still be required, Kindleberger's elasticity pessimism notwithstanding. Lags are long, transfer prices rigid, and profits unpredictably compressible; but there has been a significant rectification of the earlier flow disequilibrium, and this must be ascribed in part to the significant depreciation of the dollar in 1971-73. More important for international economic integration, there has been an ebbing of protectionist sentiment in the United States, and this has been due in large measure to the change in the competitive position of its import-competing industries, especially the change vis à vis Japan. Governments will go on making mistakes like those that led to the disequilibria of 1970-73, and changes in exchange rates will be needed to compensate for those mistakes. But floating may not be the best technique for making those changes. It may impart too much disintegrative influence to those same vagaries of economic policy which make it impossible to fix rates forever.

REFERENCES

1. Kenen, Peter B., "Monetary Reform - - You Can't Get There from Here," Euromoney, (September 1974), 19-23.

2. Williamson, John., "Exchange Rate Flexibility and Reserve Use," August 1974 (mimeograph).

OUR RECENT EXPERIENCE WITH FIXED
AND FLEXIBLE EXCHANGE RATES:
A COMMENT

Michael Mussa
University of Rochester

The papers by Professors Kindleberger and McKinnon provide much food for thought concerning our recent experience with flexible exchange rates. Indeed, there are so many tantilizing tidbits that to attempt to sample them all would put one in serious danger of indigestion. Accordingly, I shall restrict my remarks to a limited diet, focusing on three main issues. First, what can we learn from our recent experience concerning the applicability of various theories of the behavior of the balance of payments and of exchange rates? Second, what has been the role of "speculation" in influencing the movement of exchange rates and flows of funds? Third, to what extent have flexible exchange rates enhanced the capacity of individual governments to pursue independent monetary and fiscal policies and to insulate their own economies from disturbances originating in the rest of the world?

I. A MONETARY INTERPRETATION OF RECENT EVENTS

Professor Kindleberger discusses the relative merits of the elasticities approach, the absorption approach, and the monetary approach to balance of payments analysis in the light of our recent experience. I would like to take issue both with Professor Kindleberger's interpretation of the alternative approachs and with his conclusions concerning their relative capacities to explain our recent experience. My particular concern is with the interpretation of the monetary appraoch and with its capacity to explain both the events leading up to the breakdown of the fixed rate system and our recent experience with flexible rates.

The monetary approach to balance of payments analysis under a fixed exchange rate regime has three essential ingredients. [1] First, the monetary approach asserts that the behavior of the official settlements balance is essentially a monetary phenomenon in the sense that it necessarily involves an analysis of the behavior of the demand for and the supply of money. Second, the monetary approach focuses on the demand for and the supply of money as the proximate determinants of the behavior of the official settlements balance and

---

[1] A more extensive discussion of the basic features of the monetary approach is given in Mussa (1974).

analyzes the way in which various policy and parameter changes affect the official settlements balance through their effects on the demand for and the supply of money. Third, the monetary approach concentrates on the long-run behavior of the balance of payments and takes an eclectic view of the short-run processes whereby these long-run consequences are brought about. These essential features of the monetary approach do not constitute a formal model or imply particular formulas for the effects of devaluation or other policy changes on the balance of payments. Rather, they are the general characteristics of a broad class of theoretical models which share the common sense presumption that money matters, at least in the analysis of monetary phenomena.

Formal models which embody the essential features of the monetary approach have been presented in a number of recent papers. [2] By making reference to this work, it is possible to dispel some of the confusion which has arisen with respect to the monetary approach and its relationship to alternative approaches to balance of payments analysis. First, there is no conflict between the monetary approach and the absorption approach. In dealing with the process of adjustment, the monetary approach lays emphasis on the fact that any accumulation of foreign exchange requires an excess of receipts (from sales of goods and assets) over expenditure (on goods and assets). This fact is the central focus of the absorption approach. What the monetary approach adds to the absorption approach is a theory of how long the accumulation (or decumulation) of foreign exchange can go on before the consequences of changes in the stock of money choke off the divergence between receipts and expenditures.

Second, the monetary approach deals primarily with the official settlements account, and not with the current account. There has been some confusion on this issue because the current account and the official settlements account are identical in theoretical models which assume capital immobility and abstract from private and government transfers. In a world of capital mobility, however, current account deficits can be balanced by capital account surpluses, without any effect on the official settlements account. The monetary approach suggests that this is precisely what will happen as the result of a policy or parameter change, unless the change in question has a direct or indirect effect on the demand for or the supply of money. For instance, if domestic residents decide to spend more on domestic consumption at the expense of the accumulation of interest bearing assets (without any effect on the desire to hold or accumulate money), then the monetary approach would predict that the result

---

[2] See, especially, Dornbusch (1973), (1974), and (1975), Frenkel (1971), Frenkel and Rodriguez (1975), Johnson (1973), and the essays in Frenkel and Johnson (1975).

would be a current account deficit financed by a capital account surplus, with negligible effect on the official settlements account.

Third, the monetary approach is not a partial equilibrium approach. The monetary approach does focus on a single relationship as the proximate determinant of the behavior of the official settlements balance. But, this does not imply that other relationships are unimportant in the analysis. Indeed, much of the recent work in the monetary approach has dealt with the question of how the whole structure of the economy influences the demand for and the supply of money. For instance, Dornbusch's work on the role of non-traded goods, Frenkel and Rodriquez' work on capital mobility, and my own work on tariffs and commercial policy [3] all emphasize the role of "non-monetary" factors in influencing the behavior of the balance of payments.

Fourth, the monetary approach does not rely on the real balance effect as the principal determinant of fluctuations in the level of expenditure. In some early work on the monetary approach, the real balance effect was utilized as the simplest and most direct method of developing a monetary model of the process of adjustment under fixed exchange rates. However, it is possible to construct monetary models of the balance of payments in which there is no real balance effect, but in which a decrease in the real value of the money supply reduces expenditure by driving up interest rates. The most general models of the monetary approach envision a number of linkages between money and expenditure. For instance, in discussing the effects of a devaluation, monetarists would point to the direct effect of devaluation in increasing the nominal prices of traded goods, thereby reducing real money balances, and hence reducing expenditure through both a direct real balance effect and through the indirect effect of increases in interest rates on domestically traded securities. Monetarists would also point to the effects of devaluation on the relative prices of tradables and non-tradables and the tendency of a devaluation to shift expenditure in the direction of non-tradables. Further, there would be effects of portfolio adjustments as domestic residents sell off some of their internationally tradable assets in order to restore the real value of their money holdings. In addition, a devaluation would be expected to stimulate foreign demand for exportables (which are not perfect substitutes for foreign goods) by reducing their relative price in world markets. In the short run, such an increase in demand would be expected to lead to an increase in output. Provided that the short-run marginal propensity to spend is less than one, this increase in output should induce an excess of income over expenditure. Further, the increase in output would increase the

---

[3] See Dornbusch (1973) and (1974), Frenkel and Rodriguez (1974); and Mussa (1975).

demand for money, putting upward pressure on interest rates which would tend to depress expenditure.

There is little in this discussion of the channels through which a devaluation affects the balance of payments which is the unique province of the monetary approach. Indeed, at the level of general theoretical models, there is little difference between the monetary approach and the elasticities approach as represented by the work of Meade and Pearce. [4] What the monetary approach does is to focus on the behavior of critical monetary variables. The behavior of these variables, particularly the behavior of the domestic credit component of the money supply, is usually submerged in the elasticities approach behind the assumption that the monetary authorities pursue "accommodating" or "neutral" policies. Given the assumption about the response of monetary policy, the effects of, say, a devaluation are shown to depend on various "reduced form elasticities and marginal propensities" which take account of the response of monetary policy.

There are three basic objections to this procedure. First, while it is readily conceded that the behavior of the domestic credit component of the money supply is often endogeneously determined, it seems unlikely that any single policy is consistently followed in all countries at all times. For this reason, it is preferable to treat the domestic credit component as a separate variable in explaining the behavior of the official settlements balance and then to analyze why domestic credit behaved in a particular way. This procedure permits a more unified analysis of the determinants of the behavior of the balance of payments across a wide range of policies and institutional arrangements. Second, the use of "reduced form elasticities" confounds the direct effects of changes in relative prices with the induced responses of the monetary authorities. This creates the impression that monetary policy is of secondary importance when, in fact, it is the vital factor. Third, in discussions of policy and in policy oriented empirical work, the theoretical niceties tend to be forgotten. Advocates of the elasticities approach discuss "elasticity optimism" and "elasticity pessimism" and neglect the response of monetary policy. Monetarists focus on the demand for money and the supply of money and treat the concepts of elasticity optimism and pessimism as nonsense. In my view, this is the essential difference between the two approaches. To the first order of approximation, what is the critical determinant of the official settlements balance, the behavior of relative prices or the demand and supply of money?

---

[4] See Meade (1951a) and (1951b), and Pearce (1961) and (1970). Also see Tsiang (1961).

126

To provide support for the monetarist position on this question, I will analyze three recent events from the perspective of the monetary approach to balance of payments analysis: the French devaluation of 1969, the collapse of the dollar exchange standard in 1971, and the large fluctuations of exchange rates since 1972.

1969 French Devaluation

The source of the french devaluation of August 1969 was the political disturbances of May 1968. As shown in Table 1, prior to the second quarter of 1968, the Bank of France had accumulated large net holdings of foreign assets. In the second quarter of 1968, net foreign assets of the Bank of France fell by nine billion francs. Of this decline, approximately one billion francs was associated with a deterioration in the trade balance. The rest was accounted for by a capital outflow, through both the private sector and the commercial banking system. This outflow was probably the result of political uncertainty which significantly increased the desire of French residents to hold non-franc denominated assets and, in particular, to reduce their holdings of francs. Newspapers reported that people were carrying suitcases of francs into Germany and Switzerland and exchanging them for foreign money. Note, however, that the supply of reserve money did not fall. The Bank of France increased its domestic assets by seventeen billion francs, enough to provide for an unusually large increase in the money supply.

The resolution of the political crisis involved a deal in which the unions were pacified by a large wage increase together with a promise that prices would not rise by a comparable amount. The effects of this deal are also shown in Table 1: between the first quarter and the third quarter of 1968 the index of wages rose by ten per cent; consumer prices rose by two per cent; and both export and import prices fell by about two per cent. In 1968-III, the trade balance actually improved, but net foreign assets of the Bank of France fell by another five billion francs. Reserve money, however, fell by only one billion francs since the Bank of France increased its domestic assets by four billion francs. In effect, the Bank of France was financing the increase in wages at the expense of its foreign exchange reserves.

127

Table 1

France: 1967-I to 1970-IV

Billions of Francs   Indices: 1963 = 100

Quarter	Reserve Money	Domes. Net Assets of BOF	Foreign Assets of BOF	Trade Balance Surplus	Import Prices	Export Prices	Consumer Prices	Wages
1967-I	71.8	35.8	33.1	-1.4	104.1	107.9	110.6	125
II	74.2	38.5	32.9	0.0	105.6	107.0	111.0	128
III	76.1	40.6	33.3	0.2	102.3	106.4	111.8	129
IV	77.8	38.8	34.3	0.2	104.2	106.1	113.4	132
1968-I	73.8	37.8	34.0	0.0	102.9	106.6	115.0	134
II	81.2	53.6	25.3	-1.0	101.7	103.8	115.7	140
III	80.3	57.6	19.9	0.4	100.7	104.8	117.1	146
IV	83.3	61.6	18.4	-1.1	100.9	108.2	119.4	149
1969-I	82.8	63.6	16.1	-1.5	102.5	109.0	121.5	149
II	84.5	73.0	7.2	-2.1	103.3	110.7	123.1	153
III	84.1	73.9	6.6	-1.2	108.7	113.7	124.5	154
IV	82.7	72.0	9.3	-0.8	119.1	121.0	126.4	161
1970-I	80.3	64.5	13.2	-0.1	121.0	122.8	128.9	166
II	82.2	63.0	19.0	0.0	121.1	125.1	130.4	172
III	83.9	61.5	21.9	0.3	118.9	125.3	131.8	175
IV	86.4	62.4	23.9	0.6	119.1	129.1	133.3	179

Source: International Financial Statistics: 1973 Supplement,
International Monetary Fund, Washington, D.C., 1974.

In 1968-IV and the first two quarters of 1969, the trade balance deficit grew, first to one billion, then to one and a half, then to two billion francs. These trade deficits may be explained along traditional lines. Consumer prices rose relative to export prices and export prices rose relative to import prices. This is the pattern which should be expected as the increase in wages put upward pressure on the prices of French made goods, with the prices of exports held down somewhat by pressures in world markets. This change in relative prices would be expected to shift French expenditure away from French goods and towards imports, and, simultaneously, to reduce world demand for French exports. Note, however, that the emergence of a trade balance deficit required an excess of expenditure over income (in accord with the absorption approach) and that this excess was associated with an apparent willingness of the Bank of France to finance it by creating domestic credit.

In 1968-IV and 1969-I, the trade balance deficit accounted almost completely for the reduction in the net foreign assets of the Bank of France. In 1969-II the trade deficit rose to more than two billion francs while net foreign assets of the Bank of France fell by nine billion francs. This very large deficit, which was spread broadly across the trade and capital accounts, may well have reflected the political uncertainties created by the resignation of President de Gaulle, the symbol of postwar economic and political stability. Once again, the reduction in net foreign assets was prevented from reducing the supply of reserve money by a massive injection of domestic credit.

By August of 1969 the limit had been reached, and the franc was devalued by approximately eleven per cent. The response to devaluation was rapid. Comparing the quarter before devaluation, 1969-II, with the first full quarter after devaluation, 1969-IV, export and import prices rose by approximately the same amount as the devaluation. Over the same period, the general index of consumer prices rose by only three per cent. Wages more than kept pace with consumer prices, but fell relative to traded goods. Net foreign assets of the Bank of France increased by two billion francs between 1969-II and 1969-IV, despite the fact that the trade account remained in deficit (though the size of the trade deficit was reduced). By the second quarter of 1970, the index of wages had caught up with the increases in traded goods prices and far outstripped the increase in general consumer prices. Nevertheless, net foreign assets of the Bank of France continued to increase. Thus, the reduction of real wages was not critical for the success of the devaluation. What appears to have been the critical factor was the behavior of the domestic credit component of the monetary base which fell dramatically from its peak in 1969-III throughout all of 1970.

The case of the French devaluation is interesting for at least three reasons. First, the ultimate cause of the devaluation was neither a disturbance in the monetary sector nor a disturbance to relative prices and wages. The ultimate cause of the devaluation was a political disturbance. Nevertheless, the monetary approach to balance of payments analysis provides a useful framework for analyzing how the political disturbance came to be manifested in a loss of foreign assets by the Bank of France and, hence, ultimately led to a devaluation. Second, this example shows that there is no essential inconsistency between the absorption approach, the monetary approach, and the relative price approach to balance of payments analysis. Each approach plays a useful role in explaining some aspect of the course of events which followed upon the disturbances of May of 1968. Third, granting that relative prices and wages influenced the course of events, however, does not deny that monetary factors played a vital role. Between 1968-I and 1969-II, net foreign assets of the Bank of France fell by twenty-seven billion francs. If this loss had not been compensated by increased holdings of domestic assets, the supply' of reserve money would have fallen by more than a third. There can be little doubt that such a decline would have significantly altered the course of the French economy. Further, after the devaluation, the Bank of France induced (or allowed) the domestic credit component of the monetary base to decline. The contrast between the behavior of domestic credit before and after the devaluation is a vital factor in explaining the difference between the behavior of net foreign assets before and after the devaluation.

1971 Collapse of the Dollar Exchange Standard

In discussing the breakdown of the fixed rate system, Professor Kindleberger argues, "The only hypothesis which goes any distance to explaining why the United States lost exports and increased imports so abruptly is that its exchange rate had been adjusted to a dynamic comparative advantage, under which old exports losing out to imitation and United States direct investment abroad, were replaced by new products, innovated in the United States, and that this innovative process had precipitously halted." The monetary explanation of the breakdown of the dollar standard does not rely on such sudden shifts in comparative advantage. Rather, the monetary approach attributes the breakdown of the system to excess money creation in the United States during 1970 and 1971. The expansion of the money supply was motivated by a desire to stimulate domestic output and employment and was coupled with an official policy of benign neglect with respect to the balance of payments. The monetary expansion was excessive relative to the growth of the demand for money within the United States and relative to the willingness of foreigners to accumulate dollar claims. This problem was exacerbated by a downward shift in the demand to hold dollars as it became apparent that the Nixon administration would permit (and perhaps encourage) a devaluation of the dollar.

Some facts concerning the behavior of the U.S. economy from 1967 through 1972 are shown in Table 2. Table 3 shows a comparison of the two years immediately preceding the crisis of 1971 (1969-III to 1971-III) with the previous two years (1967-III to 1969-III). The earlier two-year interval was a period of rapid growth; GNP rose by 17.6%. On Keynesian grounds, one would expect that imports would tend to rise with income and hence that the trade balance would deteriorate. In fact, the cumulative trade balance surplus over the eight quarters 1967-IV to 1969-III was only 1.1 billion dollars-small relative to the normal annual trade surpluses of 4 to 6 billion which were recorded in the early 1960s. The official settlements balance from 1967-III to 1969-III showed a cumulative surplus of over 2.1 billion dollars. This was odd given the postwar record in which the official settlements balance was almost always in deficit and, particularly, given the poor current performance of the trade balance. The monetary explanation of this apparent anomaly, however, is straightforward. The money supply (currency plus demand deposits plus time deposits) grew by only 9.7% which was 7.9% less than the growth of GNP. Applying the rough rule of a unitary income elasticity of demand for money, this implies an excess of normal growth of the demand for money over growth of supply of approximately 30 billion dollars. Monetarists would argue that such a divergence should be expected to exert upward pressure on the official settlements balance.

The interval from 1969-III to 1971-III was a period of slow growth in the United States; GNP rose by only 12.9% and much of this was taken up by increases in prices. The trade balance showed slight improvement with a cumulative surplus for the eight quarters, 1969-IV through 1971-III, of almost 1.4 billion dollars. The official settlements balance, however, shows a massive cumulative deficit of 32.9 billion dollars. The deficit in the third quarter of 1971, 12.7 billion dollars, was larger than the foreign exchange reserves of any country, except the United States, prior to 1970. The monetary explanation for this deficit is two-fold: first, the money supply grew by 24.7% between 1969-III and 1971-III, far in excess of the 12.9% growth of GNP. Applying the rule of a unitary income elasticity of demand for money, this would imply an excess of growth of the supply of money over normal growth of demand of approximately 45 billion dollars, and indicate significant downward pressure on the official settlements balance. Second, as the official settlements deficits grew progressively larger and larger, reaching the unprecedented level of 6 billion dollars in 1971-II, it became increasingly apparent that a collapse of the dollar was imminent. In this circumstance, individuals, corporations, and banks began to unload dollars any way they could. The result was the huge official settlements deficit of the third quarter of 1971 which spread broadly across all items in the balance of payments, including 5 billion dollars in the category of "errors and omissions."

The official settlements deficits continued after August of 1971, though the scale of these deficits was reduced until the crisis of early 1973 in which the Smithsonian Agreement broke down. The deficits declined because the de facto depreciation of the dollar in August 1971 removed the immediate speculative

Table 2

United States: 1967-I to 1973-II

Quarter	GNP	Money Supply (M_2)	Off. Settle. Deficit	Trade Surplus
	Billions of Dollars		Millions of Dollars	
1967-I	774.4	335.0	1280	960
II	784.5	344.7	689	1307
III	800.9	351.7	39	725
IV	815.9	369.4	1390	491
1968-I	834.0	365.8	-91	261
II	857.4	373.7	-1550	438
III	875.2	380.7	-72	-172
IV	890.2	405.7	72	97
1969-I	907.0	391.6	-1711	123
II	923.5	397.6	-1204	128
III	941.7	385.8	1040	-234
IV	948.9	402.9	-825	607
1970-I	958.5	390.4	1974	661
II	970.6	406.3	2067	992
III	987.4	424.2	2612	191
IV	991.8	453.8	3186	332
1971-I	1027.2	462.0	4718	464
II	1046.9	476.4	6462	-795
III	1063.5	481.1	12704	-1071
IV	1084.2	508.5	5870	-1295
1972-I	1112.5	512.4	2506	-1566
II	1142.4	526.3	741	-1746
III	1166.5	535.5	5590	-1474
IV	1199.2	566.8	1503	-1474
1973-I	1242.5	573.8	9995	-595
II	1272.0	595.2	-804	-54

Source: International Financial Statistics: 1973
Supplement, International Monetary Fund, Washington, D.C., 1974.

132

Table 3

A Comparison of Changes Over Two Intervals

	1967-III to 1969-III	1969-III to 1971-III
% change in GNP	17.6	12.9
% change in M_2	9.7	24.7
sum of official settlements deficits	-2,126 mil. dol.	32,898 mil. dol.
sum of trade surpluses	1,132 mil. dol.	1,381 mil. dol.

Source: Table 2.

incentive to get out of dollars. The pressure of an excess supply of money, relative to normal demand, however, continued since the rate of growth of the money supply continued to exceed the rate of growth of GNP. [5] When speculation against the dollar resumed on a large scale in January 1973, the official settlements deficit grew to almost ten billion dollars. Again, this deficit reflected a generalized attempt to get out of dollars through every available channel; "errors and omissions" rose to 4 billion.

The trade balance shows substantial deficits from 1971-II throughout 1972. These deficits were remarkable relative to the normal post-war trade surpluses. However, the deterioration of the trade balance during this period was to be expected along standard Keynesian grounds. The acceleration of economic activity which began in mid-1971 would normally be expected to worsen the trade balance by driving up imports. Large trade deficits were recorded during this period because the normal tendency of the trade balance to deteriorate in the upswing of the business cycle was supplemented by large monetary pressures on the official settlements balance, some of which were reflected in the trade account.

Fluctuations of Exchange Rates Since 1972

Concerning recent fluctuations in exchange rates between major currencies, McKinnon concludes,". . . the very instability of exchange rates in the 1973-74 period militates against a pure price alignment view [of the determination of exchange rates]." These short term fluctuations, however, are consistent with the monetary approach to the balance of payments, adapted to a flexible exchange rate regime. The monetary approach emphasizes that the exchange rate is the relative price of national monies and is determined by the demands for and the supplies of these monies. The exchange rate is a relative asset price which is subject to many of the same influences as other asset prices, for instance, stock prices, and should exhibit short-run fluctuations which are similar to those exhibited by other asset prices. Further, like other asset prices, exchange rates should be highly sensitive to expectations of future exchange rates. If the monetary approach is correct, then one of the critical variables influencing expectations of future exchange rates is the expectations which asset holders have concerning the future course of monetary policy. In accord with this view, one of the reasons why exchange rates have been unstable is that the monetary policies of major countries have shown considerable instability. Changes in

---

[5] Since the official settlements deficits of the United States were almost entirely in the form of increases in foreign official holdings of dollars (rather than reductions in U.S. holdings of gold and foreign currncies), the deficits did not reduce the U.S. monetary base and, hence, did not relieve the pressure of excessive money creation.

policy have led asset holders to alter their expectations of future exchange rates, resulting in large movements in current exchange rates. For instance, while the appreciation of the German Mark relative to the U.S. Dollar in late spring of 1973 was not (at that time) thought to reflect a real change in German comparative advantage, it may well have reflected a growing conviction that monetary policy in Germany was likely to be far more restrictive than monetary policy in the United States.

McKinnon also notes that forward rates have been poor predictors of future spot rates. This too is broadly consistent with the view that short-term movements in exchange rates are determined by fluctuations in the desire to hold various national monies (relative to the stocks available), rather than by fluctuations in real comparative advantage. We also observe that in the markets for equity shares, futures prices are poor predictors of the future movements of spot prices. An explanation of this behavior can be given in terms of the "efficient market theory" of stock prices. At any moment of time, the current market price embodies all "information" available to asset holders. Prices change when there is new information. Applying this theory to the foreign exchange markets, we would never expect that future rates would predict the turning points of the spot rates. The major turning points come when there is a major change in the "information" available to the market. If this information were already embodied in the last quarter's future rate, then it would not be new information. Efficient markets theory implies that the major turning points of the current spot rate and the current future rate (the rate today for future delivery) should occur simultaneously, rather than having the turning points of the spot rate anticipated by yesterday's forward rate. This prediction is broadly consistent with the observed behavior of spot and forward rates during the flexible exchange rate period. [6]

II. THE ROLE OF SPECULATION

Both Professor Kindleberger and Professor McKinnon devote considerable attention to influence of speculation on the recent behavior of exchange rates. Kindleberger believes that there was too much speculation. McKinnon believes that there was too little. Both agree that the large up and down movements of major exchange rates is evidence that speculation was not stabilizing.

---

[6] Under the old fixed rate system, where governments intervened actively in the spot markets to hold the official rate, but did not intervene in the future markets, future rates frequently did anticipate changes in official parities. However, under a system of freely floating rates, without official intervention, future rates should not anticipate large sudden changes in spot rates. Future rates might anticipate gradual changes in spot rates. The evidence in the tables in McKinnon's paper is that asset holders have expected a gradual appreciation of the German Mark relative to the U.S. Dollar and a gradual depreciation of the Pound Sterling relative to the U.S. Dollar.

On this issue, I disagree. It is a formally established principle of economic theory, that the price of a durable asset which is determined in an efficient market (subject to stochastic shocks) must have certain stochastic properties; in particular, it must be a martingale. The time path of an asset price which satisfies these properties will inevitably exhibit up and down fluctuations. Thus, the existence of such fluctuations is not evidence that speculation is destabilizing or that the market is in any way inefficient.

On the other hand, the large movements of exchange rates which have occured over periods of a quarter undoubtedly have generated real costs for the reasons discussed by McKinnon. Hence, even if the exchange markets are "efficient" in the sense that current exchange rates fully reflect the "information" currently available to asset holders, the question remains of why the movements of rates have been so large and what can be done in the future to reduce these movements. McKinnon suggests that one of the reasons for the short term variability of exchange rates "...is that the supply of private capital for taking net positions in either the forward or spot markets is currently inadequate." I believe that this explanation may be correct with respect to the day to day movements of exchange rates, but it does not explain the large quarter-to-quarter swings in the dollar-mark rate. The short-term smoothing of exchange rates is accomplished by specialists who stand ready to buy when the price goes down and sell when the price goes up. They balance the expected profit from buying low and selling high with the risk of being caught on the wrong side of the market when the movement of the rate is permanent rather than temporary. The evidence of the widening of bid-ask spreads (see McKinnon) and the differences in the experiences of First National City Bank and the Franklin National Bank suggests that both the returns to supplying the service of exchange rate smoothing and the risks from doing so have risen. It may well be that the expected return more than compensates for the increase in risk. If so, then we should expect that the supply of capital to this activity will increase as asset holders come to recognize the gains which can be made from investing in this particular activity.

The large quarter-to-quarter movements in the dollar-mark exchange rate cannot be attributed to an insufficiency of speculative capital. The evidence from the crises which occured at the end of the fixed exchange rate period is that it takes billions and billions of dollars to hold the dollar-mark exchange rate to a value which most of the market believes is inappropriate. The reason why the mark went up 25 per cent relative to the dollar between May and July of 1973 and then fell by the same amount by January of 1974 was that what was believed to be the appropriate exchange rate changed radically over a period of seven months. I believe that there were two reasons for such fluctuations. First, as discussed by McKinnon, the period of the last three years has been a period of remarkable turmoil in economic affairs with the breakdown of the old exchange rate system, the increase in oil and food prices, the pursuit of stop-go policies by many governments, and the acceleration of world inflation followed by the onset of world recession. All this turmoil has clearly generated great uncertainty which has been reflected in the markets for all types of assets, including the foreign exchange markets. Second, for a number of major currencies there was no well established bench mark for the appropriate value of the exchange rate at the start of the flexible exchange rate period. For instance, for the dollar-mark rate and the dollar-yen rate, it was widely believed that the old fixed parities were inappropriate, but there was great uncertainty concerning what the appropriate rate was. This is precisely the circumstance in which large swings in these rates should be expected as speculative opinion shifts first in one direction and then in another. In contrast the market seemed to have fairly firm beliefs about the rates of change of exchange rates, given that the levels were appropriate. This was reflected in the fact that the mark remained at a forward premium relative to the dollar despite the large fluctuations in spot rate between the dollar and the mark. This forward premium apparently reflects the belief that the gradual appreciation of the mark which has persisted throughout the post-war period is likely to continue into the future. Another interesting case is the exchange rate between the Canadian Dollar and the U.S. Dollar. One hundred years of experience with an exchange rate that never deviates far from par has apparently provided the market with a reasonable bench mark for the exchange rate, and this rate has shown much smaller fluctuations than the dollar-mark rate or the dollar-yen rate. Perhaps as the market gains greater experience, similar bench marks will be established for the rates between other major currencies, and there will be some moderation in the quarter-to-quarter movements of exchange rates.

Two sorts of policies might be pursued to reduce the fluctuations in exchange rates: policies which limit the movements of short-term capital or which limit its impact on exchange rates such as dual exchange rates; and policies which increase the information available to participants in a manner which helps them to establish the appropriate exchange rate. An argument for the first type of policy seems to be implicit in Professor Kindleberger's suggestion that speculation has been "both destabilizing and profitable" and that "central banks and other official operators do not have profits, but the public good of stability, in their objective functions." In this connection, however, it is well to remember that what matters is not the objective of particular economic agents, but rather how the behavior which is motivated by this objective affects the overall behavior of the economic system. The experience of the last ten years, both with fixed and flexible exchange rates, does not support the hypothesis that benevolent and omniscient governments have always acted so as to move exchange rates toward their equilibrium levels. On numerous occasions, the private market recognized that an exchange rate was out of equilibrium and forced adjustment on reluctant official agencies. During such episodes, speculation against the policy of the authorities was always attacked as "destabilizing." But, by any reasonable standard of judgment, it was the actions of the authorities in attempting to hold a disequilibrium rate which were destabilizing, and the speculative movements of private capital were stabilizing. Of course, on some occasions, the authorities were proved right by the course of later events. However, a record which shows that sometimes the authorities were right and private speculators were wrong does not provide a convincing case for interfering with private capital markets.

Policies which increase or improve the information available to private speculators are strongly advocated by McKinnon. In support of this view, I would add that in the foreign exchange markets, governments are in a uniquely good position to provide such information since one of the critical variables influencing the relative price of national monies is their relative quantities. If monetary policies were more stable and if asset holders' expectations of future monetary policies were more stable, then exchange rates would probably be more stable.

III. THE ADVANTAGES OF FLEXIBLE EXCHANGE RATES

The way to provide the greatest information concerning the appropriate values of exchange rates is for governments to adopt a system of fixed rates and to pursue policies which are consistent with maintenance of those rates. The exchange crises which occured at the end of the fixed rate period show that to maintain fixed rates, individual national governments must surrender a significant amount of control over their individual national money supplies. If asset holders suddenly decide that they want to hold fewer U.S. Dollars and more German Marks, then the supply of marks must be permitted to expand relative to the supply of dollars. Under fixed rates, the world supply of money can be controlled as a policy instrument, but the distribution of world money between individual national currencies must be left to the preferences of private asset holders.

On the questions of the desirability and feasibility of a return to a system of fixed rates, Kindleberger argues that such a move is both desirable and is feasible, at least for the dollar, the mark and the yen. McKinnon believes that a return to fixed rates is "out of the question, unless it were preceded by domestic monetary reforms and international monetary cooperation of a far-reaching kind..." I agree with McKinnon that the prerequisites for a successful return to fixed rates are not likely to be met in the near future.

Concerning the desirability of a return to fixed exchange rates, I have been forced to modify my views in the light of recent experience. A number of the arguments in favor of flexible exchange rates which I had previously accepted now appear to be either invalid or irrelevant. The principal argument in favor of flexible rates is that they permit individual countries to pursue independent monetary policies and, to some extent, insulate national economies from disturbances originating abroad. Recent experience does not suggest that the way in which independent monetary policies have actually been used has contributed to greater stability of most national economies. The phenomenon of world inflation followed by world recession does not suggest that the degree of insulation provided by flexible exchange rates, as they actually function, is very great. Further, the short term movements of exchange rates which have occured, given the actual functioning of the exchange markets, appear to have generated greater costs than were usually envisioned in arguments in favor of flexible rates. If this continues to be our experience with flexible rates, then many governments may reach the conclusion that the gains from exchange rate flexibility and monetary independence are not worth the cost. If governments are willing to sacrifice monetary independence, then a return to a viable system of fixed rates would be possible. For, unlike government attempts to fix the interest rate or the price of wheat or the price of natural gas, fixed exchange rates can be made to work. Governments cannot control the real demands or the real supplies of credit, wheat, or natural gas, but they can decide to let the relative supplies of national monies respond to preferences for holding various national monies. Hence, the operative question is not whether fixed exchange can work, but whether governments are willing to undertake the policies required to make them work.

On the other hand, it may well be the case that the instability of the world economy and the instability of exchange rates during the last three years were due to the peculiar events of that period. In the longer term, if governments pursue more stable policies and if there are no large exogeneous shocks such as the oil price increase, the exchange markets may settle down. In any case, greater stability and greater consistency of national monetary policies is a prerequisite for a successful return to fixed rates. Thus, we shall have a good deal more experience with flexible rates before a return to fixed rates becomes a realistic possibility.

REFERENCES

1. Dornbusch, R., "Money, Devaluation and Nontraded Goods," <u>American Economic Review</u>, Dec. 1973.

2. _____. "Real and Monetary Aspects of the Effects of Exchange Rate Changes," in R.Z. Aliber (ed.), <u>National Monetary Policies and the International Financial System</u>, Chicago: Univ. of Chicago Press, 1974.

3. _____. "A Portfolio Balance Model of the Open Economy," <u>Journal of Monetary Economics</u>, Jan. 1975.

4. Frenkel, J.A., "A Theory of Money, Trade and the Balance of Payments," <u>Journal of International Economics</u>, May 1971.

5. Frenkel, J.A. and H.G. Johnson. <u>The Monetary Approach to the Balance of Payments: Chicago Studies</u>, London: Allen & Unwin, forthcoming.

6. Frenkel J.A. and C. Rodriguez, "Portfolio Equilibrium and the Balance of Payments: A Monetary Approach," <u>American Economic Review</u>, Sept. 1975.

7. Johnson, H.G., "The Monetary Approach to Balance of Payments Theory," in M. Connolly and A. Swoboda (eds.), <u>International Trade and Money</u>, London: Allen & Unwin, 1973.

8. Kindleberger, C.P., "Lessons of Floating Exchange Rates," Carnegie-Rochester Conference Series, III.

9. McKinnon, R.I., "Floating Exchange Rates 1973-74: The Emporor's New Clothes," Carnegie-Rochester Conference Series, III.

10. Meade, J.E. <u>The Balance of Payments</u>, London: Oxford Univ. Press, 1951a.

11. _____. <u>The Balance of Payments: Mathematical Supplement</u>, London: Oxford Univ. Press, 1951b.

12.   Mussa, M.L., "A Monetary Approach to Balance of Payments Analysis," <u>Journal of Money, Credit and Banking</u>, Aug. 1974.

13.   Pearce I.F., "The Problem of the Balance of Payments," <u>International Economic Review</u>, Jan. 1961.

14.   _____ . <u>International Trade</u>, London: Macmillan, 1970.

15.   Tsiang, S.C., "The Role of Money in Trade Balance Stability," <u>American Economic Review</u>, Dec. 1961.

SOME CURRENTLY SUGGESTED EXPLANATIONS AND CURES FOR INFLATION

Gottfried Haberler

Professor Emeritus, Harvard University

Resident Scholar, American Enterprise Institute

I. INTRODUCTION

I take it for granted that inflation is a monetary phenomenon in the sense that there has never been a serious inflation without an increase in the quantity of money and that a serious inflation cannot be slowed or stopped without restrictions on monetary growth. Recognition of this fact does not, however, imply the assumption of a strict parallelism between changes in M and P, however these terms may be defined. Nor does it preclude going behind changes in M and analyzing the economic, social and political forces that shape the observed changes in M, in other words, identifying causes of inflation more remote than changes in M. Nor does it mean that anti-inflation policy must be confined to monetary policy, i.e., measures to restrict monetary growth. Changing or eliminating some of the factors which cause excessive monetary growth may be an indispensible ingredient, along with monetary restraint, of an economically effective and politically feasible anti-inflation policy.

Monetarists are fully aware that the parallelism between M and P is not quite strict. There is in the short-run a sizable and variable lag between changes in M and P; and there are longer-run, structural changes in the correlation. In other words V, the velocity of circulation of money, although neither a volatile nor a plastic magnitude as Keynesians assume, is subject to change. It changes cyclically and it seems to have a secular downward trend; occasionally it displays longer swings. For example, during World War II, price control, rationing and a sharply reduced supply of durable goods induced a sharp increase in consumer savings; and a decrease in consumer credit depressed V to an abnormally low level. This was followed by a longish period of rising V after the war. Prolonged inflation naturally has the effect of speeding up velocity, as recent developments have again demonstrated. The rise in V in an inflation [1] is a very important matter to which I shall briefly return later. Here I note that it marks one way by which "inflation feeds on itself" and that it has given rise to a dispute and confusion among monetarists: I am referring to the controversy on whether nominal or real balances are the proper target for monetary policy.

---

[1] The magnitude of this rise depends on the precise definition of M. It is pronounced for M_1 but not for M_2 because the latter comprises interest bearing financial assets.

I do not propose to pursue the subject of the precise correlation between M and P any further. Suffice it to say that it is only in rare, extreme circumstances that V moves out of a fairly narrow range. [2] Such extreme cases apart, changes in V are sufficiently large to create policy dilemmas and opportunities for confusion, but they do not destroy the basic connection between changes in the quantity of money and changes in the price level.

It is easy to point to certain latter day economic, political, social and intellectual developments that help to explain the modern proneness to inflation. The rise of Keynesian thinking, preoccupation with full employment and growth, and intolerance to comparatively low levels of unemployment have without doubt greatly increased the propensity to inflate. Today a slight increase in slack and unemployment which might have gone unnoticed in former years is enough to trigger loud demands for expansionary monetary and fiscal measures to speed up growth and increase employment. The recent anti-growth movement and rising concern about the environment and pollution have not reduced but increased the pressure; for environmental concerns express themselves largely in measures that reduce output, increase cost and require additional expenditures to protect the environment.

A related development that is often mentioned as a source of inflation is the enormous growth of the public sector in all countries.[3] In the broad sense, this includes increasing interventions in, and regulations of, private business, rapidly growing transfer payments (for social security and welfare purposes, subsidies of all kinds, etc.) and a growing number of firms and industries owned and operated by the government.

Still another change, largely a consequence of government policies, is the rise of monopoly or market power, labor unions and big business. It is a widely held view that wage-push by powerful unions and monopoly pricing has made inflation much more intractable than it used to be in former years.

[2] As is well known, such a rare case was the hyperinflation in Germany after World War I when V rose to fantastic heights and real balances - - expressed in gold or general purchasing power - - fell to a small fraction of their normal level. I have discussed that case in some length in my Theory of International Trade London-New York 1936. First German edition Berlin 1933.

[3] Britain has been leading the way. The Economist of London recently (November 15, 1975, p. 18) reported about a study by two Oxford economists (Robert Bacon and Walter Eltis) which reaches the conclusion that "Britain's [economic] disaster in the past decade . . . has been that . . . in 1961-1973 the numbers of men employed in industry fell by 14% . . . . The emigration has been into the public sector employment, where the marginal productivity of labor is often tiny or nil, with a . . . 53% increase in local government employment . . . and a 14% increase in central government employment." Their study was summarized in three articles in the Sunday Times (London), November 2, 9, and 16, and will be published in full by Macmillan (London) later this year.

The same alarming development threatens Italy. Guido Carli, the former governor of the Italian National Bank, has warned that the government deficits in Italy have now grown beyond the capacity of the economy to absorb them, crushing the economy and cutting living standards. These deficits result from the growth of the bureaucracy, generous social security and health insurance payments, liberal unemployment benefits and the massive cost of what Carli calls "concealed unemployment," that is, workers producing goods, at public expense, for which there is no demand. (See New York Times, December 9, 1975.) The United States is moving in the same direction. (See Warren Nutter, "Where Are We Headed?" Reprint No. 34, Washington, D.C.: American Enterprise Institute, 1975.)

Each of these various developments has, no doubt, some bearing on inflation. But the important thing is to identify the channels through which they exert the inflationary pressure.

If we accept the proposition that there can be no serious inflation without an increase in the quantity of money, it follows that these various developments operate via inducing monetary expansion. Some of the factors mentioned merely explain why there is greater readiness on the part of the monetary authorities actively to expand, or passively to permit an increase in the money supply. Larger government deficits due to the growth of the public sector provide a powerful inducement for monetary expansion. Cost-push by unions and monopolistic price rises, by threatening unemployment, are perhaps an even stronger pressure to expand the monetary circulation. (I realize that this is a controversial statement and shall come back to it presently.)

There is still another channel through which inflationary pressure may be exerted. A sharp reduction in output (aggregate supply or real GNP) could lead to a price rise. (This could be an exception to the rule that no serious inflation is possible without an increase in M.) "Special factors" such as the oil price rise, a poor crop, the disappearance of the anchovies from the coast of Peru which have been said to have greatly contributed to the price explosion in 1973 and 1974, belong to this category. As I shall try to show, the depreciation of the dollar is analytically closely related to the special factors just mentioned.

I take it for granted that any inflation, however it is brought about - - by credit expansion for private business, government deficit, wage push, "special factors" or what not - - can be slowed or stopped by monetary restraints. But the side effects on overall activity, on particular sectors and on long-run growth will be different. For brevity let me concentrate on overall activity (unemployment and idle capacity) and mention sectoral and long-run side effects only in passing.

I shall now discuss the different cases starting with (1) what is often called the "classical" case of demand inflation, and cost- or wage-push inflation, (2) "special supply-reducing factors," and (3) international aspects ("imported inflation"). Actually the different factors usually operate concurrently. Demand and cost inflation are especially difficult to separate, but it is sometimes possible to find periods when the one or the other factor was dominant.

II. DEMAND INFLATION AND COST INFLATION

There is agreement, shared by monetarists and anti-monetarists, such as James Tobin, that monetary restraint is the specific cure for demand inflation as

145

distinguished from a cost- or wage-push inflation. That holds for an inflation which has its root in expanding bank credits to private business as well as for one which finances a government deficit. If the monetary authorities stand firm, a government deficit will drive up interest rates and "crowd out" private investment. Alternatively, a deficit can be eliminated by raising taxes or cutting government expenditures. As far as the effect on overall activity is concerned, there is probably not much difference between fighting a government-induced inflation by monetary policy (higher interest rates), raising taxes or cutting expenditures. But the sectoral impact (e.g., on the construction industry) and long-run effects on productivity growth will of course be very different depending partly on which taxes are raised and which expenditures are cut. [4] It is often assumed that the transition from an inflationary to a non-inflationary (or less inflationary) situation can be accomplished without side effects on overall activity if it is brought about by fiscal rather than by monetary measures. [5] I cannot see the difference - - apart from the different sectoral or long-run impact.

But how do we distinguish a demand-pull inflation from a cost-push inflation, conceptually and in reality? The standard phrase which has been used again and again by economists and policy makers in the course of the current inflation is that when "excess demand" has been "squeezed out," but prices continue to rise, demand inflation has been transformed into a cost inflation. But this is a very misleading expression. What is "excess demand?" Whenever the price level rises, aggregate demand rises faster than aggregate supply. In that sense demand is excessive whenever there is a rise in the price level. A better description is the Keynesian term "profit inflation," used in The Treatise on Money. What is being squeezed (though not squeezed out) is profits.

Let us speak then of a demand-pull inflation when prices stay ahead of wages, salaries and often costs so that profits continue to rise. A demand inflation is, thus, an essentially unstable disequilibrium situation. Sooner or later wages and other incomes will adjust, and inflationary profits will be whittled down. But while it lasts, a demand inflation is comparatively easy to stop by monetary restraint with only mild repercussions on economic activity because inflationary profits act like a cushion. When profits have been sufficiently re-

---

[4] Differential impact on different sectors conceivably could have different secondary effects on overall activity through precipitating the collapse of some large firms. It is the task of the monetary authorities to contain the consequences on overall activity of such accidents.

[5] The theory of the differential impact of monetary and fiscal measures on prices and quantities has been more clearly spelled out for the problem of fighting recession (deflation) than for counteracting inflation. R. Mundell, ("The Dollar and the Policy Mix: 1971," Princeton Essays in International Finance No. 85, May 1971) has argued that an easy money policy for stimulating a stagnating economy merely drives up prices while an expansionary fiscal policy will result in higher output and employment. Presumably he would apply his theory also to the case of cooling an inflationary economy. Mundell's theory seems to be based entirely on the assumption that easy money engenders inflationary expectations. Even if one is prepared to put so much store in assumptions on how price expectations will be influenced, it is difficult to see why a large budget deficit too should not stimulate inflationary price expectations.

duced, but wages and other incomes and prices go on rising we have a case of cost-push inflation. Obviously it is often difficult to identify a period of rising prices as being definitely a case of cost or demand inflation. But the price explosion in 1973 had nothing to do with a wage-push, while in 1974 the inflation clearly acquired a strong cost-push element (and was aggravated by supply scarcities). It is no longer a profit inflation. There is general agreement, I believe, that profits have fallen to a very low level if the inflationary factor (insufficient depreciation of fixed capital and inventory adjustments) is eliminated.

What is the role of labor unions and other monopolies? For brevity I shall express my views somewhat dogmatically and shall concentrate on unions, saying a few words about other monopolies later. This is a highly controversial question. While many economists from different camps have reached the conclusion that in many democratic countries unions have become a major threat to price stability, some monetarists - - Milton Friedman, Harry Johnson and their numerous followers - - flatly deny that unions have anything to do with inflation. There are strange agreements and unexpected disagreements on this issue. For example, Friedrich v. Hayek and Lord Balogh agree that unions have become a major inflationary force. Herbert Giersch is a monetarist who in his theory of inflation [6] allots to monopolies including labor unions a large role. On this point I have a longstanding disagreement with Johnson and Friedman.

But the disagreement should not be exaggerated. There is full agreement that a wage-push inflation, too, requires permissive monetary policy. There is also agreement that the recent militancy of unions, in Great Britain and elsewhere, is largely a consequence of inflation and that the upsurge of inflation in 1973 was a case of demand inflation (aggravated by "special factors" which I shall discuss presently) and had nothing to do with wage-push; in fact, unions, like everybody else (including most monetarists I believe) were taken by surprise and reacted surprisingly late. Another very important point of agreement is that any once-for-all increase in monopoly or market power of unions as well as a monopolization of business will push up the price level. This happened on a large scale when the New Deal in the early 1930s , through the Wagner Act, AAA and NRA, greatly strengthened union power and fostered business monopolies. The consequence was that an abnormally large part of the sharp increase in money GNP from 1933-1937 went into prices and a correspondingly small part into output and employment. This was indeed an extreme case of a monopoly and wage-push inflation in the midst of very high unemployment. I would add that, if unions are able to push up wages in a deep depression, they are in an even stronger position without any further increase in monopoly power, when there is little unemployment.

[6] "Some Neglected Aspects of Inflation in the World Economy" in Public Finance, Vol. 28, The Hague: 1973, esp. pp. 204-208.

There is furthermore agreement I believe, that labor unions have made money wages almost totally rigid in the downward direction. This is, in my opinion, a very important matter which makes stabilization policy much more difficult. It is true that even in the absence of unions, in a free competitive labor market wages display a certain stickiness compared with commodity prices. Wages will not immediately fall to the market-clearing level when demand declines, because workers will take their time to look for a suitable job before they accept a wage cut. [7] But unions have made money wages completely rigid.

Where is then the disagreement? Briefly it is this: monetarists say there is no such thing as a continuous push for higher wages by unions. When a union is first created or when its monopoly power is increased, there will be a once-for-all increase in wages and labor cost and presumably a larger spread between union and non-union wages, but there is no continuing upward pressure. Applied to the present situation, the monetarist will say that there has been recently no increase in monopoly power of unions similar to what happened in the early 1930s. The percentage of the labor force that is unionized has not increased; it is still around 20-25 percent. Furthermore the monetarist will point to the fact that, in the short-run, union wages are sticky even in the upward direction, so that on several occasions non-union wages have risen faster than union wages.

I find these arguments unconvincing for the following reasons. Although there have been no additional legal immunities and privileges granted to the unions since the New Deal, there have been very important changes in public policy and attitudes which have given the unions much more power to press for higher wages than they used to have. Most important, much more liberal unemployment benefits and welfare payments make it possible for unions to hold out in long crippling strikes to obtain large wage increases. In fact, to a large extent, the government finances strikes; in some states the strikers themselves are eligible for unemployment benefits if the strike lasts longer than a certain number of weeks.

The fact that, compared with other countries, in the United States only a small part of the labor force is unionized, does not prove the unimportance of unions. For one thing, higher union wages obtained by threat of strike spread more or less rapidly to the rest of the labor force. Non-union firms and industries are under strong pressure to match union wages for workers of similar skills; for in order to maintain morale and efficiency and to prevent unionization,

---

[7] These things have been analyzed at great length in the modern theory of the Micro-Economic Foundations of Employment and Inflation, edited by E.S. Phelps, New York, 1970. This analytical work is very useful and has greatly enriched our understanding of the working of the labor market. But in my opinion it has gone much too far in obliterating the distinction between (a) a free, competitive labor market and a union-dominated one, and between (b) frictional unemployment and unemployment due to deficient demand combined with wage rigidity ("Keynesian unemployment"). Furthermore I find the reinterpretation of Keynes' theory of involuntary unemployment (Leijonhufvud, Tobin) quite unconvincing. (See my Economic Growth and Stability: Appendix B, "Some Recent Developments in the Theory of Unemployment." pp. 205-210.)

employers find it necessary not to let the spread between wages of unionized and non-unionized workers and of workers of different skills, etc., become too large.

Another very important recent development is the spread of unionization to groups that were not unionized in the past, to public officials and employees in all levels of government. Today teachers, policemen, firemen, civil servants and so on are organized in unions and do not hesitate to use the strike weapon to boost their salaries. True, these developments have been speeded up, if not originally caused by inflation; but there can be no doubt that they are here to stay even if inflation abates.

That union wages in the short-run are usually stickier than non-union wages and therefore on some occasions have lagged, is an unimportant frictional phenomenon which occurs because union wages are determined by a cumbersome and time-consuming process of collective bargaining and are thus fixed in contracts which run for several years. In a prolonged inflation, however, such lags and frictions are quickly eliminated.

On another occasion I have tried to formulate the problem in static, monetarist terms as follows. Unions (and other monopolies) increase what Milton Friedman calls the "natural rate of unemployment," defined as the rate which "would be ground out by the Walrasian system of general equilibrium equations provided there are imbedded in them the actual characteristics of the labor and commodity markets" including the existing labor unions and other monopolies. [8] It is surely not far fetched to assume that the "natural" or "equilibrium" rate of unemployment is thereby raised to a level which modern society does not accept without fighting back by means of expansionary policies.

It is true that this merely explains a once-for-all effect. But we should keep in mind that ours is not a Walrasian world where general equilibrium is instantaneously reached, but one where equilibrium is merely approached (without ever being fully realized) by the interaction of many markets with different, overlapping lags. In such a world, what in static theory looks like a once-for-all change becomes a multi-ratchetted, self-propelling, dynamic process which for all practical purposes is equivalent to a continuous push. The situation would perhaps be different, if labor were organized in one large union and the overall wage level were determined in one, country-wide collective contract. In that case the connection between wage levels, price levels and employment would be much clearer than it is now, and unions might moderate their demands. But we do not live in this kind of a world.

How about monopolies other than labor unions? In principle what was said of labor monopolies also holds for business monopolies; they too tend to

[8] See Friedman, "The Role of Monetary Policy," 1969.

raise the level of natural unemployment. But for reasons which I have explained elsewhere [9] and shall not repeat here, I believe that outside the public utility area - - transportation, communication, etc., - - business monopolies are not a serious threat to price stability - - except when they are created and protected by government policies.

Government regulations, restrictions and subsidies are a very potent source of inflation. They operate like private monopolies, by raising prices, making them rigid downward and reducing output. In many cases where private producers, for example, farmers, are unable to organize themselves in effective monopolies, the government steps in and in effect makes them behave more or less like monopolists. This is being achieved in many ways, by import restrictions including anti-dumping and countervailing duties, export subsidies, farm price supports, the so-called "voluntary" restrictions forced on foreign exporters, government guaranteed loans to producers to prevent a fall of livestock prices, regulation of wellhead prices of natural gas,[10] minimum wages which cause high unemployment among underprivileged workers etc. Hendrik Houthakker, Thomas Moore and Murray Weidenbaum [11] have presented a long list of such cases. Ironically the regulatory agencies themselves, which are supposed to prevent public utilities from exploiting their monopoly positions, have in many cases become their powerful protectors who shield them from competition.

Wage-push by labor unions and pressure exerted by various groups, through government restrictions, regulations and subsidies, to increase their rewards help to explain why inflation, once it has continued for a while, always tends to accelerate. The acceleration mechanism is so well known that I need not elaborate. Suffice it to say that there would be acceleration even in a competitive economy. Interest rates rise, people reduce the size of their cash balances in relation to their income by spending money faster, so that the velocity of circulation of money goes up as was already mentioned, etc. But it stands to reason that price setters - - monopolists of all description - - are in a better position to anticipate expected price increases than price takers under competition.

Saying that inflation tends to accelerate does not imply that every creeping inflation inexorably must become a trotting and eventually a galloping one. What it does mean is that an expected and anticipated inflation loses its stimula-

---

[9] See my Economic Growth and Stability, pp.114-116.

[10] This particular measure resembles a monopsony because it keeps the price below the competitive level in the interest of some consumers. But since it restricts output and distorts the efficient distribution of gas - - intrastate sales are not subject to federal regulation - - the effect is in the end inflationary.

[11] H. Houthakkar, "A Positive Way to Fight inflation," Wall Street Journal, July 30, 1974. T.G. Moore, Flexible Transportation Regulation and The Interstate Commerce Commission, Washington, D.C.: American Enterprise Institute, 1972. Murray L. Weidenbaum, Government Mandation Price Increases: A Neglected Aspect of Inflation, Washington, D.C.: American Enterprise Institute, 1972.

ting power unless it is allowed to accelerate beyond the expected rate and that, at a later stage, slowing down the rate of inflation has the same depressing effect on economic activity as stopping it altogether would have had earlier. This is, I believe, the real meaning of stagflation. We have reached a stage in the process where measures to slow down the rate of inflation, or perhaps merely to reduce the rate of acceleration, produce slack and unemployment. If we do not act now to curb inflation we merely postpone the day of reckoning. Those who clamor for expansionary measures now in' the midst of a two digit inflation close their eyes to the virtual certainty that if we follow their advice in a year's time, although unemployment may be lower, the rate of inflation will be still higher and the pains of stopping it correspondingly greater. [12]

Looking at the whole picture - - labor unions and other pressure groups trying to increase their share in the national product [13] and the government itself increasing its demands steadily - - one is lead to regard inflation as society's method of reconciling and scaling down inconsistent claims of the various groups on the national product.

Although this way of looking at inflation is not incompatible with monetarism, monetarists often reject it. They believe that a tolerable amount of unemployment for a not too lengthy period would induce unions and other pressure groups to moderate their demands. Some anti-monetarists take an equally relaxed position. Tobin clearly sees the problem but says complacently "there are worse methods of resolving group rivalries and social conflicts than inflation;" inflation has the great advantage that it works "blindly, impartially and nonpolitically." [14] He visualizes a steady, or at least a non-accelerating inflation that keeps unemployment permanently lower than it would be with stable prices. But it is difficult to believe that the various monopolies and pressure groups would not raise their monetary claims when they see their expectations again and again frustrated by inflation.

Even in a largely competitive economy it is not always possible to stop a prolonged serious inflation without a temporary rise in unemployment and

---

[12] The next stage in the evolution of the inflationary process would be that an increase in the rate of inflation, by adversely affecting inflationary expectations and creating uncertainties, ceases to be a stimulant and becomes a depressant. Some analysts, for example Alan Greenspan, believe that we have already reached that stage. That is probably too pessimistic in the short-run, but if inflation is not stopped soon we probably shall reach this stage. (See also Postcript to this paper.)

[13] It is, of course, not necessary that the various pressure groups actually think in these terms, although one encounters more and more frequently policy statements of labor organizations and other pressure groups which couch their demands in terms of a larger share.

[14] See his presidential address, "Inflation and Unemployment," American Economic Review, March 1973, p. 13.

idle capacity. [15] But the existence of labor monopolies and numerous other pressure groups and the absence of an adequate buffer of profits makes the job undoubtedly much more difficult.

I wish - - and hope - - that the optimists, Tobin and the monetarists, are right. But I am afraid there is much truth in what the pessimists, such as F.A.v. Hayek and Friedrich Lutz (both closely allied in many respects with the monetarists) say. v. Hayek recently expressed the view that inflation can be "successfully" stopped "only in collaboration with the unions." [16] Lutz believes that tight money, in the present environment, does not prevent price increases any more, but produces unemployment on top of inflation. The only way to solve the inflation problem would be to dissolve the pressure groups and make the economy more competitive. But only a strong government could do that and democracy is likely to perish in the process. [17]

III. "SPECIAL FACTORS"

The price explosion of 1973-1974 is widely assumed to have been sharply aggravated, if not caused, by special factors - - the sharp rise in food prices due to a poor crop and wheat sales to Russia, the disappearance of, the anchovies off the coast of Peru (which drove up soybean prices because soymeal is a close substitute for fishmeal), the depreciation of the dollar and later the oil price rise. [18]

The situation is often referred to as a "commodity inflation" or "raw material inflation." But this is a sloppy and misleading expression. In every

[15] There have been cases where an inflation has been stopped without any prolonged recession. The German hyperinflation after World War I (1923) and the repressed inflation after World War II (1948) were followed by rapid expansion. But both were very different from our present inflation. The hyperinflation was an uncontrolled profit inflation, prices running ahead of wages. (The same was true of the other less-than-hyperinflations in France, Italy and elsewhere.) And the inflation after World War II was a repressed inflation; the symptoms of inflation were suppressed by tight controls and economic activity was strangled in the process. When the money overhang was removed by the currency reform in 1948, Ludwig Erhard abolished all controls at one stroke. Naturally the economy responded with sustained expansion. Our present inflation is very different and it is therefore unconvincing to argue (e.g., J.K. Galbraith, "Inflation: A Presidential Catechism," The New York Times Magazine, September 15, 1974) that it can be stopped quickly without recessions as were the inflations in Germany and in France after World Wars I and II. In recent years, the country that has been most successful in containing inflation, West Germany, has consistently refused to use either price or wage controls, even under a social-democratic government.

[16] "Zwölf Thesen zur Inflationsbekämpfung," Frankfurter Allgemeine Zeitung, August 19, 1974.

[17] Friedrich Lutz, "Dilemmasituationen Nationaler Antiinflationspolitik," in 25 Jahre Marktwirtschaft in der Bundesrepublik Deutschland, Stuttgart: 1972. Other pessimists are George Terborgh, Control of Home-Grown Inflation, Washington, D.C.: 1972 (mimeographed), W. Hutt, The Strike-Threat System - - The Economic Consequences of Collective Bargaining, New Rochelle, N.Y.: 1973 and Emerson P. Schmidt, Union Power and the Public Interest, Los Angeles: 1973.

[18] In 1973, at first, the price rise was attributed by practically all journalists and by many economists to decontrol (transition from Phase I to Phase II). Post hoc ergo propter hoc! But that explanation is so blatantly inadequate that it is hardly mentioned anymore. Fads come and go very fast in economics, especially in troubled times. Controls are now thoroughly discredited, but I am afraid they will come again and will have to be discredited once more, unless inflation is stopped soon.

inflationary boom, raw material prices rise faster than the general price level. There is nothing special about that, and it is not surprising that raw material, food and fuel price rises account for a large part - - 50-60 percent - - of the rise in the CPI and the WPI in 1973-1974. There was after all a world boom not just an American one. What is "special" with respect to the inflation problem about the factors mentioned, including the dollar devluation as we shall see in the next sections, is that they imply a reduction in real GNP or more precisely in aggregate domestic supply of goods and services.

Forgetting about the anchovies (which have returned in the meantime, although, unlike their disappearance, their reappearance was not played up), the quadrupling of crude oil prices by OPEC means that we have to export more and/or import less to pay for the oil. This is a subtraction from aggregate available supplies. A crop shortfall too reduces real GNP and, in addition, implies a not insignificant internal income transfer from the urban population to the farmers. The impact of these factors on our domestic inflation is usually described in these terms: fuel prices and food prices are driven up. True, the price level could have been kept stable by tight monetary and fiscal policies, but this would have required a sharp reduction of prices other than those of food and fuel (and imports), which surely would have caused a serious recession.

I believe that, in principle, this argument is correct. It can be strengthened by pointing out that an internal income transfer from the urban population to the farmers and producers of oil has the same inflationaryeffect, given the fact that urban workers (or income recipients in general) are unwilling to accept a reduction of their money wages or even insist on their customary money wage increases. [19] It also should be kept in mind that the (monetary and real) size of the internal income transfer depends on the elasticity of demand. [20] But I do believe that the actual impact of the "special" factors on inflation in a trillion dollar economy is small compared with the other, "general" inflationary factors (demand-pull stemming from loose monetary and fiscal

[19] It is very important to realize that this could not happen in a competitive market, i.e., in the absence of labor unions. What could happen in a competitive market when the real wage is reduced by a rise in food prices is that the supply of labor declines resulting in a rise of wages. But that would not constitute involuntary unemployment. (If one wants to call it unemployment, it would be voluntary unemployment which does not count.) Moreover, depending on the shape of the supply curve of labor, the reaction could be the opposite, namely an increase in the supply of labor and a fall of wages.
All this applies also when real income is reduced by higher taxes, union dues or any other levies. In the literature on inflation it often is said that workers look increasingly at their net income (take-home-pay) and react to increased taxes and other levies by raising their wage demands. But in a competitive labor market this would reflect reduced supply of labor ("voluntary unemployment") and the result could be, depending on the shape of the supply curve, "larger employment" and lower money wages.

[20] We have here an example of Charles L. Schultze's inflation mechanism. Shifts in demand jack up the price level because the prices of products toward which demand has shifted rise, while under a regime of rigid wages the prices of the products from which demand is diverted fail to decline. See Schultze's study Recent Inflation in the U.S., Study Paper No. 1. Materials prepared in connection with the Study of Employment, Growth and Price Levels directed by Otto Eckstein, Washington, D.C., 1959. Schultze's theory was anticipated by F.A.v. Hayek, "Inflation from Downward Flexibility of Wages," in Problems of U.S. Economic Development, Committee of Economic Development Vol. 1, pp. 147-152, New York: 1958. Reprinted in F.A.v. Hayek, Studies in Philosophy, Politics and Economics, Chicago: 1967.

policies and wage-push). The impact of the special factors has been greatly exaggerated by the more or less explicit suggestion that its magnitude is indicated by the above-mentioned large share (50-60 percent) of food and fuel price rises in the increase of the CPI or the WPI from 1973 to 1974.

A simple mental experiment should convince the reader that the impact of the special factors on inflation cannot have been very large. Assume that there had been no "general" inflationary influences such as demand-pull or cost-push (however they may be defined or explained); in other words, assume that apart from the operation of the special factors, the price level would have remained stable, that aggregate monetary demand would have matched aggregate supply. Now the special factors reduce supplies. Hence demand exceeds supply; and with a constant volume of expenditures, prices have to rise. By how much? Clearly in proportion to the reduction of supply. But this reduction is really quite small, not much more than 2 percent. (It would be a little larger if we add the impact of the dollar devaluations to which we come in the next section.)

I conclude that only a small part of the actual price rise of over 10 percent from 1973 to 1974 can be attributed to the "special" factors, probably not more than one and a half or two percentage points. The rest is due to the "general" factors - - demand-pull, cost-push or whatever one likes to call it. It is needless to add that for many other countries the oil price rise is a much more important factor than for the United States.

It can be argued, however, that indirectly the impact of the special factors is much larger. The rise of the oil price will stimulate investment to develop substitutes; but this cannot yet have been an important factor. Or more important, the price rise of imported oil will lead to a similar rise of domestic oil. This, by itself, does not reduce aggregate supply but it implies an internal income transfer from the population at large to the oil producers. Given wage rigidity and wage-push (unwillingness of some oil consumers to accept the reduction in their real income implied by the rise in the price of oil) the income transfer may well produce unemployment and a rise in the price level. Or, since the special factors have burst onto a highly inflationary atmosphere, they may have further stimulated inflationary expectations. Another indirect effect would result from full indexation (see next section). Analytically closely related to indexation is the possibility that labor unions and other pressure groups will resist any reduction in their real wage and try to offset it by increased money wage demand. This would be an extreme case of wage-push. It has, in fact, been suggested that this often is the case. v. Hayek has made the point long ago that unions increasingly bargain in terms of real wages and that consequently

Keynesian policies will not work anymore.[21] However, all these indirect effects of the "special" factors presuppose and depend on the operation of the "general" inflationary forces - - monetary expansion, demand-pull and wage-push, however one wishes to describe them.

IV. INTERNATIONAL ASPECTS

Owing to the large size of the American economy and the comparatively small ratio of trade to GNP, the United States and the dollar occupy a very special position in the world economy. The United States enjoys a greater degree of national autonomy with respect to macroeconomic policies than any other Western country. This does not mean, of course, that foreign trade is unimportant. Obviously it is vitally important as a provider of essential materials and its help in maintaining a healthy state of competition in many areas is indispensable. Furthermore, relative autonomy does not mean that there does not exist a definite though changing equilibrium relationship between the U.S. price level and the world price level in the sense of the complex of price levels of other countries. What it does mean is that, even under a regime of fixed exchange rates, the U.S. price level is largely determined by U.S. policies and other countries do most of the adjusting. Floating further increases the relative autonomy.

With this background in mind I now first discuss the impact of the dollar devaluation on the U.S. inflation in 1972-1974 and, second, make a few remarks on the implications of different exchange rate systems for world inflation.

The devaluation of the dollar was one of the special factors that, along with oil price hikes and poor crops, were blamed for the price explosion in 1973. I said earlier that analytically the impact of the depreciation on inflation was similar to that of the oil price rise and the harvest shortfall. What I had in mind is this: the dollar had to be devalued because the United States suffered from a fundamental disequilibrium in the balance of payments. When the dollar was overvalued, the U.S. could supplement the domestic supply of goods and services by additional imports and by diverting exports to the home market. Contrariwise, the improvement in the trade balance following the depreciation of the dollar constitutes a subtraction from aggregate domestic supplies just as a smaller crop and the larger exports required to pay the larger oil bill do. It follows that the magnitude of the inflationary impact of this special factor has to be mea-

---

[21] F.A.v. Hayek, "Unions, Inflation and Profits," in The Public Stake in Union Power edited by Philip D. Bradley, New York: 1949, reprinted in v. Hayek, Studies in Philosophy, Politics and Economics, London and Chicago: 1967. It is interesting to observe that writers (e.g., H.G. Johnson) who reject the idea of a wage-push as cause of inflation, tacitly make use of it in other connections. For references see my book Economic Growth and Stability, Los Angeles: 1974, pp. 271-273, footnote 37.

sured by the improvement in the balance of goods and services which from 1972 to 1973 amounted to about $10 billion. [22] The reader will understand that no precise evaluation of the real burden of the dollar devaluation is attempted, but merely an indication of the order of magnitude. [23] In a trillion dollar economy the magnitude is quite small on any kind of reckoning. All three "special" factors together - - oil, crops, dollar devaluation - - account probably for not much more than, say, 2-3 percent in the 12-14 percent price rise. The rest must be attributed to the "general" factors (demand-pull and cost-push both countenanced by monetary policy). [24]

Let me restate the results of our analysis in other words: the "special" factors caused approximately a 2-3 percent reduction in real GNP. If money GNP remains unchanged, the required contraction of real GNP is brought about by a 2-3 percent rise in the price level. If the price level were to be kept stable, money GNP would have to be deflated by 2-3 percent. The monetary authorities may justly plead that they did not want to do that because it would create unemployment. That means, to put it crudely, that the special factors provide a good excuse for two or three percent inflation. But for the remaining seven or eight percent the monetary authorities have to assume full responsibility.

Several economists have pointed out that if in the last few years we had had literal and immediate full indexation of all incomes, our economy would have exploded in hyperinflation (or, it should be added, sunk into depression in the event that the Fed had prevented the price explosion by tight money). I do not believe, however, that this is a reductio ad absurdum of the indexation idea. For nobody has seriously recommended anything coming near to full indexation.

I come to the impact on world inflation of different exchange rate regimes. It has been argued by R. Mundell and A. Laffer and repeated by others that floating which became widespread in 1973 was responsible for the price explosion in the same year. Post hoc ergo propter hoc. [25] I think the opposite

---

[22] To this could be added a slight deterioration in the terms of trade over and above what is already accounted for by the larger oil import bill.

[23] We need not, therefore, go into the question whether one should use the current balance or the balance of goods and services and whether and how capital flows influence the outcome. Obviously the inflow of "petrodollars" alleviates the overall burden, at least temporarily. The deflationary effect of the internal drain, consumers having less to spend on other things because they have to spend more on gas and oil, which has been greatly played up in the literature, should be regarded as a modest contribution to the fight against inflation. It may cause some unemployment and slack like any other measure (such as tight money) to cool the economy. If that has to be prevented at all cost, (i.e., at the cost of perpetuating the inflation) easier monetary policy can do it; no other special measures are required.

[24] Again it is possible to argue that indirectly the devaluation had a much larger effect on the price level. For example, when import prices go up, the price of domestic substitutes, too, will rise. This constitutes an internal income transfer which, given wage rigidity and wage-push, could result in unemployment, if an attempt were made to keep the price level stable.

[25] In reality it was not even post hoc. Inflation had started to accelerate earlier.

is true. World inflation, proximately due to excessive money creation in all countries, makes floating necessary. How can exchange rates remain fixed when prices rise by close to 20 percent in the United Kingdom and Italy, 15 percent in France, less than 7 percent in Germany and 24 percent in Japan, to mention only a few contrasts? What is true is that, under fixed exchanges, inflation necessarily spreads from country to country. Under modern conditions any system of fixed or semi-fixed exchange rates, even the gold standard, if it could be resurrected, must have an inflationary bias. This follows from the fact that nowadays no country, literally none, is willing to undergo a real deflation in the sense of accepting a period of falling price levels. The consequence is that balance of payments disequilibria cannot be eliminated, as during the era of the gold standard, by deflation in the deficit countries and inflation in the surplus countries. Rather, they can be eliminated only by inflation in the surplus countries - - or by exchange rate changes (or by controls, but I will not discuss controls in this paper).

Balance of payments discipline enforced by fixed exchange rates does not exist any more, at least not to the extent - - and that is enough for my argument - - that a country could be induced by a deficit to undergo a real deflation in the sense of falling prices or declining money GNP. (There are, of course, cases of deflation in the sense of unemployment and declining real GNP.)

Advocates of floating have argued that the floating system provides some inducements of its own to resist inflation. For one thing, a falling exchange rate is a clearer signal that something is wrong than a declining reserve which can be more easily hidden from the public eyes. In addition, under fixed rates a country with a sufficient reserve can alleviate its inflation by stepping up imports and diverting exports to the home market, financing the deficit by drawing on its reserve; in other words, by "exporting" some of its inflation to others. Under floating each country has to swallow the inflation which it generates by loose monetary policy. This is a strong inducement to resist inflation.

These conjectures of theorists have been recently confirmed "from the horse's mouth" so to speak. Arthur Burns, not an enthusiastic floater, pointed out that under floating "faster inflation in the U.S. than abroad would tend to induce a depreciation of the dollar, which in turn would exacerbate our inflation problem." He drew the conclusion that "under the present regime of floating it is more necessary than ever to proceed cautiously in executing an expansionary policy." [26] He also noted that "no such intensification can take place under a regime of fixed exchange rates as long as international reserves remain sufficient to obviate the need for devaluation." This is often regarded as an advantage of

[26] Statement before the Subcommittee of International Finance of the Committee on Banking and Currency. House of Representatives, U.S. Congress, April 4, 1974.

the system of fixed exchange rates. But the other side of the medal should not be forgotten, namely that if any country alleviates its inflation by exporting some of it, inflation is intensified abroad. True, situations are thinkable in which deficit and surplus countries both would profit from the reserve flow under fixed exchanges. This would be the case if the surplus countries suffered from unemployment (recession) while the deficit countries are under inflationary pressure. But these are exceptional circumstances among independent countries. If such circumstances happen to exist at any moment, they are not likely to last for any length of time. [27] It should be added perhaps that the fact that floating provides a strong inducement for monetary policy to resist inflation, does not guarantee that inflation will in fact be curbed. A strong inducement to disinflate may well be overwhelmed by an even stronger propensity to inflate.

Policy makers in countries which have been more successful in holding down inflation than their neighbors are fully aware that they could not do it with fixed rates. Dr. O. Emminger, Vice President of the German Bundesbank has repeatedly declared that, without the shield of floating, Germany could not have kept her inflation rate at less than one half of that in many other important countries. In a recent speech he referred to the current discussion on floating and mentioned that some "well-known economists" and "even central bankers" criticize floating not only as "a factor of general instability but also as one of the principal sources of inflation." He added politely, "For us, who date the beginning of our effective anti-inflation policy at March 1973 when we stopped pegging to the dollar, this view sounds rather strange."[28]

I conclude once more that under fixed rates (and convertibility) inflation spreads from the inflating countries to the four corners of the world. Advocates of fixed rates sometimes object on the ground that a country can spread the infection only so long as it has a sufficient reserve. True enough, the spread of inflation stops when the inflating country runs out of reserves or exhausts its credit-line and is forced to devalue, (quod erat demonstrandum). Frequent exchange rate changes or floating are indispensable if some countries are to live without inflation in an inflationary world. But it is only a necessary, not a sufficient condition of price stability.

---

[27] For further details and references to the literature see my Money in the International Market, second edition, Cambridge, Mass.: 1969, pp. 16-17, and my contribution, "The International Monetary System: Some Recent Developments and Discussions," in Approaches to Greater Flexibility of Exchange Rates: The Burgenstock Papers, edited by George N. Halm, Princeton: University Press, 1970, pp. 113-123. See also my "Comments" on A. Laffer's paper, "Two Arguments for Fixed Rates," in The Economics of Common Currencies, ed. H.G. Johnson and Alexander Swoboda, London: 1973, pp. 35-45. There I have tried to demonstrate that the exceptional cases where deficit and surplus areas alike profit from reserve flows are more likely to occur between regions of a single country with unified monetary policy than between independent countries.

[28] Speech, March 5, 1974, in Mainz, Reported in Deutsche Bundesbank Auszüge aus Presseartikelm, No. 57, September 9, 1974, p. 3.

Is it really possible for any country, even with floating rates, always to resist inflationary pressures from abroad? For small countries there surely are problems. The smaller the size, the greater the inconvenience of fluctuating rates. Large countries, on the other hand, can get out and stay out of an inflationary world trend if they let their currency float. The United States surely could go it alone, if it wanted to. If we were able sharply to reduce our rate of inflation, the dollar would appreciate in the exchange markets and become more attractive for others to hold. But many countries would continue to peg to the dollar. A few might drop out from the existing informal dollar block but others would probably join it.

There is however one qualification to be made. The dollar is still the world's foremost reserve currency. Foreign central banks and other official national and international institutions hold close to $80 billion as reserves and there are many more billions held privately which may find their way into official reserves. This creates the theoretical possibility that the United States might be subjected to inflationary pressures from abroad if many foreign dollar holders get into balance of payments difficulties and use their dollar reserves to finance their deficits (our surplus) to alleviate their own inflation. To put it differently, they may be tempted to "re-export" the inflation to us which we "exported" to them when we had our large deficits. The potential threat would become greater, if the monetary gold price were raised to the free market level and if the United States were called upon to finance other countries' oil deficits by accepting their gold, by liberal foreign lending through special swaps, "special oil facilities" arranged by the IMF, IBRD, BIS or any other of the innumerable international agencies. Arthur Burns probably had this danger in mind when (according to news reports) he told a Congressional committee that the word "recycling" should be banished from our vocabulary. Extensive borrowing in the Eurodollar market or directly in the United States by some countries operates in the same direction. The governments of Great Britain, Italy and France have borrowed huge sums, either directly or through nationalized banks and enterprises, to finance their trade deficits and alleviate their inflation.

It should be observed that if it comes to pass that through these various channels the United States is subjected to strong inflationary pressures from abroad, it would not be due to a malfunctioning of the system of floating exchange rates, but on the contrary to the legacies of the period of fixed rates (accumulated dollar balances abroad) and to attempts to prevent the floating system from working. Collectively the foreign dollar holders have it in their power, for a period of time, to stabilize the dollar exchange rates. I do not believe that we are in imminent danger of being put under inflationary pressure by large foreign dollar holders going on a spending spree. But we should be alert to the possibility.

V. SOME POLICY CONCLUSIONS

Monetary Policy. Restraint on monetary growth is indispensable to fighting inflation. I have nothing to add to what the monetarists have been saying on that subject. The dope should be withdrawn gradually, not abruptly. Monetary restraint should not be abandoned as soon as there is slack. The consequence would be that in a years' time inflation will be still higher and the cure more painful. The present inflation cannot be stopped without a recession, hopefully, a mild one. I would not favor, however, fixing a rigid limit on monetary growth. Situations may arise when a temporary increase in the rate of monetary growth is necessary, e.g., if unemployment gets very high or if a run on some banks develops.

Fiscal Policy. It would be most desirable to support monetary policy by a tight fiscal policy, that is to say, by running a surplus by means of raising taxes or cutting government expenditures. This would relieve pressure on the capital market, reduce interest rates and make more funds available for housing and productive private investment. Sooner or later raising additional revenue through higher taxes will probably become unavoidable. Reducing government expenditures is a slow process and it is very likely that certain expenditures will go up, e.g., for unemployment relief and public service employment. A gasoline and fuel oil tax (plus an import duty on oil to stimulate the production of domestic substitutes) would be a very good method. To make it more palatable it could be combined with a reduction of the income taxes, perhaps through indexation. (See below.)

Government Regulation. Elimination of the innumerable government regulations which restrain competition, keep up prices and reduce output, as recommended by Hendrik Houthakker, Thomas Moore, Murray L. Weidenbaum and others, would be most desirable. Since far reaching deregulation will require legislation, it will take a long time to put it into effect; special interests will fight it tooth and nail. Deregulation is, in practice, a long-run measure, although once put into effect its impact on prices would soon become visible. No quick impact on inflation can be expected from a more vigorous antitrust policy nor from measures to stimulate productivity growth.

Indexation. I am lukewarm about indexation. For wages it will come anyway if inflation continues, but I would not go out of the way to push it. However the income tax should be indexed. Indexed savings bonds with lower interest yield would be desirable. Indexation of government bonds would be a most effective measure to forestall a possible gold rush by American savers. I am not sure, however, that I would recommend general indexation of govern-

160

ment bonds. Indexation might make it easier to stop a future inflation. But I cannot see how indexation can help stopping the current inflation, since it cannot be introduced retroactively. As mentioned, indexation might be used as a bait to make other measures acceptable.

Wage Policy. This presents a most intractable problem. How can inflation be brought down to, say, 3 or 4 percent, when wage rates are rising as they now do by more than 10 percent? If the price level miraculously could be stabilized first, unions would presumably moderate their demands. If wages stopped rising for a while, the price level would gradually stabilize. A severe recession would probably in the end do the trick. But this cure is hardly acceptable. A temporary wage freeze could lead in a year or two to an equilibrium with stable prices. But this again is impossible, at least without a simultaneous price freeze. Although that prospect makes me shudder, I am afraid it will happen if inflation goes on at a high rate one more year.

Would it not be possible to reach an agreement with organized labor to reduce wage demands by offering tax concessions, for example, through indexing the income tax? Union leaders are afraid of inflation and are aware of the connection between prices and wages. Mr. I.W. Abel, President of the United Steel Workers, was reported to have warned that unless labor moderates its wage demands, "the economy might go to hell." I have a sneaking hope (although I do not really expect it) that the monetarists' optimism may prove to be justified after all and that in the end a tolerable amount of unemployment will be enough to moderate union wage demands sufficiently.

If I were a dictator. Theoretically, from the economic standpoint it would be possible to reduce labor costs and prices without at the same time reducing effective demand. If all money wages, salaries and other contractual incomes were lowered a little, or at least frozen for a while, and simultaneously interest rates and taxes were reduced, we would subdue inflation and guard against recession at the same time. Of course, an across-the-board reduction or freeze of all wages and salaries is politically out of the question and would be an awfully crude method. A selective freeze or reduction of wages and salaries in industries where unemployment is large or rising or threatening would be much more effective and efficient. That is how a competitive market would work.[29]

International measures. Floating should be continued. We should go slow on official recycling. If this was done on a large scale, it would result in the United States financing other countries' oil deficits. This could lead to

---

[29] Keynes was of the opinion that, "There are advantages in some degree of flexibility in wages of particular industries so as to expedite transfers from those which are relatively declining to those which are relatively expanding." (The General Theory, p. 270.) Keynes did add that "the money wage level as a whole should be maintained as stable as possible." This implies that wages should not be entirely rigid downward.

inflationary pressures via an improvement in our trade or current balance. Similarly, a general upvaluation of monetary gold and acceptance of foreign gold in payment for exports could produce inflationary effects. All this would mean that the dollar is stabilized by the action of other countries and would amount to abandonment or at least temporary suspension of floating. But these dangers are not acute.

Liberalization of imports through lower tariffs and elimination of import quotas would help. This would be an important part of the policy of deregulation mentioned earlier.

Public Service Employment and Public Works. I have not discussed these in my paper. It is not an anti-inflation measure but rather the opposite and could be justified only as part of a comprehensive anti-inflation package designed to make the whole policy politically acceptable. I suspect that the administrative difficulties and costs of public service employment would be very high. It probably would lead to a permanent further growth of the public sector.

POSTSCRIPT TO PITTSBURGH PAPER*

When this paper was written, in October 1974, the recession was well under way; but in the fourth quarter of 1974 it spiralled much faster than most economists, including the monetarists, expected. It is a sobering and embarassing fact that neither the inflationary explosion in 1973 nor the sharp downslide in the fourth quarter of 1974 was foreseen by economists in and outside the government. Naturally those who have been all along more afraid of unemployment than of inflation have been quicker to perceive the accelerating decline.

What we should not forget is that every recession or depression (and every boom for that matter), if it lasts long enough, becomes cumulative and feeds on itself. Milton Friedman puts it as follows:

> There are such things as chain reactions and cumulative forces
> . . . [An] economic collapse often has the character of a cumu-
> lative process. Let it go beyond a certain point, and it will tend
> for a time to gain strength from its own development and as its
> effects spread and return to intensify the process of collapse....
> Because no great strength would be required to hold back the
> rock that starts the landslide, it does not follow that the land-
> slide will not be of major proportions. [30]

---

* This Postscript was written after the Conference (May 18, 1975) and was not commented on by the discussants.

[30] Milton Friedman and Anna J. Schwartz, Monetary History of the United States 1867-1960, New York: 1963, p. 419. The authors speak of the liquidity crisis and the collapse of the American banking system in the early 1930s. But recessions and depressions become cumulative long before they generate into a collapse.

It follows that once the landslide has assumed major proportions, great strength will be required to stop it.

I would not call the slide since last fall a "landslide of major proportions" comparable to the Great Depression, but that it is larger than the earlier post-war recession and has become cumulative, can hardly be doubted.

In such a situation the economic and political risks of relying entirely on monetary policy and the automatic stabilizers to stop the recessionary spiral become too large and a tax cut is in order. [31] No doubt an expansionary monetary policy and the automatic stabilizers, weakened though they have been by inflation, would in the end turn the economy around. But this may take too long, unless the monetary expansion is very drastic, which would have highly inflationary consequences in the future.

But two things should be kept in mind: first, that we still have a high rate of inflation; and second, that a tax cut will have an inflationary effect, at least in the sense that without it inflation would recede more quickly. As mentioned in the text above, the momentum of the downward movement may be such that its delayed effect on prices will reduce the rate of inflation for a while, even if the decline in real activity is brought to an end by fiscal measures. In other words, deficit spending is not necessarily inflationary in the sense that the rate of inflation will immediately increase, but it surely is inflationary in the sense that without a tax cut the inflation would taper off faster.

If at present we had an old fashioned recession or depression with a declining price level, anti-recession policy would be easy. Any expansion of monetary demand, whatever its method, would alleviate the recession and merely stop the decline of the price level or, at worst, produce a mild price rise. Unfortunately we suffer from stagflation which poses a basic dilemma for macroeconomic policies. An anti-recession policy of increasing monetary demand tends to intensify the inflation; an anti-inflation policy of reducing monetary demand tends to intensify the recession. A change in the fiscal-monetary mix cannot solve this dilemma. However, in view of the rapidly spiralling recession I conclude that we should take some chances with inflation. But we should do it in full consciousness of ths risks involved.

Why not rely on monetary policy alone? Because monetary policy alone acts too slowly. For any given increase in M (in this context the precise definition of M does not matter) in the short-run we get a larger increase in aggregate demand if the Fed finances a Government deficit, than if the same increase in M is the result of open market operations. Monetarists will say that this is true

---

[31] The economic risk is that a large monetary overhang may develop which, later on when the economy turns up again, would give rise to much inflation. This could well happen even if from now on the monetarist prescription of a steady monetary growth were followed to the letter.

only temporarily; in the end what matters is the change in M and not whether it is effected by open market operations or by financing a deficit. I agree as far as the statics of the problem are concerned - - apart from some minor qualifications such as that a higher interest rate associated with deficit financing may increase V. But in the present situation the short run dynamics are important; quick action is of the essence, from the economic and political standpoint. Therefore deficit financing is in order. [32]

If the cumulative process of recession is brought to a halt, we can count on an automatic rebound: inventories will be replenished, a backlog of demand for houses and other durable and semi-durable goods will provide additional stimulus, etc. This has been stressed by William Fellner in several papers. It is overlooked by those who argue that, what they call the "passive deficit," i.e., a deficit caused by the automatic stabilizers, does not count, because at best it merely stops the downslide and does not carry the economy closer to full employment. The automatic rebound following the halt in the downswing will carry the economy further along whether literally to full employment or only part of the way is another question which need not be discussed here. [33]

Another issue which I do not further discuss here is that the force of the automatic stabilizers has been weakened, though not fully eroded, by the inflation and that the "fiscal drag" will require tax reductions when the economy approaches full employment. Indexation of the tax system would take care of these problems.

It seems now probable that the inflation will recede much faster than foreseen in the gloomy official forecasts of the Budget message. But if we are lucky and, under the impact of the fiscal stimulus, the recession turns out to be V-shaped, the chances are that the inflation, too, will be V-shaped. High unemployment will probably prevent the early wage explosion which has been widely feared. But the wage bomb has not been permanently defused. Unions will surely try to make up for time lost when the economy goes into higher gear.

The danger is great that we shall start the coming cyclical upswing with a substantial inflation rate, say, 5 or 6 percent. Since inflationary expectations have not been subdued (in other words since "money illusion" has not been restored) during the recession, inflation may well accelerate quickly and go to a much higher level than in the last upswing. The reaction will probably be to

---

[32] It could be argued that a deficit brought about by an expenditure increase would act faster than a tax cut. But expenditure increases (public works) are subject to administrative lags and have undesirable long-run side effects. I have discussed this issue in Economic Growth and Stability, 1974.

[33] It is in this connection that the concept of the "full employment surplus or deficit" becomes relevant.

hold inflation down by a tight monetary policy. This will result in slowing down the recovery. This in turn, is likely to trigger an irresistible demand for controls.

The only real cure for stagflation is to make the economy more competitive. Macroeconomic policies should be supplemented by microeconomic measures. These measures have been detailed by Hendrik Houthakker, Thomas Moore and Murray Weidenbaum. Arthur Burns, when he recommended an "incomes policy" to assist monetary policy, had such measures in mind.[34]

---

[34] I have called this type of policy "Incomes Policy Two" to distinguish it from the usual type of incomes policy in the sense of price and wage guidelines and the like. (See Haberler, Economic Growth and Stability, 1974 and Haberler, Incomes Policies and Inflation: An Analysis of Basic Principles, Washington, D.C.: American Enterprise Institute, 1971.)

APPENDIX A

INFLATION AND PARITY CHANGES: SOME RECENT
THEORIES AND PROPOSALS

It is interesting to recall that two prominent British economists, Sir Ralph Hawtrey and Sir Roy Harrod have in numerous writings throughout the postwar period blamed the inflation in Great Britain on the misguided policy of repeated devaluations of the pound. In their opinion the devaluation of 1949 as well as that of 1967 was entirely unnecessary and the subsequent inflation simply was the gradual adjustment of the internal value of sterling to its depreciated external value. Their view was not widely accepted. It was convincingly refuted by Sir Dennis Robertson. [35] He pointed out that purchasing power parity calculations, on which Harrod and Hawtrey based their argument, were not a suitable method for determining the equilibrium exchange rate when comparisons had to be made over a longish period (from before the war to twenty years later), during which there had occurred enormous changes in international demand and in the structure of the British balance of payments.

It can be argued, however, that there was a grain of truth in the Harrod-Hawtrey theory in the following sense. Under the adjustable peg system there is a natural tendency for a devaluing country to devalue too much in order to make sure that the painful operation has not to be repeated in the near future. It is therefore quite possible that especially the 1949 depreciation of the pound was too large.

At any rate the British devaluations were much larger than the dollar devaluation. Foreign trade looms much larger in the British economy than in the American economy and the British economy has a much lighter weight in the world economy than the American. Hence it makes more sense to find in the devaluation of the pound an important autonomous inflationary factor than in the dollar devaluation.

Some writers have suggested that "the obvious and only means of coping quickly and effectively with the present inflation" in the United States is to "write up the dollar in relation to other currencies." [36] Under certain conditions this policy might help. If the world were still on the dollar standard and meekly accepted our decision on exchange rates and if other countries were prepared to finance our deficit which would develop by adding unlimited amounts

---

[35] In the first report of the Council on Prices, Productivity and Incomes, ("Cohen Council") of which Robertson was a member. (London: H.M.St.O., 1958, p. 70.)

[36] Bent Hansen, letter to The New York Times , September 20, 1974.

of dollars to their reserves - - under these circumstances we could by appreciating the dollar step up imports, divert exports to the home market and so alleviate our inflation. The trouble is that other countries too suffer from inflation and would not take kindly to our attempt to export our inflation to them. Moreover in the United States all those who are more afraid of recession than of inflation would not like it either.

It is intereting to observe that Bent Hansen's proposal is in line with the prescription of the so-called New School of Keynesian economics (N. Kaldor and R.R. Neild) which is that the exchange rate should be used to preserve internal equilibrium (counteract inflationary and deflationary developments) and the government budget to equilibrate the balance of payments. One trouble with that policy is that it cannot be applied universally when all countries suffer from inflation or deflation. In a two country model the two countries cannot both appreciate or depreciate their currencies; in other words they cannot both pursue a beggar-thy-neighbor policy.

APPENDIX B

SOME REMARKS ON FLEXIBLE EXCHANGE RATES AND THE RECYCLING OF PETRODOLLARS

It is often said that a country which is confronted with a sudden deterioration of its balance of payments - - due for example to a crop failure or an abrupt rise in oil prices - - cannot rely on flexible exchange rates to restore equilibrium. This view seems to be based on the assumption that according to standard theory, which concentrates on the current balance and neglects capital flows, under flexible rates the current balance is continuously kept in equilibrium; this, it is said, may not always be possible and is at any rate not desirable.

But this is not how floating works nor what standard theory says about how it works. [37] It is like arguing that a free market for wheat cannot work because it would continuously equate consumption and production, thus exposing a country to the danger of extreme hardship or even famine and leading to excessive seasonal and erratic price fluctuations. Actually in a free market stocks are being held by private traders. These stocks are continuously adjusted to changing current circumstances and changes in expectations with respect to future developments. It is possible to argue that the market sometimes makes mistakes and that therefore the government should stockpile to guard against emergencies and promote greater stability. (Whether the government does a better job than the market is very doubtful but need not be discussed here.) Similarly, under flexible exchange rates, private business will hold stocks of foreign moneys and maintain credit lines, but it can be argued that even under floating the monetary authorities should keep an ample international reserve in order not only to smooth out day-to-day fluctuations but also to damp down, although not suppress, medium term movements. (However I shall not discuss

---

[37] The charge that standard theory overemphasizes the current or trade balance and neglects induced capital flows has been recently made by F. Modigliani and H. Askari in their paper "The International Transfer of Capital and the Propagation of Domestic Disturbances Under Alternative Payments Systems" (Banca Nazionale del Lavoro Quarterly Review, No. 107, Rome: December, 1973). However, the point has been made before, for example in Robert Triffin's paper "National Central Banking and the International Economy" (in International Monetary Policies, Postwar Economic Studies No. 7, Washington, D.C.: Board of Governors of the Federal Reserve System, September 1947, pp. 46-81). In my comments on Triffin's paper (1947, pp. 82-100) I show, quoting J.S. Mill, R.G. Hawtrey and J. Viner, that the influence of changes in exchange rates and monetary policy on capital flows have often been taken into consideration in the literature. It has been recognized by the writers mentioned and many others that induced capital flows may change the sequence of events with respect to price movements, etc., that one would expect if there were no induced capital flows. In my book Prosperity and Depression, Chapter 12, "International Aspects of Business Cycles," I tried to analyze the adjustment mechanism under flexible exchange rates with and without capital mobility. Egon Sohmen in his well-known monograph, Flexible Exchange Rates, presents a general equilibrium model in which capital movements are treated as an endogenous variable. (See Revised Edition, Chicago, 1969, Chapter V, Section 2.)

here the problem of managed versus free or clean versus dirty floating. I have expressed my views on this problem elsewhere.) [38]

Take the case of Italy which is often mentioned in this connection. Floating has not prevented Italy from borrowing large sums, over $10 billion, in the Eurodollar market and elsewhere to finance a large trade deficit, thus cushioning and spreading out the impact of the sudden rise in oil prices on the standard of living. In addition, Italy has applied a stiff dose of direct controls of imports in violation of the IMF, GATT and EEC regulations. [39] These restrictions could have been avoided by letting the lira float down. While running a trade deficit financed by borrowing can be defended on the ground that it helps temporarily to keep down inflation and keep up the standard of living, import restrictions do neither; they are a messy kind of disguised depreciation. The reason for using controls was probably the wish to protect certain branches of industry and agriculture from foreign competition. Protectionist measures can conceivably be justified on terms of trade grounds or unemployment or external economies, but not on balance of payments grounds. [40]

There are, of course, limits to the amount that any country can borrow from abroad through the market. That is why there is so much demand for official lending called "recycling" through special oil facilities provided by the IMF, IBRD, BIS, etc., or by special swaps between central banks. Floating, it is said, can make no contribution to the settlement of oil deficits; non-oil deficits often necessitate depreciation or floating, but oil deficits call for recycling.

This argument is vitiated by the failure of making a vital distinction: are oil exporting and importing countries each group taken as a unit, or is the differential impact of the oil price rise on different oil importing countries considered?

When treating oil exporters and importers as units, it makes indeed little or no sense to propose that the transfer problems should be solved by depreciating the currencies of the oil importers collectively vis-a-vis the currencies of the oil exporters. In that respect the popular analogy with the case of the German

---

[38] See my "The Case Against Capital Controls for Balance of Payments Reasons," Geneva Conference on Capital Movements and Their Control, Forthcoming.

[39] These restrictions were later removed (under prodding from EEC, GATT and IMF) when the balance of payments improved because the Banca d'Italia applied the monetary brake.

[40] The relative merits of import restrictions and exchange rate changes have become a hot issue in Great Britain. Import restrictions, in preference to devaluation or floating are being strongly urged by labor unions, the left wing of the labor party and advocates of comprehensive planning. See for example, Economic Policy Review No. 1, University of Cambridge, Department of Applied Economics, February 1975, and the devastating criticism that this plea for restrictions has received in Import Controls versus Devaluation and Britain's Economic Prospects by W.M. Corden, M.M.D. Little and M.F.G. Scott, London: Trade Policy Research Center, 1975.

reparations in the 1920s obscures the problem. For unlike the recipients of the German reparations, the oil exporting countries, especially the Arab ones, are highly specialized, wide-open economies. The governments receive the oil income and must decide how much they want to use it for additional imports; as for the rest they have no choice but to invest in one form or another in the oil-importing countries. Under these circumstances the transfer problem, as distinguished from the problem of raising the money in local currency, would be easy - - much easier than it was in the German case - - and it would make not much sense to appreciate the Saudi riyal or the Kuwaiti dinar vis-a-vis the dollar.[41]

The situation is, however, quite different when we consider the differential impact of the oil price rise on different importing countries. Some are hit much harder than others in three different respects: first, the burden of having to pay more for imported oil; second, the opportunity to pay for part of the higher oil bill by exporting more to the oil countries; and third, the chance of receiving investment funds ("petrodollars") from the oil countries.

The basic burden of having to reduce other expenditures in order to pay more for imported oil is, of course, very different for different countries. For the United States it is, though not negligible, surely not a heavy burden, less than two percent of GNP. For other industrial countries the burden is heavier but not crushing. For some less developed countries it may be really crushing. However, I confine my discussion to the problems of the industrial countries.

If the oil price does not come down some belt tightening is unavoidable. But for no industrial country is the burden so high that it cannot be taken care of by one or two years' normal annual growth of GNP. For the United States it is perhaps one half of a normal annual increase in GNP. In other words, in a short period of time GNP and the standard of living could be back where they were before the oil price was raised and growth could be resumed, provided the adjustment to the new situation including the transfer can be made smoothly.[42]

---

[41] It could be argued, however, that appreciating the riyal would be one way to let the Saudi population share in the windfall by making imports cheaper. For oil countries with a more diversified economy and larger populations such as Iran or Venezuela an appreciation makes more sense. But both countries seem to prefer inflation to appreciation as a partial solution of their surplus problem. Since this was written the Iranian surplus has largely disappeared. Ten OPEC countries turned out to be better spenders than the experts assumed.

[42] These guesses have been confirmed by Hollis B. Chenery's analysis, "Restructuring the World Economy," Foreign Affairs, January 1975, pp. 242-263.

To the extent that oil countries use their new incomes not to import more but to invest abroad, the basic burden on the oil importing countries is postponed and spread out. [43]

Everybody knows that the oil importing countries collectively have to accept a deficit in their current balance to match the surplus of the oil exporting countries. But the petrodollars will not be distributed among the importing countries in proportion to their oil-created balance of payments gap (additional cost of oil imports minus additional exports to the oil countries), let alone in proportion to the basic burden (additional cost of oil imports in percent of GNP). Suppose that all petrodollars go to one country. Then, in the absence of recycling, this country would enjoy a temporary reduction of the basic burden. Theoretically the burden could initially even become negative, more petrodollar investments being attracted than the additional cost of oil imports. This fortunate country would have to accept a current account deficit equal to the current surplus of the oil countries and the other oil importing countries would have to develop an export surplus vis-a-vis the sole recipient of the petrodollars equal to their oil deficit matching the corresponding surplus of the oil countries.

It stands to reason that in the process of allocating the collective current account deficit among the oil importing countries, unlike the case where the importers are treated as a unit, exchange rate changes and floating cannot be excluded. In fact, in our hypothetical example, an appreciation or upward float of the currency of the sole recipient of the petrodollars might be the easiest method of adjustment.

It is widely assumed that the United States will receive the lion's share of the petrodollars and it is concluded that it should share its riches with other countries through official recycling. Nobody can know beforehand, however, how large the lion's share will be, and even ex post it may be difficult to ascertain its magnitude. Oil-related deficits and non-oil deficits are not easily separable. Floating surely should not be ruled out as a mechanism of adjustment. But floating does not exclude that a country may borrow abroad to stretch out the burden of adjusting to the high price of oil. Some countries, especially Great Britain, have made extensive if not profligate use of this opportunity. [44]

True the possibility to borrow abroad is not unlimited, but the barrier to further borrowing is not rigid but elastic, depending largely on the policies pursued by

---

[43] It is conceivable that the burden be permanently reduced (not only spread out). This could be the case if the petrodollars are productively invested and become a net addition to the annual investment stream which would, of course, require that the consumers of the oil importing countries (including the government) cut down their consumption rather than their savings to pay their increased oil bill. Whether and to what extent this will actually happen depends, as Thomas Willett has pointed out, on the domestic policies in the oil importing countries. It does not require that the petrodollars be invested in equities.

[44] The British policy could be characterized as "dirty fixing" rather than as "dirty floating."

the country in question. With prudent internal policies, many countries should be able to attract a good share of petrodollars either directly from the oil countries or in some round about way. Great Britain, if she could manage her inflation, would be in an especially favorable position in that respect, owing to the efficient financial machinery of the City of London and the historical ties with the principal oil producers.

The question whether recycling of petrodollars should be done mainly through the market or through official channels raises many difficult questions, some of which go beyond technical economics. Only a few will be briefly discussed here. There is the political question as to whether the large recipients of petrodollars have some sort of obligation to share them with less fortunate countries. It is difficult to see why oil should be treated differently from all other commodities. But even if the question is answered in the affirmative, as many people would find reasonable, it does not necessarily follow that the redistribution - - recycling - - should be done mainly through official lending. It could be argued that, given the complexity and uncertainties of the situation, the market will do a better job of the recycling that may be needed or desirable than national or international official agencies. Among the questions involved here is the capacity, or readiness, of the Eurobanks and U.S. banks to handle such a large job of intermediation. As indicated above, this will to a large extent depend on how the countries concerned manage their internal economic problems. Countries that manage well without much inflation would attract petrodollars directly or through the intermediation of Eurobanks and U.S. banks. Domestic policies, in turn, may be influenced by the method used for recycling. Easy availability of official financing may well foster laxity of national stabilization policies. On the other hand it could be argued that international financing through the IMF can effectively be used to induce the borrowing countries to put their financial houses in order. If the Euro-dollar market becomes saturated with petrodollars, interest rates will decline and the petrodollars will be diverted into other assets. This process has already started.

Whatever the final solution of the recycling problem, floating of some currencies as a method of balance of payments adjustment surely cannot be excluded. Even if the flow of petrodollars is fully and equitably redistributed through the market or official recycling and assuming that there are no non-oil deficits to adjust, floating of some currencies is almost certain to be required to effect the transfer of that part of the additional oil bill which is settled by larger imports of the oil countries. The reason is that the increased exports to the oil countries, in general, will necessitate some reshuffling of trade between the oil importing countries, because we would not want a bilateral settlement; that is to say it would be inefficient if each oil importing country tried to reach a bilateral equilibrium with the oil exporting countries in the sense that for each oil importing country the additional oil bill equals its own additional exports to the oil countries plus its share in the pool of petrodollars. A multilateral settlement implies that some oil importing countries will export more to the oil countries, others will export less than their share in the total additional exports to the oil countries. In other words some oil importers will run a deficit, others a surplus with the oil countries, these surplusses and deficits being matched by corresponding balances between oil importing countries. Nobody can tell beforehand what the equilibrium pattern of trade surplusses and deficits will be. But if each country keeps its own overall balance in equilibrium, the general equilibrium will be established by the market. This will surely require that some currencies be allowed to float, especially if we keep in mind that oil and non-oil deficits coexists and are difficult to disentangle ex post and practically impossible to separate ex ante. Fortunately there is no real need to separate them for there is no economic justification for treating oil and non-oil deficits differently.

REFERENCES

1. Chenery, Hollis, "Restructuring the World Economy," Foreign Affairs, (January 1975), 242-263.

2. Corden, W.M., Little, M.M.D., and Scott, M.F.G. Import Controls versus Devaluation and Britain's Economic Prospects. London: Trade Policy Research Center, 1975.

3. Economic Policy Review No. 1, University of Cambridge, Department of Applied Economics, February 1975.

4. The Economist, November 15, 1975, p. 18.

5. Emminger, Otman, Speech. March 5, 1974 in Mainz. Reported in Deutsche Bundesbank Auszüge aus Presseartiklen No. 57, September 9, 1974, p. 3.

6. Friedman, Milton and Schwartz, Anna J. Monetary History of the United States 1867-1960. Princeton: Princeton University Press, 1963.

7. Friedman, M., "The Role of Monetary Policy," American Economic Review, Vol. 58, (March 1968). Reprinted in the Optimum Quantity of Money and Other Essays. Chicago, Illinois: Aldine, 1969.

8. Galbraith, J.K., "Inflation: A Presidential Catechism," The New York Times Magazine, September 15, 1974.

9. Giersch, Herbert, "Some Neglected Aspects of Inflation in the World Economy," Public Finance, 28, 1973.

10. Haberler, G. Economic Growth and Stability: An Analysis of Economic Change and Policy. Los Angeles: Nash, 1974.

11. _____. Theory of International Trade. London: Hodge; New York: Mac Millan, 1936. First German edition, Berlin: Springer, 1933.

12. _____. Prosperity and Depression: A Theoretical Analysis of Cyclical Movements. 4th ed. Cambridge: Harvard University Press, 1964.

13. Haberler, G., "The Case Against Capital Controls for Balance of Payments Reasons," <u>Geneva Conference on Capital Movements and Their Control</u>. Forthcoming.

14. _____ · <u>International Monetary Policies.</u> Post-war Economic Studies, No. 7, Washington, D.C.: Board of Governors of the Federal Reserve System, September 1947, 82-100.

15. _____ , "Comments on A. Laffer's paper: 'Two Arguments for Fixed Rates,' " in <u>The Economics of Common Currencies</u>, (ed. H.G. Johnson and A. Swoboda), London: Allan & Unwin, 1973.

16. _____ . <u>Incomes Policies and Inflation: An Analysis of Basic Principles</u>. Washington, D.C.: American Enterprise Institute, 1971.

17. _____ , "The International Monetary System: Some Recent Developments and Discussions," in <u>Approaches to Greater Flexibility of Exchange Rates: The Bürgenstock Papers</u>, (ed. George N. Halm), Princeton: Princeton University Press, 1970.

18. _____ . <u>Money in the International Market</u>. 2nd ed., Cambridge, Mass.: Harvard University Press, 1969.

19. Hansen, Bent, Letter to the <u>New York Times,</u> September 20, 1974.

20. v. Hayek, F.A., "Zwölf Thesen zur Inflationsbekampfung," <u>Frankfurter Allgemaine Zeitung</u>, August 19, 1974.
    Recently v. Hayek has restated his views on inflation and recession in <u>Full Employment at Any Price?</u> London: Institute of Economic Affairs, 1975. This pamphlet also reprints his Nobel Memorial Lecture, "Pretence of Science," Stockholm, 1975.

21. _____ , "Unions, Inflation and Profits," in <u>The Public Stake in Union Power</u>, (ed. P.D. Bradley), Charlottesville: Virginia University Press, 1949. Reprinted in v. Hayek, <u>Studies in Philosophy, Politics and Economics,</u> Chicago: Chicago University Press, 1967.

22. Houthakker, H., "A Positive Way to Fight Inflation," <u>Wall Street Journal,</u> July 30, 1974

23. Hutt, W., The Strike - Threat System: The Economic Consequences of Collective Bargaining. New Rochelle: Arlington House, 1973.

24. Lutz, Friedrich, "Dilemmasituationen Nationaler Antiinflationspolitik," in 25 Jahre Marktwirtschaft in der Bundesrepublik Deutschland. Stuttgart: Gustav Fischer, 1972.

25. Modigliani, F. and Askari, H., "The International Transfer of Capital and the Propagation of Domestic Disturbances Under Alternative Payments Systems," Banca Nazionale del Lavoro Quarterly Review, No. 107,(December 1973).

26. Moore, T.G. Flexible Transportation Regulation and The Interstate Commerce Commission. Washington, D.C.: American Enterprise Institute, 1972.

27. Mundell, R., "The Dollar and the Policy Mix: 1971," Princeton Essays in International Finance, No. 85,(May 1971).

28. New York Times, December 9, 1975.

29. Nutter, Warren, "Where Are We Headed?" Reprint No. 34, Washington, D.C.: American Enterprise Institute, 1975.

30. Phelps, E.S. (ed.). Micro-Economic Foundations of Employment and Inflation. New York: Norton, 1970.

31. Robertson, D.H., The first report of the Council on Prices, Productivity and Incomes. London: H.M.St.O., 1958.

32. Schmidt, E.P. Union Power and the Public Interest. Los Angeles: Nash, 1973.

33. Schultze, C.L. Recent Inflation in the U.S. Study Paper No. 1. Materials prepared in connection with the Study of Employment, Growth and Price Levels, directed by Otto Eckstein for the Joint Economic Committee, 86th Congress of the United States, 1st session, September 1959.

34. Sohmen, Egon. Flexible Exchange Rates. Revised Edition, Chicago: Chicago University Press, 1969.

35. Terborgh, G., "Control of Home-Grown Inflation," Washington, D.C.: 1974, (mimeographed).

36. Tobin, J., "Inflation and Unemployment," American Economic Review, (March 1973), p. 13.

37. Triffin, Robert, "National Central Banking and the International Economy," in International Monetary Policies, Post-war Economic Studies, No. 7, Washington, D.C.: Board of Governors of the Federal Reserve System, (September 1947), 46-81.

38. Weidenbaum, Murray L. Government Mandation Price Increases: A Neglected Aspect of Inflation. Washington, D.C.: American Enterprise Institute, 1975.

SOME CURRENTLY SUGGESTED EXPLANATIONS AND CURES FOR INFLATION: A COMMENT

Franco Modigliani

Massachusetts Institute of Technology

Somewhat to my present surprise, I found Professor Haberler's analysis of inflation - - the great problem of the day - - not very different from my own. I was especially relieved that he too does not believe that the problem can be quickly dismissed by pointing the finger at an excessive growth of the money supply. But, more generally, I find that the areas of agreement far exceed those of disagreement. Thus, my remaining comments largely deal with details and even questions of semantics.

One such question is whether one can usefully distinguish between demand pull and cost push inflation and if so, how. I tend to differ somewhat from the author in that I have concluded that the behavior of wages and prices can be most usefully approached with the help of the so-called search theory (particularly in the form elaborated by C. C. Holt), and an oligopolist mark-up model: aggregate demand determines the available jobs, which together with the labor force, determine vacancies and unemployment and hence wages and finally prices. In terms of this model (almost) every increase in the prices of domestic output is cost push, because it reflects increased wages and other costs; but at the same time, a faster rate of growth of prices can always be traced back to demand pull, in the sense that every increase in demand causes a faster rate of growth of wages. Yet I believe that a distinction between the two types of inflation is useful in so far as they call for different remedies. Accordingly I suggest labeling demand pull a situation in which monetary and fiscal policies create a level of aggregate real demand (job openings) and a related level of vacancies and unemployment larger than is consistent, in the medium run, with an "acceptable" rate of inflation. Note that, in view of the delayed response of wages to unemployment, of prices to wages, and finally of wages to prices and so on, when demand pull first occurs, the rate of inflation may, initially, remain below the acceptable level. Furthermore, it need not be true that prices stay ahead of non-profit incomes, unless capacity utilization is also significantly strained.

When demand pull in the above sense prevails, the appropriate remedy is clearly to change the monetary-fiscal mix so as to reduce aggregate demand. To be sure, the above criterion of classification is somewhat vague both because what is "acceptable" is a value judgment and because the implied warranted level of unemployment will change over time with the composition of the labor force and is, in any event, somewhat uncertain at any point of time. In particular, one may, or not, be prepared to accept as relevant the notion of a vertical Phillips curve, in which case the warranted rate would be unique, though still uncertain. But I am afraid that this vagueness and room for divergent views is a fact that should not be hidden either to ourselves or to the laymen. Furthermore, the "vagueness" is not too great. I suspect that most economists would agree that demand pull prevailed at least in '66, '68-'69 and again in '73 - - with the problem in the latter year compounded by the fact that, as the critical zone was being approached, demand was rising much too fast.

By contrast, I would label as cost push a situation in which aggregate demand (unemployment) is at or below (above) the warranted rate, and yet wages and prices rise faster than the target rate. A most common case of cost push is as an aftermath of demand pull; because of the long and complex lags referred to earlier, the process of inflation, once put into motion, will go on for some time, feeding, as it were, on itself.

The appropriate remedy in such a situation is unfortunately much less obvious, and therefore the area of disagreement, understandably, much wider. My own prescription is that, once aggregate real demand has been brought back to the warranted level, estimated rather conservatively, one should just wait for the inflationary process to die down gradually. This implies avoiding the temptation of speeding up the process either with a "right" maneuver of breaking sharply and letting the unemployment rate go much above the warranted level, unnecessarily punishing ourselves for past sins, or with a "left" manuever of wage price controls, which are likely to create more harm than good, except possibly under very special circumstances. Note that if the above prescription is followed, then the required rate of expansion of the money supply is likely to stay for a while above the norm, given roughly by the sum of the target rate of change of prices and real rate of growth of the economy. But it would be wrong to say that this abnormal rate of growth is the cause of inflation and more accurate to characterize it as the effect.

The above discussion of demand pull, subsequent cost push, and proper remedies may perhaps be clarified by an analogy. Consider a car driven by a hurried driver, on a flat road subject to a speed limit. Clearly he should aim to keep the car at the speed limit. There is some position of the gas pedal which will result in this speed. If by error, the driver pushes the pedal beyond this "warranted" position, the car will exceed the speed limit - - the analogue of my demand pull - - and the correct response is to reduce the pressure on the pedal at least back to the warranted position. However, when this is done, the car will continue for a while to exceed the speed limit - - the analogue of cost push - - though it will eventually get back on course. Finally, to see the parallel with the money supply behavior, note that since the wheels are connected with the motor, while the car is slowing down, the motor will be running too fast; but it is the wheels that push the motor, not the motor that pushes the wheels.

The duration of a cost push situation depends on price-wage rigidities - - the speed with which they respond to an easy or tight market. I would agree, with Haberler, partly on the basis of some still unpublished empirical work, that unions contribute significantly to such rigidities - - while they tend to slow down the response to excess demand, they slow down the return to equilibrium, once the excessive demand stimulus has been eliminated. However, there are indications that rigidities have increased substantially over recent decades while, as Haberler acknowledges, the importance of unions has not changed appreciably in the U.S. In this sense, it seems hard to attribute to unions a significant portion of post-war inflationary tendencies. On the other hand, one factor that may have contributed significantly is minimum wage legislation, which he does not mention explicitly in this paper, though he has done so on many previous occasions. The above mentioned empirical study indicates that attempts at narrowing wage differentials by pushing up the lower end of the scale, and pegging it, tend to be followed by a reappearance of the differential at a higher overall level.

While demand pull is the most common, it is not the only possible cause of cost push. One other cause is that of "inconsistent claims of the various groups on national product," to which Haberler refers. I doubt that this mechanism has been important in the U.S. except quite recently (see below). Trade unions may be important contributors to this mechanism in other countries in which they cover a much greater fraction of the labor force and play a pace-setting role. The dilemma for policy makers may be especially unpleasant in this case, for, in order to redimension wage demands to realisitc levels, as is necessary to stop inflation, there may well be no alternative but to increase, at least temporarily, the target level of unemployment.

The U.S. inflation of 1974 is clearly of the cost push variety, by my definition, since prices are rising at two digit rates while unemployment has already reached the area of 6%, which is widely agreed to exceed, at least moderately, the warranted rate. Yet it cannot be fully accounted for either by previous excess demand nor by inconsistent claims - - though both factors play some role. One must also take into account a set of "special factors" - - oil, poor crops, devaluation - - whose essence according to Haberler, "is that they imply a reduction - - in aggregate domestic supply of goods and services." This is an interesting way of looking at the problem for it calls attention to the connection, which in my view also is very important, between the current inflation and the painful process of adjusting to a loss of real income. I fear, however, that Haberler pushes his approach too far when he suggests that the direct <u>price</u> impact of the special factors can be measured by his "mental experiment." Indeed, it can be verified that his proposed measure reduces to the change in a price index in which prices are weighted by <u>current</u> quantities (Paasche index), on the assumption that (i) all quantities other than the "special" goods are constant and (ii) the total value of the basket is the same before and after the reduction of some supplies. For the case in which only the quantity of the commodity s is curtailed by ΔQ_s, Haberler's measure of direct impact reduces to:

$$
(1) \qquad \Delta P^* = \frac{P^o_s \, \Delta Q_s}{Y_o} \equiv H
$$

where P^o_s and Y_o denote respectively the price of s and the value of the commodity basket (aggregate supply) before the reduction. Thus Haberler's measure, H, is simply the value of the reduction in supply at pre-reduction prices, relative to total supply. By this measure, he concludes correctly that the direct impact is fairly negligible even if we add together oil, crops, and devaluation. The trouble with his measure is that it does not take properly into account the "importance" of the commodity for the economy: (i) by assuming all other outputs constant, it fails to allow for reductions in output of complementary commodities; (ii) by relying on the initial price, it misses the full impact on the consumers as measured by the loss of consumers surplus or, more operationally, by the elasticity of demand (η). Indeed, H would have the same value whether the reduction of 1% in volume is due to a failure of the strawberries crop or to the oil embargo!

It is easy to show that if one repeats Haberler's mental experiment but then chooses to measure the direct impact by a conventional Laspreyre index, one finds

$$
(2) \qquad \Delta P^* = H(1 + \frac{\Delta P_s}{P_s}) = H(1 - \frac{1}{\eta}\frac{\Delta Q_s}{Q_s})
$$

which is necessarily larger than (1) especially if in ΔQ, we now include the secondary loss of output. But even (2) still assumes, like (1), that all prices are perfectly flexible, and on the whole, adjust promptly downward - - as they must if expenditure is to remain constant and the demand for the special commodity is inelastic. If one measures the impact effect on the assumption that all other prices are constant, the Laspeyre measure is

$$(3) \qquad \Delta P^* = H \frac{1}{\eta}$$

which is even larger than (2) if $\eta < 1$. And even (3) underestimates the full effect since it neglects the likely rise in prices of close substitutes.

I would thus conclude that the "direct impact" of the special factors of '73-'74 is a good deal larger than suggested by Haberler's mental experiment. Still I am inclined to agree that the most serious effect of the "special factors" may well come from the general endeavor to resist the unavoidable loss of real income through wage escalation, which raises prices, and so on. This adds an element of "inconsistent claims" to the direct effects and to the cost push process already in course as a result of the demand pull of '73. One interesting implication of this situation is that the public is by now thoroughly convinced that it is worse off because of the inflation, whereas it is more nearly true that the high rate of inflation is a consequence of their being worse off, the result of a fruitless endeavor to avoid the unavoidable loss of real income. Educating the public on this point, which no official has tried to do, might concievably help to cut short the cost push process without plunging the economy into deep recession.

Haberler devotes one section to the great debate about the relation between inflation and alternative exchange rate systems. I will refrain from extensive comments since, in my view, the debate is getting sterile. It all comes down to the simple proposition that flexible exchange rates (i) provide the opportunity for insulating the country from outside inflation but also (ii) permit the country to pursue or not resist inflationary tendencies free of the potential restraint imposed by the balance of payment, under fixed rates. Each side of the debate chooses to emphasize one of these two implications. I doubt, however, that one can establish a universally valid ranking since clearly neither alternative totally dominates the other.

On the issue of recycling, I would like to take exception to Haberler's assertion that "there is no economic justification for treating oil and nonoil deficits differently." To the contrary, I would argue that, at least to a first approximation, for the major developed countries, the target deficit on trade account should be commensurate to their oil deficit. The basis for this proposition is straightforward: there is at the moment extreme uncertainty as to how the current dislocation in balance of trade will eventually find a "permanent" solution, e.g., by a substantial reduction in oil countries' surplus, whether due to a lower price or to a shift in output away from the countries with the highest propensity to run a surplus; or by increased commodity imports; or by massive investments in the LDC's, and so on. Until this uncertainty is resolved, and a new permanent pattern of trade develops, it would be wasteful for countries to engage in large scale re-allocation of resources merely for the purpose of temporarily reshuffling the deficit among them. If this reasoning is accepted, I would go on to suggest that the exchange rate pattern appropriate to the above balance of trade targets is almost certain to require extensive intervention by central banks, financed, one would hope, from a cooperatively established oil facility.

Coming finally to touch briefly on policies to deal with the current inflation, my recommendation, as already indicated, is to aim for a conservative target rate of unemployment - - somewhere between 5 1/2 and 6% - - and stick to it until the inflation has abated (or the approach has clearly proved a failure). Simulation with the MPS model suggests that this policy would require a significantly larger rate of growth of M_1. It would also require other measures such as raising the ceilings on deposit rates at thrift institutions to revive housing, and some fiscal stimulus. Like Haberler, I can see little point in a public employment program aimed at re-absorbing those pushed out of private employment by our own deflationary policy. I would rather favor a reduction in payroll taxes which would have beneficial effects on prices - - much like a cost push in reverse. Finally, I would favor measures designed to reduce the greatest discomfort of a protracted period of inflation. These might include a reform of the mortgage instrument and possibly of savings deposits through indexation or other equivalent devices which would help home buyers, the housing industry, and the small savers. (To fully accomplish this task, some form of subsidization of the thrift institution may be necessary to take care of their seasoned portfolio.)

If one holds that these remedies are too slow in reducing inflation, then, rather than pursuing what seems to be the present policy of stern deflation with the result of a serious depression, one should try a new round of incomes policy - - say a ceiling on wage increases with the commitment that if the rate of change of prices exceeds some limit, then there will be some reduction in taxes. This should be accompanied by an educational campaign to persuade the public that a fall in real income is unavoidable and the only choice is between getting there through a wage freeze or through a painful depression.

THE SOCIAL COSTS OF THE RECENT INFLATION:
THE MIRAGE OF STEADY "ANTICIPATED" INFLATION*

Benjamin Klein
University of California
at Los Angeles

I. INTRODUCTION

Much of the discussion of the recent inflationary experience fails to recognize a fundamental contradiction between professional economic opinion and general public attitudes concerning the harmful effects of inflation. Economists distinguish between anticipated and unanticipated inflation and, within the context of commonly accepted economic theory, assert that the sole cost of fully anticipated inflation is that it leads individuals to economize on real cash balances. Inefficiencies are thereby created as individuals substitute real resources for money and reallocate resources towards the production of less cash intensive commodities. The public, on the other hand, seems to regard inflation as per se evil. [1] In particular, this paper presents some evidence which indicates that the current inflation is extremely steady and, therefore, may be considered largely anticipated; yet public opposition to the recent inflation appears to be deep and widespread. This is difficult to explain solely on the grounds that inflation is an inefficient excise tax. [2]

---

*I am especially indebted to Armen Alchian and also to Phillip Cagan, Stephen Ferris, Milton Friedman, Levis Kochin, Roger Kormendi, Anna Schwartz, and Paul Wachtel for rewarding discussions. Useful comments were also supplied by participants at seminars at the VPI Center for Study of Public Choice, at UCLA, at the University of Chicago, at the Federal Reserve Bank of San Francisco, and at the Board of Governors of the Federal Reserve System. Able research assistance was provided by Irene Abramson, Stephen Ferris and Laura LaHaye. H. Irving Forman and Scott Harris drew the charts. The paper was begun during 1971 while I was a postdoctoral Fellow at the National Bureau of Economic Research. I am also grateful to the Foundation for Research in Economics and Education for research support. I, of course, remain solely responsible for the opinions expressed and for any errors.

[1] An observable political implication of this attitude is the finding by Stigler (1973) that although the unemployment rate has no influence on national voting patterns, the rate of inflation is negatively related to the incumbent's share of votes.

[2] Since there is evidence that market-determined interest payments are being made by commercial banks on some demand deposits cf. Klein (Dec. 1974), the empirical importance of this argument is reduced. The payment of competitive interest on deposits may also explain the general opposition by commercial bankers to inflation. The banking system does not share the proceeds of the inflation tax but is merely forced to pay the tax on their large high-powered money holdings.

In addition to assuming that interest is not paid on money, the usual argument that anticipated inflation is an inefficient tax also assumes that (a) real cash balances are costless to produce and that (b) a more efficient alternative source of government revenue exists. But the monetary confidence capital that must "back" money does not have a zero cost of creation and maintenance, cf. Klein (Nov. 1974). And given the transaction costs of levying and collecting taxes and the relatively low price elasticity of demand for real cash balances, an excise tax on money may be an efficient element in an optimal tax package (see Phelps 1972, ch. 6).

Current policy discussions usually ignore the theory and accept the general public attitude by implicitly or explicitly entering price change in a social welfare function, i.e., by assuming inflation is a social "bad" which should be avoided and traded off against other social costs such as involuntary unemployment. But this general practice should leave us somewhat uneasy. Have we economists failed in our educational task and merely reinforced an irrational belief? Or does the current opposition to inflation rest on rational grounds and is it the analysis that is deficient?

My answer to this question can perhaps most usefully be placed in the context of the "new inflationist" answers supplied, for example, by Gordon (1971) and Tobin and Ross (1971). Since the current inflation is steady and, consequently, largely anticipated, they argue, it entails little or no uncertainty cost. Hence, economists must educate the public that government policy should be geared solely to permitting individuals to more costlessly adjust to and live with inflation, e.g., by eliminating maximum interest rate restrictions and adopting escalator clauses, rather than reducing the inflation rate and thereby creating increased unemployment. In the discussion which follows I attempt to demonstrate that this analysis is incomplete and that there may be a rational explanation for the general public opposition to the current inflation.

The paper is an empirical examination of the movement of prices and of changes in the implied underlying monetary framework in the United States over the last century. Using annual inflation rates, 1870-1972 (listed in the Appendix, Table A1), I try to make some historical comparisons and general observations regarding the crucial differences in the behavior of prices over the last fifteen years compared to the previous seventy-five. The particular narrow question I focus upon is whether price changes are more predictable now than they were previously, for example, at the turn of the century.

My initial, somewhat superficial, analysis is consistent with the "new inflationist" argument that since the current inflation is relatively predictable, the social costs of continuing it are small. However, once the recent inflationary experience is put into historical perspective, the current inflation can no longer be described as almost perfectly predictable. I present evidence, some of it weak but all of it consistent, which clearly suggests that we have only very recently moved to a fiduciary-monetary standard where the long-term trend in prices is no longer presumed to be zero and where large price changes in one direction are not expected to be reversible. When all this evidence is taken together, a persuasive case can be made that under this new standard the variance of estimates of the price level expected in the future (e.g., five years from now) may be relatively high. Therefore, although variability in the annual rate of price change is now relatively low, long-term price unpredictability is significant, and the uncertainty

186

costs associated with the current inflation no longer seem to be trivial.

II. PREDICTABILITY OF THE PRICE LEVEL

Traditional economic theory emphasizes the <u>predictability</u> and not the <u>stability</u> of price change as the primary determinant of the real monetary service flow from money. Unanticipated price changes decrease the usefulness of money as a store of value and unit for long-term contracts by redistributing income and wealth among individuals and by introducing a random element in all monetary agreements for future payment. The added uncertainty of an increase in the expected value of unanticipated price changes, i.e., of an increase in the variance of the prior probability price change distribution, leads individuals to devote increased quantities of scarce resources to attempting to predict future price movements and, as Fisher stated so well in <u>The Purchasing Power of Money</u>, discourages the formation of long-term contracts.

It is important to explicitly note how "unpredictability" of price change is used in this paper. Most discussions of inflation implicitly assume a degenerate prior probability price change distribution. Individuals are assumed to estimate an "expected" rate of price change (which can be thought of as the mean of the prior probability distribution), but the confidence interval on this estimate (the variance of the prior probability distribution) is ignored and implicitly assumed to equal zero. It is useful, however, to distinguish between two separate questions: (a) does the current actual rate of price change, in fact, equal the mean of the expected or predicted price change distribution, i.e., assuming that contracts were adjusted to this mean, does the inflation produce any wealth redistribution effects? and (b) how much uncertainty now exists regarding future price changes i.e., what is the variance of the expected price change distribution? I am here concerned with the latter question and therefore with the variance of the underlying prior probability price change distribution individuals believe they face. The actual rate of price change may equal the mean expected rate of price change (and we can therefore call this price change "fully anticipated") yet there may exist a great deal of price change uncertainty. Zero information costs would imply not just that, ex post, the actual rate of price change equals the mean predicted rate of price change but also that the prior variance of the predicted rate of price change equals zero, i.e., <u>perfect accuracy</u> and <u>perfect certainty</u>. The rate of price change may not equal the mean predicted rate of price change and therefore be "unanticipated" yet may be "expected" (if, say, the actual is within one standard deviation of the mean). The variance of the prior probability distribution can therefore be thought of as a measure of how much "unanticipated" price change is "expected." [3]

To get some idea of the historical movement of the unpredictability of price change and therefore of the costs of uncertainty associated with price change, Chart 1 (solid line) shows the variability of the annual rate of price change over the period 1880-1972. Variability is measured by the six-term moving standard deviation of the annual rate of change of prices. [4] If price anticipations are assumed not to be formed regarding the acceleration of price change (or of any higher derivatives), this series may be regarded as an operational measure of the amount of unanticipated annual price change over the past six years and the amount of unanticipated price change (or price uncertainty) expected for the immediate future. [5] This measure clearly indicates that the unpredictability of price change has been extremely low over the past fifteen years. Although there is a positive relationship between the mean annual rate of price change and the variability of the annual rate of price change in some countries at some times, it seems not to be the case now for the United States. The average rate of price change over the last decade has been very high by historical U.S. standards, but the variability in the annual rate of price change is seen to be extremely low. [6] It is necessary, therefore, to consider the transaction costs

---

[3] Explicitly introducing the variance of the prior probability of price change distribution, i.e., risk considerations associated with the future real value of money, requires that the usual demand for money and "optimum" quantity of money" analysis be modified. See Klein (1972) where a price variance term is entered into the demand for money function.

[4] This is similar to the concept used by Friedman and Schwartz (1969) as a measure of the variability of money and income. I first computed logarithmic first differences of a price index series centered in mid-year and then computed moving standard deviations from these year-to-year percentage rates of price change for six terms and dated the result as of the final year. The vertical scale on the chart is logarithmic to minimize the heteroscedasticity problem (cf. Friedman and Schwartz, 1969, p. 202). The price series is the implicit national product deflator using Gallman's annual NNP estimates for 1874-1909 and Kuznets' annual NNP estimates, adjusted in wartime, for 1910-1946 and an annual average of the Commerce Department's quarterly GNP estimates for 1947-1972.

[5] This is a crude measure of price unpredictability. A more complete analysis might contain an explicit model of the formation of price expectations based on the stochastic properties of the series and a measure of price change unpredictability based on the deviations of actual from expected price changes over time. But merely fitting a Box-Jenkins ARMA model (or an adaptive regression model) to past rates of price change to make price forecasts at every point in time will yield misleading results. A major point of this paper is that the public considers other information when forming price expectations, such as the nature of the underlying monetary institutions. And the problem is one of explicitly considering shifts in these other factors without relying at any point in time on price information not yet experienced. Variability is, however, a good measure of unpredictability if the underlying stochastic structure is assumed to be one of a constant mean plus some random disturbance. Some evidence presented below (Chart 1, fn. 9 and Table 1) suggests that the assumption of a constant (zero) mean works reasonably well until 1955 and therefore substantiates my implicit model of the formation of expectations at least up to that point.

[6] Joseph A. Livingston conducts a semi-annual survey of price predictions of economists which has been reported in the Philadelphia Bulletin since 1946. The standard deviation of these (mean) predictions across individuals (which is not necessarily equal to my concept of the standard deviation of a representative individual's expected price change distribution) coincides remarkably closely to my variability measure. Both series fall over the postwar period and reach a low point in the early 1960 s (0.62 percentage points in 1963 for the Livingston series and 0.24 percentage points in 1964 for my variability series), and then both rise to a peak in the early 1970 s (1.56 in 1971 for the Livingston series and 1.30 in 1970 for my variability series). The correlation between the two series over the 1947-72 period is .77. I am indebted to Paul Wachtel for making the Livingston data available to me.

associated with predictable price changes as a rationale for the public opposition to the current inflation.

III. STABILITY OF THE PRICE LEVEL

Traditional theory emphasizes price predictability but does not ignore price stability. Even if perfectly predictable, there may be information and transaction costs associated with changing prices. Fisher (1920), in a largely unknown popular tract published nine years after The Purchasing Power of Money, modified his position noted above and emphasized the calculation costs which exist when prices change. By drawing an analogy between the dollar and other measures such as the inch he advocated a policy of "standardizing" the dollar by varying its gold content to produce a stable and not solely a predictable price level. The greater the rate of inflation, the more rapid is the depreciation of unadjusted price information and therefore the greater the economic incentive to discount monetary magnitudes. Since discounting is costly, inflation thereby decreases the usefulness of money as a measure of value. It is also important to recognize that there are adjustment costs of altering prices. Some prices are less than perfectly (i.e., costlessly) flexible in the face of changing anticipations because they were previously fixed by long-term contracts and the renegotiating costs are significant. "Even in the absence of explicit contracts, prices may be kept from adjustment by implied understandings and by the mere inertia of custom" (Fisher, 1911, p. 185). Our tax code, accounting conventions, legal system and other long-term institutional arrangements are also far from perfectly flexible. In addition, the costs of changing price signs, labels, catalogs, bookkeeping entries, coin vending machines and currency denominations may be significant. [7] Therefore, inflation, even if perfectly predictable, increases the cost of monetary exchange. Such an inflation produces both more frequent price changes and greater discrepancies from "equilibrium" prices (i.e., prices that would prevail in the absence of adjustment costs) and reallocates resources toward industries in which prices and factor payments can be adjusted more cheaply.

---

[7] It is important to note in this context that the commonly made distinction between open and repressed inflation which is usually defined in terms of the extent of government intervention in the market place that prevents prices from reaching their equilibrium values should more generally be made in terms of the degree of price adjustment costs present in a particular market. Given costs of changing prices, all prices will not be fully adjusted at all times to anticipations and hence can sometimes be said to be "repressed." Prices fixed by law may be extremely rigid, but the evasion or alteration of governmental regulatory constraints is just one type of the more general price adjustment costs present in all markets. The costs of adjustment in the political market place are not infinite and may be in some cases less than in some private markets. For example, a primary motivation for the 1969 income tax modifications may have been the political disequilibrium produced by inflation given our progressive income tax structure, and the recent Social Security adjustments may have been similarly motivated. On the other hand, an obvious example of very slow (costly) adjustment of governmentally controlled prices can be found in some of the legal fines and penalties which now give a convicted defendant a grossly unbalanced choice between days in jail and a monetary fine (e.g., 30 days or $250). Lack of upward adjustment of these monetary fines over time is one of the factors that has led to the recent Supreme Court decision that the few poor defendants "forced" to go to jail are treated unequally under the law.

To get some idea of the historical movement of these transaction costs associated with anticipated inflation, Chart 1 (dashed line) shows the extent of annual price change over the period 1880-1972. The variable plotted is the log of the six-term moving average of the absolute annual rate of change of prices. This series can be regarded as an operational measure of the transaction costs associated with annual price change over the last six years. (The six year moving average of the absolute value of the annual rate of change of prices is used since the transaction costs associated with anticipated inflation considered above are also present with anticipated deflation, i.e., price change per se is what is costly.)

IV. PREDICTABILITY VERSUS STABILITY

The most obvious fact about Chart 1 is that the moving standard deviation of the rate of price change and the moving average absolute rate of price change coincide remarkably well. Although there is no necessary identity between them, large annual price changes in a six year period have historically been closely associated with highly variable price changes in the same period. Both of these series are measures of variability - - one is the square root of the average of squared deviations around the mean; the other is the average absolute deviations around zero. And the average absolute deviations around zero can usefully be thought of as a mixture of the standard deviation (σ) and the mean (μ) of the underlying population. For example, for a normal distribution the absolute annual rate of change of prices can be approximately estimated by:

$$(1) \qquad E(|x|) \approx .7\sigma + \mu(2p-1),$$

where p is the probability that an observation will be positive, or the integral of the normal curve above zero which is itself a function of (μ/σ). [8] The closeness in the levels of our two time series therefore suggests that μ has generally been constant and statistically near zero,[9] and hence, that large annual rates of price change have generally been largely unanticipated. It is, therefore, understandable why stability is often identified with predictability when individuals contemplate the evils of inflation.

But after 1955 a wide separation appears in the two series, and it is crucial that the distinction be explicitly made when analyzing recent experience. This unprecedented separation is produced by the combination of two historically

---

[8] I am indebted to Milton Friedman for this formulation.

[9] The average rate of change of prices during the 1880-1915 period is close to zero (.0064), implying that the first term in expression (1) dominates our estimate of $E(|x|)$. Although there is a significant increase in the average rate of price change during the 1916-55 period (to .0242), a very large increase in σ occurred during the period causing p to remain not very different from one-half. The first term of (1) therefore continues to dominate and the two series continue to be merely alternative measures of σ through 1955.

Chart 1. Variability and Extent of Annual Rate of Price Change, 1880-1972.

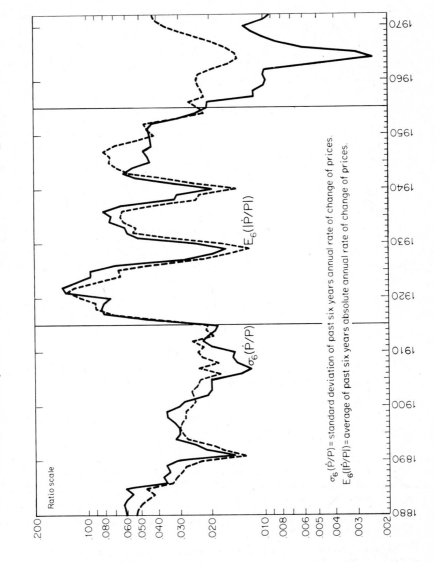

$\sigma_6(\dot{P}/P)$ = standard deviation of past six years annual rate of change of prices.

$E_6(|\dot{P}/P|)$ = average of past six years absolute annual rate of change of prices.

unique characteristics of our present monetary situation: a relatively high level in the average rate of change of prices and a very low variability of price change around that level, or a high μ relative to σ. [10] The only other time interval of similar length that compares with the most recent period in terms of a continuous upward trend in prices is the pre-World War I gold inflation of 1897-1914 when prices rose at an average annual rate of nearly two percent. But this 18 year period follows a long period of deflation and includes three years when prices actually declined. The last twenty years is the only such period in our recorded history without a single year in which prices fell. This is reflected in the moving standard deviation of prices, which is significantly lower during the last fifteen years than in any other period, reaching an historically unprecedented low level of .0024 (i.e., .24 percentage points) in 1964. [11] That we are experiencing a significant steady inflation for the first time in our recorded history may lead us to assume that this inflation is largely anticipated. [12]

Examination of Chart 1 seems to suggest uneasy acceptance of the conclusion that if the present opposition to inflation is "rational," it must be based on the somewhat vague calculation and adjustment costs associated with price change and not on the costs of price uncertainty. While the moving average absolute rate of price change variable is now relatively high by historical standards (reaching .0413 in 1972) and is rising, the moving standard deviation variable is now exceptionally low. Although the moving standard deviation has risen since 1964, it is unlikely that this recent increase in the unpredictability of prices is the basis of the recent opposition to inflation. The level of the moving standard deviation was still very low by historical standards at the 1970 peak (.0130) and by 1972 was less than one percent (.0091). [13] Therefore, unless the public's tolerance of price level unpredictability has fallen drastically, the figures seem to indicate that a satisfactory explanation for the continued opposition to the U.S. inflation cannot be based on the fact that the inflation is now largely unpredictable. However, under the more complete analysis that follows, this conclusion will be shown to be incorrect.

---

[10] That is, although the post-1955 period is not very different from the earlier 1916-55 period with regard to the mean rate of price change (.0279), it is dramatically different with regard to the ratio of μ to σ. After 1955, μ rises significantly relative to σ and therefore p rises significantly above one-half and the estimates of $E(|x|)$ become dominated by the μ term in expression (1).

[11] Note, however, that part of the secular decline in the variability of price change may be due to the statistical improvement over time in our price measures.

[12] The only other period of fairly steady moderate inflation occurred briefly during 1902-1907, producing a large gap in the two series in 1907. But the post-1955 inflation has, by comparison, been higher, less variable and of much greater duration.

[13] If the series are extended with the 1973 observation, the moving standard deviation remains unchanged at .0091 while the moving average absolute rate of price change continues to increase to .0450.

V. A NEW MONETARY STANDARD

It is useful to compare the annual rate of price change and the movement of the two derivative variables plotted in Chart 1 over different time periods. The total period covered in the chart can be conveniently divided into three sub-periods: (a) the "gold standard" period from 1880 to 1915; (b) the "transitional" period from 1916 to 1955; and (c) the "new standard" period from 1956-1972. The corresponding average level of the moving standard deviation variable over each of these subperiods is: (a) .0310; (b) .0569; (c) .0095. The transitional period has the largest average standard deviation. Since this period contains the Great Depression, the two World Wars and the Korean War, comparisons with the other two periods are not entirely relevant. The comparison between the latest period and the gold standard period, however, is striking. The average standard deviation was more than three times as great during the gold standard period than during the recent period. This merely confirms the argument of the previous section regarding the historically unique character of the extremely low level of price unpredictability which now seems to exist.

But comparison of the recent period with the earlier "gold standard" period in terms of a moving standard deviation as a measure of the predictability of prices is misleading. The post-1952 period contains only positive price changes while the earlier time period contains positive and negative price changes. And although price changes were previously unsteady, price changes of similar magnitude but of opposite sign occurred temporally close to one another, i.e., the variance of the absolute rate of change of prices was low. During the 1880-1915 period the mean of the moving six-year average $\underline{absolute}$ annual rate of change of prices was near three percent (.0284), but the mean of the moving six-year average annual rate of change of prices was very close to zero (.0017). This explains the closeness during this period of the two series plotted in Chart 1. At any point in time the average absolute rate of change of prices, $E(|X|)$, is mathematically related to the variance of the rate of change of prices, $V(X)$, by:

$$(2) \qquad [E(|X|)]^2 = V(X) + [E(X)]^2 - V(|X|),$$

where $E(X)$ is the average rate of change of prices and $V(|X|)$ is the variance of the absolute rate of change of prices. During much of the gold standard period, $E(X)$ $\underline{and}$ $V(|X|)$ were both close to zero. That is, during the gold standard period annual price changes were highly variable but the absolute annual rate of price change was extremely steady, and the average rate of price change was near zero. If, for example, an eight percent inflation rate occurred in a particular year, an inflation rate of approximately minus eight percent would likely occur a short time later (within six years). [14]

This gold standard phenomenon can perhaps be seen most clearly by examining the sample autocorrelations of the annual rates of price change presented in Table 1. Each of the first two subperiods has been further divided into two twenty year periods. [15] There are thus five periods of similar length over which autocorrelations have been calculated. The first two gold standard periods are quite distinctly different from the final new standard period. The autocorrelations during the gold standard periods are generally negative or close to zero while the autocorrelations during the most recent period are positive, in fact quite strongly positive for the one- and two-year lag terms. [16] The gold standard can be considered to have been a period of mean reversion in the rate of price change while the current period is one of persistence or long-term mean revision in the rate of price change. Hence, the current rate of price change is now a good indication of what the rate of price change will be in the immediate future while under the gold standard the relationship between the current rate and future rates was negative and weaker. [17]

----

[14] The prominent peaks and troughs in the two series on Chart 1 during the 1916-55 period consist of large (small) price changes in one direction which are frequently closely followed by large (small) price changes in the opposite direction, a pattern one would also expect under a commodity standard. For example, the peak in the early 1920 s includes the large World War 1 and post-War inflation and the large 1921-1922 deflation; the peak in the mid-1920 s is due to the unusually large price decreases in 1931-1932, followed by a fairly rapid inflation; and the sharp troughs in 1929 and 1940 are due to very brief periods in the late 1920 s and 1930 s of fairly steady mild inflation and deflation. Only the peak in the mid-1940 s can be ascribed solely to price changes in one direction, with the unsteadiness of the large reported price increases during and after World War II possibly due to the existence of price controls.

[15] The gold standard subperiod happens to be divided at the point where the post-Civil War deflation can be thought of as turning into a period of gold inflation. That is, although the average rate of change of prices over the entire subperiod is close to zero, in terms of the average inflation rate it really consists of two rather distinct periods.

[16] Because the rate of price change data in the most recent period are annual averages of quarterly observations, there is an aggregation bias in the first-order serial correlation (cf. Working, 1960). If the serial correlation of the quarterly data is zero, there is a positive bias of .227; with positive serial correlation in the quarterly data, the bias is lower than .227; with negative serial correlation, the bias is higher than .227.

[17] The new standard period, however, is not strictly one of a martingale in the rate of price changes since, as can be seen in the following table, the first year autocorrelation of the acceleration of price change is not zero but positive. The autocorrelations of the acceleration of price change in the earlier periods are generally zero or negative.

Sample Autocorrelations of Annual Rates of Price Acceleration

lag 1876-95	1896-1915	1916-35	1936-55	1956-72
1. -.496*	-.647*	-.398	-.001	.527*
2. .109	.244	-.079	-.431	.006
3. -.053	.162	.182	-.145	.008
4. -.188	-.474*	-.406	.150	-.150

*indicates autocorrelation significantly different from zero at the .95 confidence level.

Table 1

Sample Autocorrelations of Annual Rates of Price Change

lag	1876-95	1896-1915	1916-35	1936-55	1956-72
1.	.027	-.357	.421	.487*	.857*
2.	-.009	.058	.211	-.039	.598*
3.	-.258	.032	.071	-.146	.342
4.	-.461*	-.527*	-.229	-.090	.012

*indicates autocorrelation significantly different from zero at the .95 confidence level. (The asymptotic standard error of each sample autocorrelation is $1/\sqrt{n}$, where n is the number of observations in each time period under the null hypothesis that the true autocorrelations are zero, cf. Box and Jenkins (1970, ch. 2). All autocorrelations within each time period are calculated using data only from that indicated time period.

Under a commodity standard, therefore, an average of past price changes has no direct _positive_ relationship with long-term price anticipations, and so the standard deviation of the annual rate of price change variable cannot be regarded as a complete measure of the unpredictability of prices in such an economy. Although annual rates of price change may have been highly variable, the price level expected in five or ten years may have been more predictable during much of our early history than now. The historically unique characteristic of the inflation of the last 15 years represented by the separation of the two series in Chart 1 is not that we are experiencing a predictable price movement, but that we have moved fully to a new monetary standard where the long-term trend in prices is not expected to be zero and where large price changes in one direction are not expected to be reversible.

VI. PUBLIC RECOGNITION OF THE NEW MONETARY STANDARD

Realization that we were on this new monetary standard, where rapid inflation would not likely later be followed by deflation, must have occurred very gradually over the last twenty-five years. There is evidence which suggests that although the U.S. went off the gold standard _de jure_ in 1933, the gold standard mentality (where large or unanticipated price changes in one direction are expected to be reversible) persisted _de facto_ into the 1960s. In the immediate post-World War II period a deflation was generally expected. The Livingston survey data on price anticipations noted above (fn. 6) indicates a forecasted rate of change of the CPI for the following year which, except for the Korean War period during 1951 and early 1952, was consistently negative over the 1946-54 period. The reported "expected" annual rate of price decline immediately following World War II in 1946-47 was greater than eight percent. Individuals expected a postwar price reaction to wartime inflation very similar to our experience after earlier wars. Only after the post-World War II deflation did not materialize and after prices failed to fall following the Korean War or during the recessions of the 1950s and early 1960s, did the public gradually recognize that we were operating under new monetary rules. [18]

A major determinant of the fundamental policy shift to the new monetary standard was the gradual _de facto_ adoption of the international dollar standard which reduced the force of the balance of payments as a constraint on U.S. monetary policy. But even as late as 1964 firm expectations must have been held that a long-term monetary policy necessary to maintain foreign convertibility of the dollar at $35/oz. would be followed. As Table 2 shows, the index of the official commodity value of gold (the ratio of the official dollar value of gold to the

---

[18] However, even as late as a couple of years ago many individuals maintained that the current inflation was due solely to the Vietnam War. We were merely experiencing the usual wartime price increase, they claimed, without any fundamental change in the underlying ground rules.

Table 2

Index of Official Commodity Value of Gold, 1921-73

(1926 = 100)

year	index	year	index	year	index
		1938	215	1956	96
1921	102	1939	220	1957	93
1922	103	1940	215	1958	92
1923	99	1941	194	1959	92
1924	102	1942	171	1960	92
1925	97	1943	164	1961	93
1926	100	1944	163	1962	92
1927	105	1945	160	1963	92
1928	103	1946	140	1964	92
1929	105	1947	114	1965	90
1930	116	1948	105	1966	87
1931	137	1949	111	1967	87
1932	154	1950	107	1968	85
1933	194	1951	96	1969	81
1934	225	1952	99	1970	79
1935	212	1953	100	1971	76
1936	210	1954	100	1972	79
1937	196	1955	99	1973	77

Source: 1921-55 from Cagan (1965, table F7), extended 1956-73 using Bureau of Labor Statistics WPI and official U.S. price of gold. Observations are on June 30 of the indicated year.

wholesale price index) was only slightly lower in 1964 than in 1922 (after the sharp post-World War I deflation). Using this as a benchmark, as late as the mid-1960s the official price of gold was not more than ten percent too low in terms of real purchasing power. The inflation of the 1940s, the 1950s and the early 1960s merely readjusted the level of prices for the deflation and devaluation in the 1930s. It is, therefore, easy to understand why much of the public, although looking at the accumulating annual price change evidence over this period, did not clearly see the fundamental change in the monetary framework that was taking place. Since 1964, however, in spite of the recent U.S. devaluations, the purchasing power of official gold has fallen (by late 1973) an additional twenty percent. Within this context the twenty percent increase in the official dollar price of gold that has occurred since 1971 has clearly been of insufficient magnitude. But a major deflation is certainly not now generally anticipated. [19]

It is also instructive to note in this context that until very recently the ratio of the total stock of high-powered money to the official dollar value of the total U.S. gold stock has been historically rather stable. [20] The ratio of high-powered money to gold was 2.5 as late as 1960, which was very close to the average level of 2.3 during the 1880-90 period after the return to convertibility. In fact, the ratio averaged 2.2 over the entire 1880-1915 gold standard period. The ratio reached an all time low of 1.0 in 1941 after the massive gold inflows of the 1930s and a pre-1961 all time high value of 2.9 in 1893 when the Treasury experienced significant gold drains. In spite of the large increases in the official dollar value of gold, the post-1960 rise in the (H/gold) ratio has been dramatic and is currently close to 10.0. This indicates how unique the last decade has been in terms of the break of the tie between our money stock and gold and the de facto movement off the gold standard.

The substantially shorter lag of adjustment of interest rates to price level changes found by Yohe and Karnosky (1969) than that found in many earlier studies is behavioral evidence that individuals began to realize during the late 1950s and 1960s that a new pure fiduciary standard was replacing any remaining semblance of a gold commodity standard. If the Yohe and Karnosky regressions are extended backward in time from the 1952-69 period used in their study, the total effect of price level changes on long-term interest rates is much smaller and slower. The initial price change coefficients are often negative and the sum of the coefficients is often close to zero. These are results one would

---

[19] There are, however, some "prophets of doom" who continue to predict an enormous deflation and depression that, in comparison, will make the 1930 s contractions appear minor. Many of these individuals (including, for example, some neo-Austrians) make the error of implicitly assuming we are still on a form of the gold standard and therefore that eventually prices must fall. The idea that "the inflation bubble of the last thirty years must eventually be burst," of course, makes no sense under our new monetary standard.

[20] See Cagan (1965, p. 56, Chart 4, appendix table F7 and also pp. 49-67).

Table 3

Almon Lag Regressions of Monthly Rate of Change

of CPI on Long-Term Interest Rate

time period	$\sum_{i=0}^{48} \beta_i$	$\sum_{i=0}^{6} \beta_i$	mean lag
1917-33	.057	-.005	28.61
1933-52	-.112	-.022	22.41
1952-72	1.068	.577	14.86

The long-term interest rate, r_L, is the basic yield on high grade (Aaa) corporate bonds to 30 year maturity. The β_i coefficients are estimated using a sixth degree Almon lag on the current and past monthly rates of annual change in the CPI, $(\dot{P}/P)$, with the far term constrained to zero:

$$(3) \qquad (r_L)_t = a_0 + \sum_{i=0}^{48} \beta_i \, (\dot{P}/P)_{t-i} + \epsilon_t \; .$$

expect under a commodity standard with long-term expectations of a stable price level. For example, Table 3 presents regression results over three time periods of the monthly annual rate of CPI change on the long-term interest rate, using a 48 month sixth degree polynomial lag structure. [21] Both the six month and 48 month sum of price change coefficients on the long-term interest rate have risen dramatically in the 1952-72 period compared to the two earlier periods. [22]

Table 4 shows more precisely when the change in the short-run impact on the level of interest rates of a change in the rate of price change took place. This table presents decade by decade results of the sum of the first six months' coefficients for similar regressions using a 36 month six degree Almon lag of the annual rate of monthly price change in the CPI against both long and short interest rates. These results clearly indicate that a significant positive short-run impact of price change on the level of interest rates is present only in the last decade. It appears, therefore, that changes in the actual rate of price change have only very recently had a large positive impact on changes in the future anticipated rate of price change. In fact, the short-run Fisherian price anticipations effects emphasized by Yohe and Karnosky only make sense under the pure fiduciary standard of the late 1960s with its substantially greater short-run adjustment in price anticipations to rising prices. [23]

---

[21] The time period noted for these and all other distributed lag regressions refers to the dependent variable. In this case there are therefore another previous four years of rate of price change data entering each estimate.

These regressions implicitly assume that the level of the real rate of interest is statistically independent of current and past rates of price change, making it possible to treat it as a constant plus a residual term. Sargent (1973) has demonstrated that this procedure is most appropriate when the interest elasticity of demand for money is zero, a condition that makes some theoretical sense when competitive interest payments are made on money (cf. Klein, Dec. 1974). But, in any event, I am merely comparing the effects of current and past price change on interest rates over different time periods and need only assume that whatever short-run changes in the real rate do occur have not changed over time.

[22] These results are to be expected from the sample autocorrelations of Table 1 and the efficient markets hypothesis. The autocorrelations imply that the current rate of price change contains information about future rates of price change and the results indicate that the capital market adjusts to this information. It is important to recognize that the efficient markets hypothesis implies adjustment of relative prices of storable assets. Therefore bond prices (the price of money today relative to tomorrow) will adjust to the future price change information embodied in the current rate of price change, but other current nominal prices will not adjust to this information. The current price of a house, for example, will not increase with an increase in the anticipated rate of change of prices since future housing rental prices and the interest rate will both rise, leaving the asset price in current dollars unchanged. The existence of significant positive autocorrelation in the rate of price change variable is therefore not inconsistent with the efficient markets hypothesis. Although we may now have information that general prices will be higher next period, it will not pay to carry those goods in the GNP basket which are storable over to the next period because the real value of these goods is not anticipated to rise. The efficient markets hypothesis implies zero serial correlation around trend, which in this case is the now higher interest rate. Significant positive serial correlation in the rate of price change merely indicates the presence of positive autocorrelation in monetary policy.

[23] This explains why the St. Louis macroeconomic model has a dummy variable for the post-1960 period in the interest rate equations. Yohe and Karnosky note that the larger and more rapid effects of price level changes on interest rates during the 1960 s may be due to "institutional changes." But, in a listing of the plausible explanations for a shift in the underlying framework, they never suggest that the complete movement from a commodity to a fiduciary monetary standard may be a major force explaining the shift in behavior.

The fact that comparative historical results such as these have not been emphasized in the literature is likely due to selective reporting by investigators. Without a theoretical understanding of the underlying institutional framework, the pre-1960 results appear meaningless.

Table 4

Six Month Impact of One Percentage Point Change in Rate of Change of

CPI on Level of Interest Rates

time period	r_L	r_S
1920-30	.0048	.0029
1930-40	-.0641	-.1021
1940-50	-.0048	.0057
1950-60	-.0318	-.0068
1960-70	.2083	.7246

The long-term interest rate, r_L, is the basic yield on high grade (Aaa) corporate bonds to 30 year maturity. The short-term interest rate, r_S, is the yield on 4-6 month NYC commercial paper. The elements in the table are $\sum_{i=0}^{6} \beta_i$ from the regression:

$$(4) \qquad r_t = a_0 + \sum_{i=0}^{36} \beta_i (P/P)_{t-i} + \epsilon_t,$$

where the β_i are estimated using a sixth degree Almon lag with the far term constrained to zero.

201

An alternative way of describing these results is by claiming not that in the 1960s price expectations adjusted faster to past actual price changes but that changes in price expectations merely had a larger and more rapid impact on interest rates during the 1960s. Gibson (1972), using the Livingston price expectations data discussed above (fn. 6), finds a much greater effect on this particular expected rate of price change variable on the level of interest rates after 1959 than before. [24] Gibson "explains" (p. 863) the fact that price predictions were more inaccurate before 1959 (and therefore given less weight by rational market participants) by asserting that "information costs made predicting inflation less rewarding for the market before 1959." This tautology is then fleshed out with two possible hypotheses: (a) since the actual inflation rate was lower before 1959, the benefits from accurately predicting it would also be lower; and (b) it became cheaper to predict prices after 1959. Unfortunately, hypothesis (a) ignores the fact that price uncertainty and the gains from increased accuracy are related to the variance and not the mean of expected price change. And Gibson suggests no reasons why hypothesis (b) may be correct, i.e., why the production function regarding future price level information shifted up the 1960s. The analysis of this paper suggests that the 1950s were part of the transitional phase of final adjustment to the new monetary standard. Since market participants were not yet fully aware of the fact that the gold standard, in the sense of relative stability in the long-term trend of prices and short-term reversibility of large price changes, was nearing its demise, less accurate price predictions should be expected.

VII. LONG-TERM PRICE PREDICTABILITY

A measure of longer-term price unpredictability than that plotted in Chart 1 may be conveniently defined if stability is assumed in the underlying process generating the annual rates of price change in each of the five time periods isolated in Table 1 and if these sample autocorrelations are considered as the best point estimates of the true autocorrelations of the underlying statistical processes. Consider the six-term moving standard deviation of the rate of price change variable, denoted σ_S, as a measure of short-term price unpredictability or uncertainty in next year's rate of price change. To derive a measure of price uncertainty over a longer time period, consider the annual rate of price change expected for each future year as a random variable and merely use the formula for the variance of the sum of n random variables:

$$(5) \quad \text{Var} \left(\sum_{i=1}^{n} x_i \right) = \sum_{i=1}^{n} \text{Var}(x_i) + \sum_{i} \sum_{j} \text{Cov}(x_i, x_j).$$

---

[24] His regressions begin in 1952. If he took them back to 1946, when the Livingston data begin, the difference of the results between the early and later periods is even much greater.

Uncertainty of the rate of price change over the next five years, for example, may be measured by the sum of our σ^2_S variable over the current and previous four years plus a term to measure twice the expected covariance of the annual rate of price change over these five years, $\sum_i \sum_j \sigma_S(i)\,\sigma_S(j)r_{i,j}$, where the value of $r_{i,j}$ is taken from Table 1 for the year for which long-term price unpredictability is defined. This variable is divided by five and the square root taken to get a measure of <u>uncertainty regarding the average annual rate of change of prices over the next five years</u>, denoted σ_L and plotted in Chart 2. This variable can be compared to the σ_S of Chart 1. When price predictability is measured in this manner the recent "new standard" period no longer appears to be historically unique. The average level of this longer-term price unpredictability variable over each of the three subperiods is: (a) .0229; (b) .0777; (c) .0223. The transitional period, once again, has the highest average level. This period has by far the greatest degree of price uncertainty with both short-term and long-term price unpredictability, σ_S and σ_L, extremely high. But what has changed in comparison to the relative levels of our σ_S series is that the degree of price uncertainty experienced during the new standard period no longer is one-third what was experienced during the gold standard period. The average values of σ_L are approximately the same and, in fact, confining the analysis to the 1890-1915 part of the gold standard period (where σ_L averages .0157) shows that long-term price unpredictability is now somewhat higher. σ_L has risen more than a percentage point since the rapid inflation began in 1966 and now stands at slightly more than two percent, a level we remained below for the entire 1896-1915 period. And even the low level briefly reached by σ_L in 1965-67 (0.100) is above the 1909-11 trough (.0084), but, more importantly, the entire 1905-15 period averaged only slightly more than one percent (.0102).

Clearly, unlike the analysis with regard to σ_S, it cannot be concluded that under the new standard of the last fifteen years <u>long-term</u> price unpredictability has been at an historically unprecedented low level. In addition, while σ_S peaked in 1970, σ_L has continued to rise. There has been a secular upward shift in the amount of long-term relative to short-term price unpredictability. The average ratio of σ_L to σ_S over our three sub-periods is: (a) .74; (b) 1.37; (c) 2.35. At the turn of the century (σ_L/σ_S) was around .5 while now it is above 2.0. This phenomenon can be attributed to the general increase over time in the autocorrelations of the annual rate of change of prices. The σ_S variable indicates that we are less likely now than under the gold standard to experience next year a rate of price change that is more than, for example, two percentage points away from the mean estimate. But the high autocorrelations imply that if in fact we do experience such an unanticipated price change, it is more likely now to continue for a few years while under the gold standard it was likely to reverse or "correct" itself, i.e., "average out" over time.

Chart 2. Long-Term Price Unpredictability, 1880-1972.

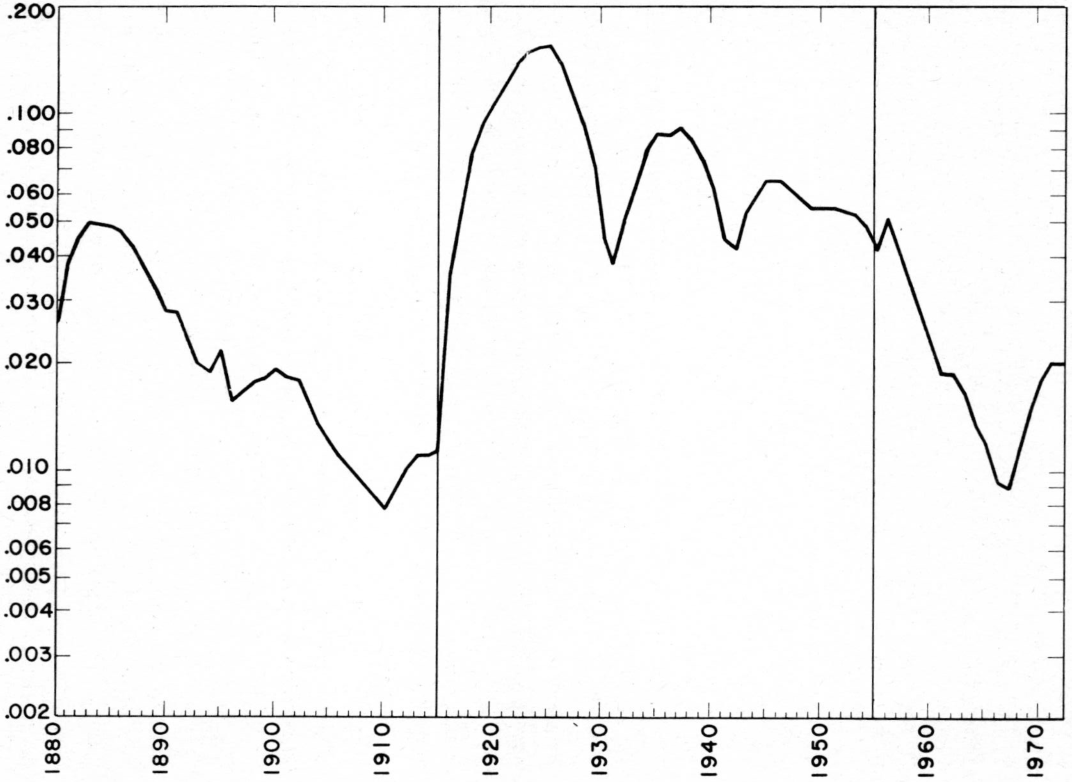

VIII. <u>IMPLICATIONS</u>

If the current period is one in which long-term price uncertainty has risen relative to short-term price uncertainty, the increase in the short-run impact of prices on interest rates would be expected to be greater for short-term than for long-term interest rates. If, for example, the σ_S and σ_L variables are measures of the underlying distribution of short-run and long-run price change individuals believe they face at each point in time, an increase in (σ_L/σ_S) will imply an increase in the weight placed on the observed sample information (e.g., six monthly observations on the annual rate of price change) for short-term relative to long-term interest rates. This is because as the variability of the underlying generating process decreases, the informational content of the given sample becomes more reliable. As shown in Table 4, the differential short-run impact of price change on short-term compared to long-term interest rates does increase as would be expected. [25]

A major implication of an increase in the amount of long-term price unpredictability relative to short-term price unpredictability concerns a change in the composition of debt. A decrease in the demand for and therefore the quantity of long-term debt relative to short-term debt should be expected. On a cursory level, this seems to be obviously true. One hundred year railroad bonds were, for example, issued around the turn of the century, while it is now quite uncommon to find a maturity of a new corporate issue that is greater than 30 years. I examine this secular movement towards shorter term corporate debt issues elsewhere. [26]

Finally, if long-term price uncertainty has increased during the recent inflationary period, increased use of price escalator clauses in long-term contracts would be expected. The general adoption of these clauses (or the adoption of a tabular standard) can, in principle, cheaply avoid the costs and riskiness of long-term commitments that are associated with price uncertainty. The fact that we do not now observe purchasing-power bonds nor escalator clauses in many long-

---

[25] The increase in the short-run adjustment of both short-term and long-term interest rates to price changes that occurred in the 1960 s does not imply, however, that the variance around the estimates of the mean rate of short-term and long-term price change (or short-term and long-term "price uncertainty") has decreased. (For example, individuals may have held the gold standard presumption of a zero mean rate of long-term price change with great conviction, i.e., with a small variance around the prior probability estimate, and therefore placed little weight on a given sample of price observations.) All the 1960 s movement means is that individuals now more easily reject the hypothesis that their mean estimate of price change is correct. This is because of the high autocorrelation of price change under our new standard.

[26] See Klein (1975).

term contracts indicates that price change uncertainty is low relative to how accurately our price indices measure the price changes. [27] If, in fact, existing price indices are rather poor measures of the purchasing power of money, [28] adoption of price escalators will reduce the variance of the anticipated real payoff only if the variance of future anticipated price change is high. This explains why such clauses are generally written into contracts only in countries such as Israel, Brazil and Argentina, that have experienced great price variability and not necessarily high inflation rates. In the U.S., which likely has the most reliable price statistics, still only relatively few contracts possess escalator clauses. For example, approximately five percent of the labor force is currently working under contracts with escalator provisions. But, use of such clauses over time is more highly correlated with measures of price unpredictability than with measures of the expected mean rate of price change. Over the 1957-71 period, the correlation of the percent of the labor force covered by escalators with the measure of short-term price unpredictability, σ_S, is .53, the correlation with the measure of long-term price unpredictability, σ_L, is .84, while the correlation with the moving

---

[27] Economists who now advocate general indexing, a policy recommendation that dates back more than a century, cf. Alfred Marshall, "Answers to Questions on the Subject of Currency and Prices Circulated by the Royal Commission on the Depression of Trade and Industry" (1926, p. 10; also p. 31), fail to recognize that our largely unused price indices have failed the market test. Since there generally are no regulations prohibiting the use of escalators, these economists must be assuming that profit motivated businessmen are ignorant in this regard.

The general benefits of indexing are based on the reduction in the time lag of nominal contract terms to changes in "the general price level," and the assumption that the subset of prices in the index has greater flexibility to changes in demand than the prices being indexed. Indexing, however, then ties one to follow changes in these particular flexible prices when relative changes in these prices would imply that other prices should move in the opposite direction to the price index change. This difficulty of confusing absolute and relative price movements is present under all indexing schemes.

[28] One of the major deficiencies in using either of the two common measures of inflation (the CPI or the GNP deflator) as an escalator in all contracts is the insufficient weight these narrowly based indices give to existing capital goods prices (cf. Alchian and Klein , 1973). The recent price controls have exacerbated the usual difficulties with these indices. I suspect that the discrepancy between quoted and transaction prices has probably widened (with, in many cases, barter transactions actually being made to hide higher transaction prices during the control period and likely substantial discounts from artificially high precautionary list prices in the post-control period). In addition, during the price control period the quality (including variety) of goods fell, while there was a substantial increase in the "indirect" or non-measured cost elements of purchases, e.g., the increase in queues and other time and inconvenience costs associated with stores "running out" of particular products, the elimination of trading stamps, and the higher inventory costs to customers due to the increase in uncertainty. (The large increase in freezer sales during the beef "shortage" and the recent gasoline "topping-off" phenomenon are dramatic cases.) Since true price change was probably understated during controls and true real income change overstated, we are now probably in a "catching up" period with regard to these indices. It is therefore likely that the high measured rate of price change during late 1973 and early 1974 is an over-estimate of the true rate of price change, and the low measured rate of real income change during this recent period is an under-estimate of the true rate of real income change. (This may partially explain why unemployment has not substantially increased in this period although measured real income growth has been far below trend.

average of the past six years' rate of price change is only .19. [29] (Since an increase in future price unpredictability should not only increase the use of escalators in long-term contracts but also decrease the fraction of workers operating under long-term contracts, the correlation with σ_L is remarkably high.) If σ_L continues to rise in the future, the use of escalator arrangements can be expected to continue to expand.

IX. SUMMARY AND CONCLUSION

The variability of annual price change series plotted on Chart 1 suggests that if unpredictability of annual price change were the only economic variable accounting for the opposition to inflation, then no attempt should be made to reduce the current rate of price rise. Such an attempt would entail transitional unemployment costs while a major deceleration of inflation would, in fact, increase the unpredictability of prices, as measured by this variable. Abstracting from the possible increased transaction costs associated with a higher rate of change of prices, maximization of the monetary service return from money would then seem to imply a policy of maintaining the inflation rate at about four percent.

But a closer historical examination of annual rates of price change indicates that the recent inflationary episode is much more unique than is commonly believed and that the moving standard deviation of the annual rate of price change variable does not measure the unpredictability of prices properly. The measure of uncertainty in the annual rate of change of prices expected over the next five years derived in this study showed a markedly different historical pattern than the measure of short-term price uncertainty. This measure of long-term price uncertainty is higher now than at the turn of the century. Under the gold standard, annual price changes were relatively unpredictable, but the price level expected in five years was relatively more predictable; and if enough information were available to obtain a measure of price uncertainty with regard to the very far future (e.g., 10-20 years), these effects would probably be increased.

In addition to a survey of price movements over the last century, the evidence presented on the adjustment of interest rates to price level changes suggests that a major institutional monetary change has occurred over the last decade and that long-term price uncertainty has increased relative to short-term uncertainty. The long-term movement of the monetary framework away from a

---

[29] The percentage of the labor force covered by escalators peaks in 1958 and declines until 1966 after which it again rises, but is now still below the 1958-60 level.

The number of workers covered by escalator clauses for the 1957-73 period is reported in Larson and Bolton (1973). This figure is then deflated by a moving average of the labor force where the current year's labor force was weighted one-half and the previous and future year's labor force weighted one-quarter each. The moving average was taken to reduce the statistical noise produced by the procyclical growth of the labor force which is to a large extent a movement of transitory workers not covered by long-term contracts. But the correlations using the current year's labor force as the deflator are nearly identical.

gold exchange commodity standard accelerated over the postwar period and has finally culminated in an irredeemable pure fiduciary standard. Although the bond markets appear to have adjusted to this new monetary standard where the long-term trend in prices is no longer presumed to be zero and where large price changes in one direction are not expected to be reversible, it is unclear whether there has been full adjustment of all contractual arrangements to this new institutional arrangement. Recognition of and adjustment to such a major alteration in the underlying monetary framework should take place very gradually.

If this delay in recognition and adjustment were the sole basis of the opposition to the recent inflation, over time the opposition would be expected to decline as more and more individuals realize that we are operating under a new monetary standard. But permanent opposition to the current inflation may rationally be based on the high and rising level of long-term price uncertainty. This is the major conclusion of the paper. Compared to the gold standard, the current standard entails the economic benefits of greater short-run price predictability but also the generally unrecognized costs of greater long-term price unpredictability. The net gain or loss crucially depends upon the importance of long-term contracts, both explicit and implicit.

The current crucial question with respect to price predictability is the credibility of the government regarding the long-term trend of price change. A commodity standard (with a low probability of change in the official price of the commodity) severely limits the possible extent of changes in the price level expected over the long-term and can be thought of as a public investment in long-term monetary trust. The price behavior since 1955 has destroyed a large part of this capital. Although the annual inflation rate over the recent past may have been steady and near, for example, four percent, there is now little public confidence that the government will maintain this rate over the next decade. While gold convertibility implied an expected long-term price trend within relatively narrow bounds, there is nothing "natural" or sacrosanct about a four or five or six percent inflation rate. In order to reduce the variance around estimates of long-term price change, what is required is a new myth to replace the now defunct gold standard mentality. Unfortunately resources and information are scarce and public confidence that the Fed will now maintain over the long-term any particular rate of price change cannot be created costlessly.

This analysis does not necessarily imply that we should move back to a gold standard since the variance of unemployment was certainly much higher during that period than it has been over the last fifteen years. But the monetary authorities should begin to take explicit account of the influence of policy on long-term price uncertainty. It is, however, very unlikely that the authorities will adopt a secular monetary policy of mean reversion around a given long-term trend, i.e., a policy designed to create long-term price predictability. The primary concern of keeping unemployment low is instead more likely to lead via a random ratchet process to ever increasing rates of inflation. As Hicks (1955) perceived nearly twenty years ago, we have permanently moved from a fixed exchange rate gold standard to a flexible exchange rate labor standard.

Table A1

Annual Rate of Change of Implicit National Product Price Deflator, 1870-1972

Date	(P/P)	Date	(P/P)	Date	(P/P)	Date	(P/P)
1870	-5.66	1897	0.45	1924	-1.30	1951	6.49
1871	1.59	1898	2.87	1925	1.99	1952	2.20
1872	-5.14	1899	2.58	1926	0.49	1953	0.90
1873	-1.21	1900	5.17	1927	-2.68	1954	1.42
1874	-1.07	1901	-0.61	1928	0.70	1955	1.46
1875	-2.34	1902	3.39	1929	-0.10	1956	3.37
1876	-4.69	1903	0.98	1930	-4.60	1957	3.69
1877	-3.71	1904	1.54	1931	-12.83	1958	2.51
1878	-7.68	1905	2.08	1932	-12.27	1959	1.62
1879	-3.59	1906	2.04	1933	-1.36	1960	1.60
1880	9.88	1907	4.13	1934	6.34	1961	1.27
1881	-1.93	1908	-0.18	1935	-1.29	1962	1.05
1882	3.15	1909	3.47	1936	4.07	1963	1.29
1883	-1.21	1910	2.52	1937	0.87	1964	1.61
1884	-5.37	1911	-0.83	1938	-0.50	1965	1.87
1885	-6.85	1912	4.26	1939	-0.75	1966	2.72
1886	-1.39	1913	0.48	1940	1.12	1967	3.19
1887	0.99	1914	1.43	1941	7.61	1968	3.92
1888	1.76	1915	3.10	1942	12.27	1969	4.68
1889	0.58	1916	12.20	1943	12.37	1970	5.41
1890	-1.95	1917	21.12	1944	7.17	1971	4.53
1891	-0.99	1918	13.97	1945	4.32	1972	3.06
1892	-4.06	1919	1.51	1946	0.87		
1893	2.45	1920	13.15	1947	11.21		
1894	-6.47	1921	-16.01	1948	6.50		
1895	-1.52	1922	-5.04	1949	-0.66		
1896	-2.89	1923	2.31	1950	1.39		

REFERENCES

1. Alchian, A.A. and B. Klein., "On a Correct Measure of Inflation," _Journal of Money, Credit and Banking,_ (February 1973), 173-191.

2. Box, G.E.P. and G.M. Jenkins. _Time Series Analysis._ San Francisco, 1970.

3. Cagan, P. _Determinants and Effects of Changes in the Stock of Money, 1875-1960._ New York: Columbia University Press for NBER, 1965.

4. Fisher, I. _The Purchasing Power of Money._ New York: Macmillan, 1911.

5. _____. Stabilizing the Dollar._ New York: Macmillan, 1920.

6. Friedman, M. and A.J. Schwartz., "Money and Business Cycles," (1963), in Friedman, _The Optimum Quantity of Money and Other Essays._ Chicago: Aldine, 1969, 189-236.

7. Gibson, W., "Interest Rates and Inflationary Expectations: New Evidence," _American Economic Review,_ (Dec. 1972), 854-865.

8. Gordon, R.J., "Steady Anticipated Inflation: Mirage or Oasis?" _Brookings Papers on Economic Activity,_ (1971:2), 499-510.

9. Hicks, J.R., "The Economic Foundations of Wage Policy," _Economic Journal,_ (September 1955), 389-404.

10. Klein, B., "The Competitive Supply of Money," _Journal of Money, Credit and Banking,_ (November 1974), 423-453.

11. _____. "Competitive Interest Payments on Bank Deposits and the Long-Run Demand for Money," _American Economic Review,_ (Dec. 1974), 931-949.

12. _____, "The Demand for Quality Adjusted Cash Balances," unpublished manuscript, 1972.

13. Klein, B. ,"The Impact of Inflation on the Term Structure of Corporate Financial Instruments: 1900-1972," in Silber, W. (ed.), <u>Financial Innovation</u>. New York: Heath, 1975, 125-149.

14. Larson, D. and L.W. Bolton., "Calendar of Wage Increases and Negotiations for 1973," <u>Monthly Labor Review,</u> (Jan. 1973), 3-9.

15. Marshall, Alfred. <u>Official Papers.</u> London: Macmillan, 1926.

16. Phelps, E.S. <u>Inflation Policy and Unemployment Theory.</u> New York: Norton, 1972.

17. Sargent, T., "What Do Regressions of Interest on Inflation Show?" <u>Annals of Economic and Social Measurement</u>, (July 1973), 289-301.

18. Stigler, G.J., "General Economic Conditions and National Elections," <u>American Economic Review,</u> (May 1973), 160-167.

19. Tobin, J. and L. Ross., "Living with Inflation," <u>The New York Review of Books,</u> (May 6, 1971), 23-26.

20. Working, H., "Note on the Correlation of First Differences of Averages in a Random Chain," <u>Econometrica,</u> (October 1960), 916-918.

21. Yohe, W.P. and D.S. Karnosky., "Interest Rates and Price Level Changes, 1952-69," Federal Reserve Bank of St. Louis <u>Review,</u> (Dec. 1969), 18-38.

212

THE SOCIAL COSTS OF THE RECENT INFLATION:
THE MIRAGE OF STEADY "ANTICIPATED" INFLATION:
A COMMENT
Jerry Jasinowski
Joint Economic Committee
Congress of the United States

Having the comparative disadvantage of not keeping up with the technical literature on inflation, I choose to review Benjamin Klein's paper in terms of its usefulness in answering certain policy questions about inflation. In my view there are four central questions. Why are people in general so concerned about inflation? What is the social cost of inflation? Are the present price indices adequate for measuring inflation? What has caused the post-World War II shift toward a higher rate of inflation? Does Klein's paper shed any light on these issues?

First, why is the public bothered by inflation? Until recently I have generally accepted the answer that their concern grew out of ignorance. People just did not understand inflation as well as economists did. Recent inflation in the United States was of the anticipated variety, I thought, with little social cost. There was always a nagging doubt about this position, perhaps because of the elitist tone of those who said the public was just confused; or perhaps my doubts were stimulated by the constant debate in Congress emphasizing the adverse redistribution consequences of inflation.

Klein's paper is quite useful because it provides an explanation for why people are bothered by inflation - - a high and rising level of long-term price unpredictability and the uncertainty costs associated with that outcome. People are concerned about inflation not so much because of its impact today, but because there is more doubt about its impact in the future. This increasing doubt arises from a decline in government's credibility with respect to maintaining price stability.

The second policy question before us is what is the social cost of inflation? The implication of Klein's paper is that the social cost of inflation is greater than previously believed, but he tells us little about the nature and dimensions of the cost. At the end of this paper he covers the question with the following sentence, "The net gain or loss crucially depends upon the importance of long-term contracts, both explicit and implicit."

Perhaps this statement is pregnant with information, but I doubt it. The economics profession seems confused on this question, and Klein has provided no illumination. I am also amused by what seem to be some rather dramatic shifts in position on this question by prominent members of the economics profession and Congress. Herb Stein, for example, testified for years before the JEC that inflation was the nation's number one problem, while Congressional Democrats argued that the Administration was taking inflation too seriously. Now Herb Stein tells another story. In a March 3, 1974 speech, he said:

> All-in-all there has been little suffering in the country as a result of the inflation. The explanation for this is simple. The high and rising prices we pay are almost all paid to other Americans and become part of their rising incomes.

Because of these disagreements, as well as the disagreements generated by Klein's findings, it seems to me we need further research on the social cost of inflation. The kind of research that seems most useful to me is empirical work that looks at recent inflation periods to determine the impact of inflation by income and wealth class.

A third major policy question that relates to both an estimate of the social cost of inflation, and to understanding how people perceive inflation, is how adequately do our published price indices measure inflation? This is not a new subject, for the Stigler Report of 1960 initiated a public debate that has continued since. In his paper Klein argues that the price indices are quite deficient, emphasizing their failure to take into account changes in asset prices. Although I can see the need to improve our data on asset prices, there are several reasons why I am not persuaded that we can or should adopt a general price index with asset prices.

First, there is the lack of empirical evidence to support the hypothesis that changes in the money supply will cause asset prices to change at a different rate than current consumption services. To believe this requires one to thoroughly accept the monetarist view about how money affects individual portfolios and asset prices. The evidence offered of a 30 percent drop in common stock prices in 1970, as a result of a small 2.9 percent increase in the narrowly defined money supply in 1969, although quite interesting, does not seem to me to be convicing. As I recall, the money supply also grew by about 8 percent in 1972; and yet stock prices tumbled in 1973. If one were to systematically look at changes in the money supply and stock prices, I wonder how consistently the theory would be validated.

Moreover, there is the problem of what factors affect the prices of other assets such as real estate and durables, and how these price changes compare with price changes for current consumption services. Until we know the answers to these questions, we are not in a position to advocate an intertemporal price index for policy purposes.

Assuming that the Klein hypothesis is valid, however, I have a second concern about how suitable such an index would be for general policy. The concern of his paper is to measure the money cost of some fixed level of welfare as prices change, with appropriate weights for assets in the typical portfolio of claims. Implicit in the word typical, it seems to me, is a normative judgment about what group (s) should serve as a national standard in measuring inflation. The current CPI uses the standard of the urban wage earner, or what amounts to a middle income family. Although my data may be somewhat dated, it seems to me that the top 20 percent of the population own about 75 percent of the assets, while the poorest 20 percent of the population have no significant assets. A general index that would include most assets could, in some cases, underestimate the impact of inflation on the poor.

If Klein's general findings are correct, a fourth major policy question is: why has there been this post-World War II trend toward a higher rate of inflation? In other words, what explains the weakening of resolve in the economy against higher prices? Klein discusses this question in terms of a fading in the gold standard mentality, which seems fine as far as it goes. Whenever we are dealing with folklore, it is difficult to be precise.

There are numerous other explanations for the growing inflationary bias of the economy. The commitment of the Federal Government to the full employment mandated under the Employment Act of 1946 may explain some of this upward bias. The increasing cost of resource extraction and production worldwide, which increases resource prices generally, is another likely explanation for this trend. In my opinion, however, much of this acceleration in inflation can be explained by a series of policy errors made by the Federal Government over an extended period of time, including excessive fiscal stimulus associated with the Vietnam War, an over-expansion in the money supply during 1971-72, and mismanagement of agricultural production and exports during 1972. All of these policy errors, along with events beyond our control, such as the oil embargo, led to an accelerating inflation that altered people's expectations about price stability. Altered expectations then became a separate source of inflation. [1]

The fundamental question posed but not answered by Klein is: what can we do to restore government credibility with respect to maintaining price stability? There is no single answer, as there may have been in the days of the gold standard, but an array of answers depending upon the nature of the inflation at a particular time and place. This means that the government must main-

---

[1] For more details on the sources of inflation see "Achieving Price Stability Through Economic Growth," a report of the Joint Economic Committee, December 23, 1974, Chapter II.

tain sensible monetary and fiscal policies relative to the capacity of the economy, but it also means that prudent micro-economic policies in both product and factor markets must complement such aggregate policies. In short, the government must become a competent eclectic in its efforts to achieve price stability.

REFERENCE

1. "Achieving Price Stability Through Economic Growth," a report of the Joint Economic Committee, December 23, 1974, Chapter II.

POLICY CONFLICTS IN THE SEPARATE CONTROL OF QUANTITY AND PRICE IN THE ENERGY INDUSTRIES*

Paul W. MacAvoy**
Massachusetts Institute of Technology

The energy sector of the American economy has long been subject to the entire range of public policy instruments. Containing markets characterized by natural monopoly, as in the distribution of electricity, and competition, as in bidding for lease rights to acreage in new oil or gas discovery regions, every type of government control mechanism has been applied in the last few years. State and local governments have experimented with policies controlling entry and location of firms, particularly with respect to the construction of new plants having effects on environmental quality. State governments have experimented with production controls for oil and natural gas. At the same time, the Federal Government has tried price controls, taxes and/or subsidies applied separately and together to particular sets of markets.

The reasons for the policies have varied as widely as the policies themselves. It is very difficult to find any resemblance between reasons given by the states for restricting the construction of nuclear power plants, and those of the AEC for subsidizing the purchase prices of nuclear fuels. But there has been a strong central thrust to the direction in which each of the various governments has been moving. For the most part, State and local governments have used output restraining policies that favored local corporations on the producing side of energy markets. But, the Federal Government including the Executive, Congress and the courts has tended to apply controls that would keep down prices to final consumers. There are important exceptions. For example, the oil import control program of the 1960s was designed to support the states in their policies to enhance the incomes of domestic petroleum producers. But in general national programs have been in conflict with state programs. The results of the conflict have been difficult to determine, at least up to 1972, but under the severe stress of the OPEC embargo the effects of inconsistent strategies have been made more clear, since they centered on the volume of imports of oil from abroad.

I. GOVERNMENT AND ENERGY MARKETS UNTIL 1972

By tradition, the workings of government on energy production have been mostly at the state or community level. The development of procedures for obtaining ownership rights to reserves of petroleum or mineral resources took

* First revision, November 10, 1974.

** Henry R. Luce Professor of Public Policy, Massachusetts Institute of Technology; on leave as a member of the President's Council of Economic Advisers, 1975-1976.

217

place in local and state courts for the most part. The applications of these procedures were carried out by local governments except when competition or technology made possible interstate evasion of local rules so as to bring forth the establishment of interstate regulation or other government policies across regions.

After World War II, the production of oil and gas in Texas, Oklahoma, and Louisiana took place under "rules of capture" which gave ownership rights to the one company of many in a field that brought the product to the surface. This way of establishing property rights tended to increase the rate of production out of proved reserves and provided strong incentives to drill too many wells in order to protect the boundaries of surface ownership from sub-surface depletion by the adjoining producer.[1] To reduce these incentives, state conservation commissions restricted rates of output from all wells in the state and set minimum well spacing rules. This was a "mistake," given that it would have been more efficient to have established one producer in each field as unit operator with power to set rates of output within the field but not between fields.[2] Mistake or not, the conservation commissions used their power to restrict outputs not only from individual wells, but also from the state as a whole. With the establishment of an interstate oil compact, oil production from the entire South Central region of the country was collectively controlled by state regulatory commissions.

Regulation by the States

The state commissions, acting under the rubric of "conservation," managed to achieve a number of goals at once. Setting limits on the output of individual wells greatly favored the smaller producers owning marginal or extramarginal capacity. The commission restrictions on rates of output, formally based on the physical concept of "maximum efficient rate" (MER), were greatest on producing properties having the highest potential. This is because the high potential wells were cut back to the lowest percentage of MER, so as to allow smaller, "high cost" wells to produce at MER. The impact of allowed well spacing was also greatest on the larger properties, given that although most land owners were small and had plots less than the minimum for a single well, they were not refused the right to drill that first well.

These production restrictions reduced the opportunity of the largest producers to exploit reserves quickly, so that "conservation" was achieved by reducing the outflow from the inventory of proved reserves. Most important,

---

[1] Cf. E.V. Rostow (1948, p. 44). Rostow asks the question: "Wouldn't the desire to prevent a neighbor from draining away one's total potential production lead to production that could not be sold at any price, and would therefore be stored as effectively as possible, so that a fraction could be saved rather than to have the total supply lost to the neighbor?" (p. 44).

[2] Cf. E.V. Rostow (1948); cf. also M.G. DeChazeau and A.E. Kahn (1959) and W.F. Lovejoy and P.T. Homan (1967).

proration developed in such a way that <u>total state production</u> was limited by the commission, so that prices were increased above levels that would have been realized without regulatory controls. [3]

By the middle 1950s most of these results had been realized. Prices of crude oil had been rising by steps since 1947, while production from the larger sources had been cut back to half and production from smaller sources (making up more than one third of the total) was at full capacity. Detailed analysis by Stephan McDonald (1947, p. 346) showed that "the price of crude oil was too high for long-term equilibrium in the fifties and [that] market-demand proration-ing made that condition possible. Without regulatory restriction of output to market demand at the going price . . . competition would have forced the price down." Mistake or not, the results protected and enhanced the value of smaller producing properties within the jurisdiction of the local commissions.

There were quite different long-term effects. The incentives to add reserves were significantly dampened by reductions in the rate of production for the larger companies, simply because "proration" cutbacks reduced the present value of revenues received from produced oil. As McDonald (1974, p. 350) found, "As spare capacity grew in the 'market demand states,' the going price proved insufficient to yield target rates of return to the integrated [larger] firms, the chief owners of non-exempt productive capacity." Given reduced exploratory incentives, the "inflow" into the reserve inventory slowed down as much as or more than the slowdown in "outflow" resulting from conservation controls.[4] By the late 1960s it would appear that, although the distributive effects in favor of small producers continued, the short-term inventory enhancing effects had given way to a significant reduction in inventories of reserves. [5]

Similar results would have followed from regulation of natural gas pro-duction as well, except for particular conditions of technology and demand in the gas industry. Natural gas production in large part has gone into large-scale inter-state transmission lines, or into local pipelines for industrial use in the South

---

[3] Cf. DeChazeau and Kahn, (1959, p. 151). It is concluded that "prorationing is a primary reason for the vastly reduced number of crude oil price changes since 1933, as well as for the timing of those that occured. Nor can it escape responsibility for holding prices at the high levels they have reached since World War II. In view of the supply inelasticity characteristic of competitive crude oil production, the smoothness of the transitions from one price to another in the long periods of intravening stability in the face of changing demand bespeaks the presence of administrative control. Only in this way could the emergency of a rapidly expanding low-cost, world source of oil in the Middle East have rolled back United States sales in Europe and penetrated domestic markets without creating more than a ripple in the domestic price. And only in this way could great new discoveries and developments of crude oil have been blended into national pro-duction without upsetting the short-run balance of supply and demand," (p. 151). Cf. also M.A. Adelman, (1964, pp. 100 et seq.) for an evaluation of the significant excess capacity while letting production in "mar-ginal" wells with limited ability to produce go to the maximum efficient rate.

[4] According to Professor Edward W. Erickson, (1968, pp. 91-92), "Market demand prorationing entails arbitrary well spacing, depth bracket allowables and production restrictions [that have] shifted the supply curve of crude oil downward."

[5] Cf. Erickson, (1968).

219

Central region. Buyers take gas on demand at a higher rate during peak heating or manufacturing production periods so that commission restrictions on outputs by day or month would have inhibited the development of markets. In fact, the regulators paid little attention to production control (for similar reasons, the well spacing rules have operated in conjunction with the growth and development of pipelines). The state commissions at various times did attempt to operate around these specific conditions in gas markets by setting minimum prices for gas moving across state lines; these attempts were thwarted by court decisions finding the minimum prices to be in violation of the commerce clause of the Constitution, even though they might help "conserve" gas at the wellhead by reducing demands. [6]

Technological and economic conditions determining the production of coal have been greatly different from those in petroleum and natural gas. There have been no political-economic problems in "capture" of the underground resource. Therefore, the state governments have not intervened directly in the production process for reasons of conservation. Without such intervention, there has been no basis for state-wide control of levels of production.

But where policies have been developed affecting production of coal, they have tended to favor the producer in the local region, focusing on the "externalities" of bringing coal out of the ground - - the safety conditions in the mines, and the environmental conditions in the neighborhood of the mine sites (particularly in strip mining). Regulations affecting safety and environmental quality that could have imposed significant costs on producers have for the most part been ineffective at the state level. In those few instances where the effect has been substantial, particularly in regard to working conditions, and where costs have been imposed on the producers, they have been imposed mostly on the smaller producers. This may seem inconsistent with favoritism towards smaller oil and gas producers, except for the strength of the miners' union in local and state politics. With larger mines unionized, and smaller mines not unionized, collective control of labor supply by the union has been attained by forcing higher costs on the smaller mines. [7]

Electric power regulation by state public utility commissions has done little more. A number of studies has been conducted of electric power regula-

<hr>

[6] "Federal Power Commission Jurisdiction over Producers," George Washington Law Review (January 1956, p. 336); W.M. Wherry (1955, p. 157). Cf. also P.W. MacAvoy (1961).

[7] Although no documentation has been provided to date, it is generally agreed among coal experts that state regulation of coal production for the purpose of preserving the environment has not been effective. Earlier work by M.S. Baratz, (1960), indicated that the union control over working conditions was operating as if to maintain control by union members of the supply of labor in the eastern United States coal markets. For the effects of legislation on small coal mines, cf. "Coal Mines Safety Deadline: Comply with Code or Close," New York Times, March 31, 1974, p. 49 and "Mine Owners Ask Delay on Safety Laws," New York Times, March 19, 1974.

tion leading to the finding that the state commissions have had insignificant effects upon the level of rates charged by the companies. But there seem to have been significant effects on the structure of charges - - favoring industrial consumers over residential consumers - - where these charges have been under the review of the state governments. As shown by Jackson (quoted in Jordan, 1972, p. 158), "The main beneficiaries of electric utility regulation were the combined industrial and commercial users." [8] Power regulation began for reasons of "establishing the franchise" or improving the quality of service as often as for "protecting the consumer." The tendency of state controls to favor industry as producer or interstate consumer extends from the fuel source to the production of power.

The Introduction of Federal Regulation in the 1960s

The actions and reactions of the Federal Government to this pattern of regulation began to appear in energy markets in the late 1950s, but did not take effect until the early 1960s. Federal oil import controls in petroleum were the product of conflicting purposes, even within the Federal Government. Energy demands had continued to grow in the 1950s, even though there had been substantial price increases. The combination of declining discovery and of depletion of known onshore resources had led to declines in levels of oil production. It was evident that imports of crude oil from abroad would increase over time, and that the price paid for foreign crude would set the national price levels since foreign sources were going to provide the marginal supplies. Arguments were made that these marginal supplies were insecure, and that there could be embargoes against the United States that would affect domestic energy prices and consequently factor costs in a wide variety of industries. The immediacy, if not the effectiveness, of the Arab embargo after the Suez war of 1956 gave this argument some cogency. At the same time, there was concern within the energy companies that marginal supplies would not be embargoed, but rather would provide essentially limitless volumes at prices significantly below those prevailing. [9] Although these

---

[8] See also Jackson (1969), Moore (1968), Stigler and Friedland (1962).

[9] The purpose of oil import controls was stated by the Cabinet Task Force on Oil Import Control in The Oil Import Question (February 1970) as "protecting military and essential civilian demand against reasonably possible foreign supply interruptions that could not be overcome by feasible replacement measures in an emergency" (p. 8). But this implied "another primary objective. . . to prevent imports from causing a decline in the petroleum sector of the U.S. economy that would so weaken the national economy as to impair the national security - - taking into account resulting employment decreases, losses of skills or investment, decreases in government revenues, 'or other serious effects'" (p. 8). The quota system, as developed and practiced, given these goals, was found by the Task Force to be "no longer acceptable" because of its inability to provide security against disruptions given the lack of inventory or excess production capacity under the program. The Task Force did not propose "complete abandonment of import controls at this time" but abandonment of controls over time coupled with appropriate Western Hemisphere preferences and "a security adjustment to prevent undue Eastern Hemisphere imports" (p. 129). The final conclusion is that the prudent course would be to adopt "a system of tariff restrictions at an approximate level of $1.45 per barrel" (p. 131).

reasons for controlling imports were inconsistent, they were reinforcing in that those concerned with security of supply were allied with those who were concerned with price reductions on the need to control imports of crude oil and petroleum products into the United States.

The quota controls placed on imports throughout the 1960s had none of the results justifying their existence for either group. The way in which the program operated did not provide incentives for holding inventories against embargoes. Quotas were extended to companies on the basis of historical production capacity, not on the basis of inventories held against embargoes or of security of the source of supply. Nor did the controls result in a floor under prices benefiting the domestic producers. Rather, the pressures on Congress from consuming states, and of academic or newspaper criticism of the restrictiveness of the program, hampered the potentially restrictive operation of the program. That is, controls turned out to be somewhat lax, first maintaining the nominal price of crude oil but then allowing these prices to slide downward. The program turned out to be no more than a "loose" freeze on current dollar prices, thereby heading off adverse reactions from consumer regions of the country but also "protecting" domestic producers from the "downturns" of one dollar per barrel or more.

At the same time, the Executive branch operated various other programs to increase the supply of domestic resources. The Eisenhower Administration, while curtailing supplies from abroad through import controls, moved vigorously to claim offshore lands for Federal ownership of crude oil and natural gas. This was to lead to production outside state proration controls and put supplies into interstate commerce to the maximum extent possible. Similarly, programs for leasing onshore Federal lands were put into effect for the purpose of adding to the supplies available from within the states.

By Federal action, a price freeze was put into operation over field sales of natural gas going into the interstate pipelines. Federal Power Commission regulation of interstate sales began in 1954, with a Supreme Court decision requiring direct control of wellhead prices on production destined for interstate consumption. This decision occurred in a case brought by the Attorney General of Wisconsin against Phillips Petroleum Company to eliminate wellhead price increases on the gas destined for retail delivery in Wisconsin. Higher prices were alleged to be contrary to consumer interests. The Supreme Court, without explicitly examining the reason for the price increases, found that the Federal Power Commission had a mandate to regulate wellhead prices and should in the future control them to "just and reasonable" levels.

For the next five years, the Commission attempted to respond to the mandate. After a number of unsuccessful trials at case-by-case decision-making, the Commission in 1961 instituted regional price ceilings that remained in effect throughout most of the decade. Temporary ceilings were set at levels established by unregulated market transactions in the late 1950s and subsequently they were made permanent (by circular reasoning, since the permanent ceilings were based upon costs incurred while the temporary ceilings were in effect). Logical or not, the frozen prices served the Commission by preserving the price level in effect when the pipelines were first built in the early or middle 1950s. Price increases were undesirable in and of themselves because they could be subject to court disapproval as being against the interests of consumers. [10]

At the same time that price ceilings were being put into effect on oil and gas, Federal tax codes containing special benefits for this industry were in full effect. These regulations included a percentage depletion allowance offering a tax deduction of 22 percent of gross income, accelerated depreciation, and liberal writeoff of the intangible costs of drilling. Altogether they constituted a significant subsidy to the production of reserves of all types of hydrocarbon products. There is some basis for asserting that they may have added to the amount of reserves as well; work by Susan Agria (1969) indicates that the ratio of petroleum investment to ordinary investment (after lease costs and severance taxes) was between 1.2 and 1.3, so that 20 to 30 percent more capital was invested in petroleum production than would have been the case without special tax benefits. These findings have been extended by the CONSAD Research Corporation (1969) to indicate that, out of the additional investment, reserve levels have been increased by approximately 5-7 percent, at annual tax expenditures in the late 1960s of approximately 1.7 billion dollars. Since the reduced taxes provided incentives not only to carry out additional investment, but also to exploit the investment as fast as possible, these were supply-increasing policies complementary to price-reducing policies.

Coal was the only major energy resource not affected by controls at the national level. To be sure, there were a number of ways in which Federal controls might have been put into effect, by setting imports or exports, or setting prices paid by the electric utilities. Possibly the strength of the miners' union, and the limited markets for domestic coal turned the attention of the Federal regulators away from price ceilings on this fuel source. The advent of the unit train and larger-scale mining activities brought forth cost reductions in the 1950s that opened up major international markets for American coal, thereby significantly increasing the demands facing American coal producers. In the 1960s foreign demand increases generated both international and domestic price increases

---

[10] Cf. P.W. MacAvoy and R.S. Pindyck (1974, pp. 10-20). This is exemplified by the 1959 case in Atlantic Refining Company v. Public Service Commission (360 U.S. 378) where it was stated that price increases were to be denied because "this price is greatly in excess of that which Tennessee pays for any lease in Southern Louisiana." Based on this case, Professor Edmund Kitch (1968, p. 261) argues that "the Court reasoned from the premise that prices higher than prevailing prices were questionable simply because they were higher."

which were not controlled at the Federal level.

At this time, the Interstate Commerce Commission allowed substantial increases in coal freight rates, particularly on bulk shipment, [11] and the domestic producers were subject to increasing Federal control over mine safety and environmental pollution, reducing both domestic supply and demand. These imposed higher costs on producers, and narrowed the domestic markets for the product. Even with these policies the cost increases did not result in a substantial disadvantage in domestic or foreign markets. But coal lost a portion of its domestic market share to oil and gas, since rising coal costs and prices were in contrast with constant or falling oil and gas prices. Contrary to policies imposed on other fossil fuels, there were more obvious direct benefits from Federal regulation to particular groups such as the coal miners and the railroads than there were to the consumer. But the consumers were left with cheap oil and gas. [12]

The Legacy of the 1960s

With conflicts between state and national regulation of oil and gas, and with different kinds of controls in coal markets, almost anything could have happened in the 1960s. As a matter of fact, both state and national controls "worked" in crude oil markets, while only Federal controls had any significant effect in natural gas markets. The results form a cohesive pattern of market performance.

Federal policies to hold the line against price increases resulted in falling real prices for both oil and gas over the decade (as shown in Table 1). With production controls operating in crude oil, and with import controls, the price freeze brought forth a 3 percent growth in domestic production per annum throughout the decade, but a 4 percent growth in domestic consumption. With no controls by the states on natural gas, but with a national price freeze, the annual 1 percent reduction in real prices for that fuel was met with a 6 percent increase in domestic production and consumption. Natural gas sold at 17¢, while oil sold at 52¢ per million Btu at the wellhead in 1961; henceforth the lower-priced fuel reduced prices more (in real terms) and increased its share of total production significantly until 1970. [13]

But all was not well in natural gas field markets. The price freeze contributed to a winding down of exploratory activity, resulting in substantial reduc-

---

[11] Cf. James Sloss (1967).

[12] This is indicated by relative prices for crude oil, natural gas and coal, all delivered for boiler fuel use in electric power plants in 1961. These prices were roughly: crude oil 35.3 ¢ per million Btu, natural gas 26.3 ¢ per million Btu and coal 25.9 ¢ per million Btu before adjustments for the superior environmental impacts of the first two fuels.

[13] Cf. MacAvoy and Pindyck, (1974, p. 21).

TABLE 1: Energy Production and Domestic Consumption, 1961-1970

Industry	Annual Percentage Change in Field Prices	Annual Percentage Change in Domestic Production	Annual Percentage Change in Domestic Consumption
Crude Oil	-0.67	+3.32	+4.03
Natural Gas	-0.71	+5.75	+5.83
Coal	+2.13	+4.27	+2.65

Source: U.S. Bureau of Mines and the Federal Power Commission. The estimates of rates of change are geometric rates of growth. Prices are deflated by the 1961-1970 Wholesale Price Index of all commodities and services.

tions in new reserves over the last half of the 1960s. Total additions to reserves declined over the period until by 1972 the national stock was only 80 percent of the 1967 peak. [14] Moreover, the decline in reserves would not have been the case if new contract field prices had been higher. Indeed "unregulated" prices could well have resulted in more than a trillion cubic feet of additional reserves each year, sufficient to prevent a drawing down of the total reserve stock. [15]

Because of the reduced discoveries, pipelines were meeting the increased demands for production by taking from their inventories of previously committed reserves. The gas industry was in effect "selling short" by meeting additional demands out of existing stocks. Established consumers with expectations of 15 years of reserves against their annual deliveries lost that backing, to the advantage of consumers receiving expanded service, at least up to 1970. By chance or otherwise, customers in the Northeast, the North Central and the West received smaller shares of the increased production as compared to customers in the Southeast and South Central regions of the country. [16] The full benefit from depleting resources was realized in the South, while those losing the reserve backing were in the North. The freeze policy in the first few years was mostly advantageous to industrial and home consumers within the producing states who were not part of the usual constituency for Federal Power Commission regulation.

Coal for domestic use expanded throughout the period, but this source of energy made up a smaller portion of total domestic consumption. This is partially a result of the substantial price increases for domestic coal relative to other fuels, and of limitations on the utilization of this fuel because of environmental quality controls late in the decade. Coal seemed to have been reduced in share by the increased costs of production (for mine safety and environmental quality), by increased costs of transportation by the railroads, and by substantially increased demands in Western Europe.

The legacy of the 1960s policy was a set of markets unable to respond flexibly to abrupt changes in foreign supply conditions. By 1971, significant shortages of natural gas had developed as rates of production reached technical limits from reduced reserves. (Although the Federal Power Commission responded to indications of shortage with large increases in prices on new contracts for gas, the lag adjustment process of discovery and commitment of reserves did not permit a quick market response.) With limits on production and with price controls, reserve accumulation in crude oil had been reduced. With coal production limited by safety regulation, and production diverted abroad, there was little

[14] Cf. MacAvoy and Pindyck, (1974, p. 44).

[15] Cf. MacAvoy and Pindyck, (1974, p. 26 and Table 1.4).

[16] MacAvoy and Pindyck, (1974, pp. 27-33).

chance that coal could expand.

Within very few additional years regulated markets required large increases in imports of crude oil and petroleum products. Between 1971 and 1973, natural gas had declined to the extent that the Federal Power Commission expected interstate gas distributors to be 10 percent short of meeting consumption demands in 1974. [17] The shortage could have been much greater than 10 percent, given that the Federal Power Commission only counts the excess demands of those already connected to the system, leaving out those who wish to connect but cannot.[18] Those not getting gas under existing contracts were, in the absence of sufficient supplies able only to go to fuel oil markets; their demands for fuel oil increased by more than 2 million barrels per day. [19] At the same time production of petroleum in the United States has been decreasing, from a maximum of 11.3 million barrels per day in 1970 to 10.9 million barrels [20] in 1973 and a forecast level of slightly more than 10.0 million barrels per day in 1974.[21] With demands for petroleum running close to 17 million barrels per day in 1973 and forecast demands to 19-20 million barrels per day in 1974, imports had to rise from 6 million barrels per day in 1973 to 8 million barrels per day in 1974. Such growth is at least partially due to the shift from gas, and to the lack of oil reserves, as a result of price and production controls.

The response of the Federal Government to these conditions in domestic markets and to the Arab embargo must have been predictable from previous policy. In the face of a potentially effective elimination of U.S. deliveries by the Persian Gulf oil countries, the Congress passed the Emergency Petroleum Allocation Act in November of 1973 setting up mandatory allocation regulations to be administered by the Federal Energy Office. These regulations controlled all petroleum prices and directed product allocation from refinery to end user, except for gasoline which was allocated only down to the wholesale level. The allocation regulations gave priority to certain industrial users and to the provision of emergency services to households. The price controls called for a freeze on crude under Phase III Price Controls, (eventually administered by the Federal

[17] Natural Gas Division, Federal Power Commission, National Gas Supply and Demand, 1970-1990 (Washington, February 1972).

[18] Cf. MacAvoy and Pindyck, (1974, p. 50). The econometric model developed in this study shows shortages of 1.7 trillion out of 26.2 trillion cubic feet of demand for 1974.

[19] A shortage of 2.6 trillion cubic feet, from which 1.8 trillion cubic feet transfers to oil markets as additional demand for crude oil or petroleum products, would be realized in demands in petroleum markets for 1.0 billion barrels more per annum. This is equivalent to more than 2 million barrels per day of demands for residual or distillate fuel oil, for all intents and purposes.

[20] Cf. Office of Economic Impact, Federal Energy Administration, The Economic Impact of the Oil Embargo on the American Economy (August 8, 1974), Table I-1.

[21] Office of Economic Impact, Federal Energy Administration (1974, p. 12).

Energy Administration after price control agencies were phased out). The freeze maintained the level of prices on producing wells, but allowed stripper and new production to go to the import price level; thus a new/old price system was put into effect, resulting in sales from a producing field at two or more prices varying from 5 dollars a barrel on the low side to 10 dollars a barrel on the high side.

The conditions reduced the ability of companies to respond to the embargo. There was no incentive for drawing down inventories to replace the reduced foreign supplies, since inventories were old oil. The rules also provided incentives for importation from abroad by companies with access to more domestic crude since "excess" domestic supplies had to be turned over to other companies unless there was a counterpart source of imports.

The actual results of the embargo have not been evident. Both domestic production and imports remained roughly constant from October 1973 to March of 1974, so that there is some basis for concluding that the quantity reduction from the embargo was limited to the growth of imports. This would be a significant effect, given that imports were expected to grow by more than 2 million barrels per day (or 10 percent of total consumption) through 1974. But changes in both supply and demand could have caused this reduction considered to be the embargo effect. Domestic supplies out of inventory did not increase by more than 1 million barrels per day, presumably because of price incentives under the freeze not to reduce holdings at that time. Demands did not increase by as much as expected, because of higher prices for foreign supplies (rolled into the frozen domestic prices). These conditions can be said to be caused only indirectly by the embargo. But in addition some part ot the demand reduction was created by uncertainty as to whether "embargoed supplies" would be forthcoming, or by queues or congestion in gasoline markets; these could be said to have been means for dealing with embargoes, so that they were results of the embargo itself. Without giving the embargo too much weight, it probably reduced domestic consumption by 5 percent on an annual basis, but the reduction was realized through excess demands that were a product of price controls and allocation regulations.

Given such output effects from the embargo, there were alleged to be short-term reactions from the economy as a whole. The quarterly econometric models indicate that real output of the economy fell in the first quarter of 1974 by 10 to 20 billion dollars concurrent with the embargo. The indication becomes blame, with the assertion that the import disruption had the effect of putting the economy on a growth path $20 billion lower than would have occurred without the embargo. But the GNP reduction was due not only to a decline in the automotive sales part of the "energy crisis" (down 27 percent from the same quarter the preceding year), but also in housing (down 32.5 percent) or other durables (down 10 percent) not related to energy. In any event actual and hypothetical growth paths should eventually converge to "make up the difference" with later purchases of these consumer goods. Thus there is little basis for attributing long-term GNP effects to the embargo.

This may not be the pattern for further embargoes occurring through the rest of the 1970s. Future political actions could be constructed to last for longer periods of time and to prevent all shipments by Arab countries to all countries. Under such circumstances, the relevant consideration is the future impacts on GNP. To date, state regulatory policies have limited domestic production capacity, while Federal policy has limited price, with the result that the country has been put in the position of expanding imports. This has made the conditions prevailing at the present time and likely to prevail in the near future favorable for imposing more effective embargoes.

II. STATE AND NATIONAL POLICIES FOR THE 1970s AND 1980s

The energy-producing companies can go on for the rest of the decade operating under state or Federal regulations, just as if no embargo would occur. Indeed, this policy of day-to-day operation is likely for the next five years. The state regulatory commissions would continue to set "allowables" for the production of crude oil. The Federal Energy Administration and the Federal Power Commission would set maximum prices for crude oil and natural gas. The public vetting of differences of opinion as to production levels between petroleum and coal companies on the one hand, and environmental groups on the other, would continue. After some delay, the United States Department of the Interior would put up for lease auction a compromise amount of Federal acreage for development - - between an amount that would have an appreciable effect on the rate of production of oil, gas and coal in the next five years, and that amount that would preserve the environment. This practice of "conflict as usual" would result in no significant changes in the rates of depletion domestically on the supply sides of energy markets. Changes on the demand sides would be negligible as well, given that taxation, or other measures for "conservation" that imply more than inflation-induced price increases for final consumers, would not be acceptable as new energy policy by the Federal Government.

With constraints on production from both state and Federal regulation, there is no chance that additional supplies would erode prices set by the Middle East countries. This is not to say that international oil prices are not within the realm of government policy, but rather that they cannot be affected by these domestic supply policies. If it is assumed that import prices remain close to 10 dollars per barrel in real terms, and thus domestic prices average 7 dollars per barrel, then the import situation in the last half would be quite similar to that in the first half of the 1970s.

There could be substantial increases in domestic output if domestic prices are allowed to increase. Assuming that domestic prices for new or additional crude oil and natural gas go up by 6 percent per annum more than the rate assumed for general inflation, then it is forecast that there will be 10.6 quadrillion Btu more energy production from domestic oil, natural gas and coal in 1980. This increase of more than 13 percent over 1973 estimated production (as shown in Table 2) is based on extrapolation of depletion and discovery patterns of the 1960s and early 1970s and as such is a product of assuming that "more of the same" can be stimulated to higher levels by higher prices and profits. With new areas of potential resources offshore to be opened up, the results most likely would be the finding of more reserves and the adding of more production than shown here. [22]

But these output increases would not be sufficient to meet all domestic demands for these fuels. Even rough judgmental estimates establish that petroleum imports will have to increase. The forecasts of a number of energy experts, made over the period 1972-1974, center on a consumption level greater than 96 quadrillion Btu for 1980 if energy prices in the United States remain at 1974 real price levels.[23] But giving due consideration to the long-term impact of these 1974 prices - - that they have been considerably higher than previously, and forecasters have not assessed their full effects - - then consumption probably should not exceed 90 quadrillion Btu by the end of the decade.[24] Meeting these demands, with domestic supplies as in Table 2 and with uranium and hydroelectric power set at 13.4 quadrillion Btu by capacity limits, requires petroleum imports to reach the level of 15.9 quadrillion Btu at 10 dollars per barrel. This is 3.1 quadrillion Btu or approximately 30 percent greater than 1973 levels of imports.[25]

Given that most of the additions to U.S. petroleum imports would come from the Middle East, approximately 3 million barrels per day or 6.4 quadrillion Btu per annum could be cut off in 1980 if an embargo were run by the

---

[22] The judgmental forecast of the margin of error is ±2 percent, even though the test emphasizes the greater probability of higher rates of growth of crude oil and natural gas. Thus the growth of supply should be between 8.1 and 10.7 quadrillion Btu.

[23] As compiled in "Energy Self-Sufficiency: An Economic Evaluation," Technology Review, May 1974.

[24] Cf. E.A. Hudson and Dale W. Jorgenson (1974). The Hudson-Jorgenson model is a production model for nine industrial sectors, combined with a model of consumer demands and a macroeconometric growth model for the United States economy. The production model is an integration of econometric modeling and input-output analysis. Altogether, the three models are used to predict economic activity and energy utilization for the period 1975-2000 under various assumptions of changes in energy policy and tax programs for stimulating conservation and reducing dependence on imported sources of energy. This model has been combined with the MacAvoy-Pindyck model described in MIT EL-74-011 to provide an integrated supply-demand mechanism for the simulations discussed below.

[25] Because of probable variations from the forecasts of both domestic supplies and demands, the size of imports could be greater than or less than 3.1 quadrillion Btu. With ranges of error of 1.3 quadrillion in supply and 1.0 in demand, these imports could increase from 0.8 to 5.4 quadrillion Btu.

TABLE 2: Initial Estimates of 1980 Domestic
Production and Imports

Industry	1973 Estimated Production (10^{15} Btu/annum)		Forecast 1973-1980 Growth (10^{15} Btu)	
Crude Oil	18.8		+3.4	
Natural Gas	22.9		+8.6	
Coal	14.4		-1.4	
Domestic Production		56.1		10.6
Petroleum Imports	**13.0**		+3.1	
TOTAL		69.1		13.7

Source: derived from "Energy Self-Sufficiency: An Economic Evaluation," Technology Review (May 1974) as explained in the text.

Persian Gulf States against the United States at the same time that similar curtailments were made to other large consuming countries. At the other extreme, given that the United States purchased from Persian Gulf producing countries only as a last resort (so that imports from that source held to 1974 levels in 1980), the embargo would be limited to 1.5 million barrels per day or 3.2 quadrillion Btu per annum. The losses incurred by the United States under these two sets of embargoed supply conditions would depend on the length of the embargo and how effective it was. Assuming conservatively the worst, the embargo might be fully effective in cutting off all such supplies for one year, so that its effect would be much greater than that achieved in the 1974 attempt to limit supplies to the United States for a few months. Over this range of sizes of embargoes, the potential loss to the economy in 1980 would be substantial.

One measure of loss is that of the Federal Energy Administration, equal to the money value of imports eliminated by the embargo. This measure assumes that the import reduction cannot be made up by short-term increases in domestic production (at frozen prices, there would be no incentive for additional domestic production). There would be no substitution for these lost imports on the demand side either. Using this measure, the losses from a year-long embargo of 3.1 quadrillion Btu would be 3.8 billion dollars, but losses from a year-long embargo of 6.4 quadrillion Btu would equal 7.7 billion dollars. That is, any embargo of such sizes and time duration would cost billions of dollars but not as much as already assessed against the shorter and more limited 1973 embargo. This could be because the lessons of the first embargo would have been learned, so that the economy would not abruptly reduce demands for automobiles and other high energy-using consumer durables when a new embargo came along.

The embargoes envisioned might actually cost less, given that "lost" imports were replaceable in various markets. Changes in demand and supply for consumption, investment, capital and labor could dampen somewhat the cost of the economy's response to such an action. Projecting a level of activity and relative prices for the products and imports in nine sectors of the economy for 1980, the Hudson-Jorgenson econometric energy policy model allows consideration of these patterns of adjustment. For an embargo of the smaller size and duration, 3.1 quadrillion Btu for the full year 1980, the real GNP effects would be 3.3 billion dollars in that year; for the 6.4 quadrillion Btu embargo, the GNP losses are forecast as 6.8 billion dollars. [26] The economy itself adjusts away 13 percent of the cost of the embargo by replacing energy with other input factors, in contrast to merely doing without production of energy using goods and services.

---

[26] This estimate, and subsequent estimates of dollars, are in 1973 Gross National Product terms.

The reaction to vulnerability has universally been to call for reductions in imports. Whether by "Project Independence" or some other plan for curtailment of demands and thus imports by millions of barrels per day, the justification is that if imports are vulnerable then they should be eliminated. The way to eliminate imports is to reduce "waste" and to require consumers to practice "restraint" in day-to-day demands for energy. Such demand curtailment policies could be worse than the status quo, because they replace any intermittent foreign embargo with a permanent embargo imposed by government on the demand side of the market. This can be seen by considering a policy requiring a one million barrel per day curtailment of consumption. This reduction of imports can be achieved by forcing speed reductions on the highway, lowering temperatures in public buildings, and rationing energy to industry. The result is forecast to be a reduction in GNP of 2.2 billion dollars (as shown by line 6 of Table 4 for the year 1980). On a five-year horizon, with a hypothetical embargo in 1980 the costs of this policy of independence are those of an additional year of embargo (as shown by "high" losses of $6.8 billion in Table 3 without the policy, and "high" losses of $2.2 billion each year and $4.6 billion during the embargo in Table 4 with the policy). A policy to curtail consumption and GNP to reduce the effect of intermittent foreign embargoes can make sense only if a permanent reduction in GNP of $2.2 billion in all years as well as a transitory $4.6 billion loss of GNP in each embargo year is somehow less harmful than no permanent reduction in GNP but a transitory $6.8 billion loss of GNP in each embargo year. That is, efforts to reduce dependence on foreign oil can be justified only by arguing that each billion dollars of transitory reduction in GNP is far more costly (in welfare terms) than each permanent billion dollar reduction in GNP. Put differently, such a policy makes sense only if it is better to fall from an uncomfortable sitting position than from a more comfortable standing position.

A more complete independence policy would have a more substantial and negative effect on GNP each year. Assume that a concerted move to independence cut off gasoline and heating fuel consumption so as to reduce demands for energy so that 1980 imports are at the 1973 level. The effects on energy consumption and GNP are shown in Table 5. The curtailment would prevent the U.S. from being exposed to a large embargo; at worst a 1980 embargo would shut off 1.5 million barrels per day (or 3.1 quadrillion Btu per year) and at best would involve only 0.5 million barrels (or 1.0 quadrillion Btu, as we replaced 1.0 million barrels of present purchases of Persian Gulf Oil with purchases elsewhere). The smaller embargo then would cost only $1.0 billion. But the policy's benefits from avoiding the embargo would have to be put against the policy's costs of the output lost each year from demand curtailment. These costs are losses of GNP from energy curtailment of $3.0 billion each year, as shown in Table 5. Once

233

TABLE 3: The Effect of Embargoes
Under 1980 Forecast Conditions

Forecast Category	Forecast Level, 1980	
	(high)	(low)
1. Energy Consumption (quad. Btu)	90.5	90.5
2. Energy Imports (quad. Btu)	15.9	15.9
3. Reduction of Imports During the Assumed Embargo (quad. Btu)	6.4	3.1
4. Gross National Product ($ billion, 1973 dollars)	1780.4	1780.4
5. Reductions in Gross National Product Consequent from the Embargo ($ billion, 1973 dollars)	6.8	3.3

Source: E.A. Hudson and D.W. Jorgenson, "U.S. Energy Policy and Economic Growth, 1975-2000." Bell Journal of Economics and Management Science (Autumn 1974), pp. 461 et seq.

TABLE 4: The Effect of Embargoes
Under the Import Reduction Program

Forecast Category, 1980	Forecast Level, 1980	
	(high)	(low)
1. Energy Consumption (quad. Btu)	88.3	88.3
2. Energy Imports (quad. Btu)	13.8	13.8
3. Reduction of Imports During the Assumed Embargo (quad. Btu)	4.2	1.0
4. Gross National Product ($ billion, 1973 dollars)	1778.2	1778.2
5. Reductions in Gross National Product Consequent from the Embargo ($billion, 1973 dollars)	4.6	1.0
6. Reductions in Gross National Product from Policy to Deal with the Embargo (line (4) in Table 3 minus line (4) in Table 4)	2.2	2.2

Source: E.A.Hudson and D.W.Jorgenson, "U.S. Energy Policy and Economic Growth, 1975-2000." Bell Journal of Economics and Management Science (Autumn 1974), p. 461 et seq.

TABLE 5: The Effect of an Embargo
Under Stronger Demand Curtailment Policies

Forecast Category, 1980	Forecast Level, 1980	
	(high)	(low)
1. Energy Consumption (quad. Btu)	87.3	87.3
2. Energy Imports (quad. Btu)	12.8	12.8
3. Reduction of Imports During the Assumed Embargo (quad. Btu)	3.1	1.0
4. Gross National Product ($ billion, 1973 dollars)	1777.4	1777.4
5. Reductions in Gross National Product Consequent from the Embargo ($billion, 1973 dollars)	3.3	1.0
6. Reductions in Gross National Product from Policy to Deal with the Embargo (line (4) in Table 3 minus line (4) in Table 5)	3.0	3.0

Source: E.A. Hudson and D.W. Jorgenson, "U.S. Energy Policy and Economic Growth, 1975-2000." The Bell Journal of Economics and Management Science (Autumn 1974), p. 461 et seq.

again, a permanent embargo in the form of demand controls prevents the unpleasant surprise of a temporary embargo, but also generates costs each year that would be incurred otherwise only during the intermittent cut-off period.

The alternative policy, termed "continuing to do the same" does not seem to be a productive path to amelioration of energy crises either. Holding prices at the equivalent of 7 dollars per barrel for oil, with gas prices considerably below this level, will bring forth less than enough supplies to keep up with growing demands. Energy imports will, if·allowed, increase by close to 3 quadrillion Btu between now and 1980 as a result. A substantial amount of these additional imports in the next few years will probably have to come from those countries able and perhaps willing to conduct lengthy embargoes against the United States. Exposure to one or two of these embargoes, of sufficient severeity to eliminate annual imports of 6 quadrillion Btu, might cost as much as $7 to $8 billion in real resource losses to the American economy, even without government reaction. And government programs to curtail consumption could add $6 billion or more to these costs. This picture, which goes beyond Tables 3-5, is forbidding enough that real alternatives to such policies should be considered. The place to begin is with present controls to determine whether changing one or the other might reduce the losses.

Federal oil and gas policies freezing prices work naturally against bringing forth additional supplies in domestic markets, but particularly so when foreign supplies are cut off. Domestic producers would not hold inventories against an embargo, when the prices to be allowed during the embargo are going to be no more than those prevailing. Therefore the ameliorative effects of inventories in compensating for temporary restrictions would be lacking under price freeze policies. More important, in the long-run, state and Federal oil and gas price controls reduce domestic reserves and replace them with foreign reserves. Changes in these policies could eliminate some of the effects of an embargo, by increasing domestic reserves and production and thereby reducing the amounts of crude oil that can be embargoed.

The most important of the price freeze policies is Federal Power Commission wellhead price controls over natural gas. The alternatives to controls include any of a variety of plans to allow new contract prices to seek their own levels after 1980, with ceilings imposed in the interim, but with the ceilings rising significantly over the period. The interim ceilings probably will not eliminate excess demand for natural gas before 1980, and thus could not provide excess gas capacity to replace all the supplies withheld under any potential embargo before 1980. But assuming that interim controls hold average wholesale prices at levels within 200 percent of the 1973 price over the 1975-1980 period, there would be substantial additional supplies available by the late 1970s and early

1980s as replacement for foreign oil. [27]

The gradual unfreezing of prices could be followed by substantially increased gas discoveries each year so that additions to reserves rise to 30 quadrillion Btu by 1980, with total reserves increasing to the level of 278 quadrillion Btu by that year. [28] The impact of the price increases would not occur immediately, but rather would be realized in increased new discoveries the second and third year after the ceilings had been raised. Production out of reserves would increase somewhat faster than reserve accumulations themselves, since production depends on price as well as the reserve level. As a result, it is forecast that production would rise from 32.5 quadrillion under FPC controls to 36 quadrillion Btu by 1980 without controls, or at a rate slightly more than 1 quadrillion Btu per annum. Since gas is a superior substitute for crude petroleum products in household heating, these additional Btu would easily replace foreign imports of 3.5 quadrillion Btu.

Allowing domestic oil prices to rise to the level of import prices would have some of the same effects on imports. Eliminating the freeze, so that all domestic prices increased to the international level of 10 dollars per barrel, is forecast to add 5 quadrillion Btu to reserves and (assuming fixed production/reserve ratios) 0.6 quadrillion Btu per annum to production. [29] Eliminating state-wide "proration" controls would increase market growth even more, although the forecast amount is highly uncertain. State controls in recent years have mostly set "allowables" at 100 percent of MER (the "maximum efficient rate" alleged to allow recovery of the greatest physical volume of production over the lifetime of the reservoir). One hundred percent has been a magic upper bound, because exceeding it would clearly indicate that more production now could be had for good economic reasons even though more output was unrecovered later. But in fact, exceeding "one hundred percent" would probably not result in any physical losses, and that would be clear once and for all. There is no engineering evidence that there would be physical losses from operating over the range of 100 to 110 percent of MER. Elimination of MER controls or production at 110 percent of MER could increase production in each of the next five-to-ten years by at least 5 percent, or by as much as 1 quadrillion Btu per annum. [30]

---

[27] Cf. P.W. MacAvoy and R.S. Pindyck, (1974, Chapter 5) for detailed simulations of additional supplies forthcoming by the late 1970s under phased deregulation.

[28] MacAvoy and Pindyck (1974).

[29] MacAvoy and Pindyck (1974).

[30] If elimination of MER regulation were to take place then, as a safeguard, the installation of unit operation in each reservoir simultaneously could also increase production further. Not only would physical loss be prevented by the unit operator running the field to maximize present value, but also improvements in well spacing and well operation could increase present output substantially as well.

TABLE 6: The Effect of Embargoes
Under Elimination of Domestic Price Controls

Forecast Category	Forecast Level, 1980	
	(high)	(low)
1. Energy Consumption (quad. Btu)	90.5	90.5
2. Energy Imports (quad. Btu)	10.8	10.8
3. Reduction of Imports During the Assumed Embargo (quad. Btu)	1.0	0.0
4. Gross National Product ($ billion, 1973 dollars)	1780.4	1780.4
5. Reductions in Gross National Product Consequent from the Embargo ($ billion, 1973 dollars)	1.0	0.0

Source: E.A. Hudson and D.W. Jorgenson, "U.S. Energy Policy and Economic Growth, 1975 - 2000." Bell Journal of Economics and Management Science, p. 461 et seq.; P.W. MacAvoy and R.S. Pindyck, The Economics of the Natural Gas Shortage (1960- 1980).

The sum total of these policy changes would be to replace the growth in imports with domestic production. Altogether, (a) phased deregulation of natural gas, (b) elimination of the price freeze on old and new oil from domestic wells and (c) elimination of state commission controls over output in crude oil, could increase domestic output by 5 quadrillion Btu by 1980, enough to replace the growth of imports over the rest of the decade. With reasonable facility in purchasing the 13 quadrillion Btu already being received from abroad - - facility in avoiding the Persian Gulf States as suppliers - - the likelihood of being embargoed could be much reduced.

At worst, however, with potential imports of 16 quadrillion Btu reduced to 11 quadrillion Btu by expanded domestic supplies, somewhat more than one quadrillion Btu could still be embargoed. The results are shown in Table 6, for the case of an embargo of 0.5 million barrels per day or 1 quadrillion Btu. The GNP costs do not exceed $0.5 billion. This is 6 to 10 percent of the costs of a "conservation" program (Table 4). The losses to the economy from periodic embargoes would be much less when the policy consists merely in tolerating them, but only if we put into place domestic productive capacity that can be justified as below the costs of alternative supplies from abroad, and free from the political disruption that characterizes the foreign supplies. This overriding consideration focuses attention upon the elimination of Federal and state controls which have the effect of reducing domestic reserve accumulation and production.

REFERENCES

1. Adelman, M.A., "Efficiency of Resource Use of Crude Petroleum," Southern Economic Journal, (October 1964), 100-22.

2. Agria, S.R., "Special Tax Treatment of the Metal Industries," in A.C. Harberger and M.J. Bailey (eds.), The Taxation of Income from Capital. Washington: Brookings, 1969.

3. Atlantic Refining Company v. Public Service Commission (360 U.S. 378).

4. Baratz, M.S. The Unions and the Coal Industry. New Haven: Yale University Press, 1960.

5. Cabinet Task Force on Oil Import Control. The Oil Import Question. (February 1970).

6. CONSAD Research Corporation. The Economic Factors Affecting the Level of Domestic Petroleum Reserves (Part 4) 1; U.S. Congress Committee on Ways and Means Tax Reform Studies and Proposals, Washington, D.C.: 1969.

7. DeChazeau, M.G., and Kahn, A.E. Integration and Competition in the Petroleum Industry. New Haven: Yale University Press, 1959.

8. Erickson, E.W. Economic Incentives, Industrial Structure and the Supply of Crude Oil Discoveries in the United States, 1946-1959. (Ph.D. dissertation, Vanderbilt University, 1968).

9. Federal Power Commission, Natural Gas Division. National Gas Supply and Demand, 1970-1990. Washington, D.C.: February 1972.

10. Gilliam, C.L., "Federal Power Commission Jurisdiction over Producers," George Washington Law Review (January 1956), 336.

11. Hudson, E.A. and Jorgenson, D.W., "U.S. Energy Policy and Economic Growth, 1975-2000," The Bell Journal of Economics and Management Science, (Autumn 1974), 461-514.

12. Jackson, R. , "Regulation in Electric Utility Rate Levels," <u>Land Economics</u> (August 1969), 372-376.

13. Jordan, W.A., "Producer Protection, Prior Market Structure and the Effects of Government Regulation," <u>Journal of Law and Economics,</u> (April 1972) Vol. 15 No. 1, 151-76.

14. Kitch, E., "Regulation in the Field Market for Natural Gas by the Federal ˙Power Commission ," <u>Journal of Law and Economics,</u> Vol. 10, (October 1968), 243-80.

15. Lovejoy, W.F.,and Homan, P.T.   <u>Economic Aspects of Oil Conservation Regulation.</u> Baltimore: The Johns Hopkins Press, 1967.

16. MacAvoy, P.W. <u>Price Formation in Natural Gas Fields.</u> New Haven: Yale University Press, 1961.

17. MacAvoy, P.W.,and Pindyck, R.S. <u>The Economics of the Natural Gas Shortage (1960-1980).</u> MIT Energy Laboratory Report No. MIT-EL74-011 (September 1974).

18. McDonald, S.L., "Conservation Regulation and the Elements of a Natural Energy Policy," in E.L. Erickson and L. Waverman (eds.) <u>The Energy Question,</u> Vol. 1, Toronto: University of Toronto Press, 1974, 331-354.

19. Moore, T., "The Effectiveness of Regulation of Electric Utility Prices," Michigan State Workshop Paper No. 6711 (March 1968).

20. <u>New York Times,</u> "Mine Owners Ask Delay on Safety Laws, " March 19, 1974.

21. _____ , "Coal Mines Safety Deadline: Comply with Code or Close," March 31, 1974.

22. Office of Economic Impact, Federal Energy Administration. <u>The Economic Impact of the Oil Embargo on the American Economy,</u> (August 8, 1974).

23. Rostow, E.V. <u>A National Policy for the Oil Industry.</u> New Haven: Yale University Press, 1948.

24. Sloss, J., "Competitive Railroad Rates and Services Applied to the Movements of Bituminous Coal." American Society of Mechanical Engineers Publication 67-TRAN-36, 1967.

25. Stigler, G., and Friedland, C., "What Can Regulators Regulate?" The Journal of Law and Economics, (October 1962), 1-16.

26. Wherry, W.M., "Can Gas Production be Regulated?" Public Utilities Fortnightly (August 1955), 157-160.

POLICY CONFLICTS IN THE SEPARATE CONTROL OF QUANTITY AND PRICE IN THE ENERGY INDUSTRIES: A COMMENT

Robert H. Rasche
Michigan State University

Professor MacAvoy reaches two principal conclusions about the regulation of the energy industries: (1) his evaluation of the most likely state of the world over the next five years is that regulation will go on pretty much as it has over the recent past and (2) that the most important consideration in putting domestic production capacity into place as an alternative to dependence on foreign sources of energy is the elimination of the existing state and Federal regulation of energy industries. I concur in his assessment that the continued existence of present regulatory practices is highly likely. I would also concur that it is highly desirable to eliminate many, if not all, of these regulatory practices. The important question, from our joint perspective on the issue, is why are we so likely to lose the battle?

The primary thesis of Professor MacAvoy's analysis is that past regulation has brought us to where we now are as far as dependence on foreign energy sources, and that continued regulation is likely to get us into even a worse bind over the next five to six years in terms of the sensitivity of production in the U.S. economy to changes in the availability (and price?) of foreign energy sources. Therefore, because of these costs, regulation should go. The problem with this view, in my judgment, is that it does not make a particularly strong case for eliminating the regulations. Consider the estimated costs associated with the embargoing of foreign energy. MacAvoy cites a $10-20 billion decline in real GNP concurrent with the embargo, (page 228), but recognizes that much of this is attributable to events not related to the energy embargo, such as the decline in housing starts and the decline in sales of non-auto durables. He feels that there is little knowledge of the importance of the long-run effects, and that it is even possible that all of the losses were potentially one-shot events with no continuing long-run effects.

What about the cost of future embargos? Professor MacAvoy has provided us with what he regards as a conservative (or pessimistic) scenario that all supplies from the Persian Gulf are successfully cut off for a period of one year. Based on the extrapolations from his econometric work, combined with that of Hudson and Jorgenson, he concludes that "any embargo of such sizes and time duration would cost billions of dollars, but not as much as already assessed against the shorter and more limited 1973 embargo," (page 232). He continues, "the embargoes envisioned might actually cost a great deal less, given that the 'lost' imports were replaceable in various markets" (page 232). His range of cost estimates, presented in Table 3 (page 234) for an embargo in 1980 is from 3.3 to 6.8 billion (1973) dollars. This is relative to an estimated base (real) GNP for the U.S. in 1980 of 1780.4 billion dollars, or from 0.19 to 0.38 percent of real GNP. These numbers hardly seem catastrophic. Yet there are several reasons why they may be overestimates of the costs of such an embargo.

First, it should be remembered that an embargo is not at all certain. We are presumably not interested in the cost of an embargo, but rather the expected cost, given some estimate of the probability that it would occur. Whatever number policy-makers would care to attach to this probability, it is certainly less than one.

Second, these cost estimates are dependent on the accuracy of the simulation results from the Hudson-Jorgenson-MacAvoy-Pindyck model. In reviewing the current paper, I have had to work with the disadvantage that I have not seen either of the two econometric models. Under these circumstances it is impossible to criticize the analysis in detail. Nevertheless, there is some information revealed in the tables of the present paper which raises some suspicions. Consider the discussion on page 230 and the associated Table 2 which indicates domestic production in 1973 and associated growth through 1980. Crude oil production estimates for 1973 are given as 18.8 quadrillion BTU/Annum. In Table 1, below, data are presented on the "real" price of domestic crude for the period 1970-1973, and for one month in early 1974. These data are compiled using both the wholesale price index for industrial commodities and the wholesale price index for all commodities as the deflator. In both cases the price is remarkably stable, varying between 2.00 and 3.00 1967 dollars per barrel. By March 1974, the nominal price had jumped to 6.33 dollars and the real price was up to 4.45 1967 dollars. As I understand the assumptions in the MacAvoy projections, it is assumed that this increase in the real price of crude which took place during late 1973 and early 1974, is projected to remain through 1980 (see pages 229-30). This represents a 41 to 44 percent increase in the real price of crude over the levels which had prevailed for the four years ending with late 1973. The question is what long-run price elasticity of supply should be applied to this change in real price to get an estimate of the increase in rate of crude production?

There are a number of estimates of the long-run elasticity of crude supply in existence, at least some of which predate the crisis of the past year. Three of these are cited by L. Cookenboo. [1] They are drawn from studies by CONSAD Research Corporation, CRA, and Standard Oil of New Jersey. The elasticity estimates are, respectively .125, 1.0 and 1.67. The CONSAD results strike me as totally implausible. The Standard Oil results were considered at the time they were developed from engineering studies to be completely plausible by

[1] L. Cookenboo, "Economic Significance of Petroleum Tax Provisions," Chapter 7 in Tax Incentives, Tax Association of America, Heath Lexington, 1971, pp. 105-111.

TABLE 1

CRUDE OIL PRICES

	Price of Crude[1] ($ Per Bbl) (1)	Wholesale Price Index (1967 = 1.0) Industrial Commodities (2)	"Real" Price Crude (1) ÷ (2) (3)	Wholesale Price Index (1967 = 1.0) All Commodities (4)	"Real" Price Crude (1) ÷ (4) (5)
1970	3.23	1.100	2.94	1.104	2.93
1971	3.41	1.140	2.99	1.139	2.99
1972	3.45	1.179	2.93	1.191	2.90
1973[2]	3.87	1.253	3.09	1.339	2.89
1974[3]	6.33	1.424	4.45	1.154	4.18

[1] Source: Survey of Current Business

[2] January-October Average

[3] March Only

industry spokesmen, but it should be recognized that they were talking about price fluctuations over a much narrower range than we are considering here. The CRA estimate is supported by a more recent discussion of the supply response. If we assume that unity is a reasonably accurate estimate of the long-run supply elasticity of domestic crude production, then by 1980, if current real prices are maintained, we would expect about a 40 percent increase, or about 7.5 quadrillion BTU/Annum increase in domestic energy production from this source alone. This contrasts with the MacAvoy conclusion that there would be a 10.6 quadrillion BTU/Annum increase from oil, natural gas, and coal combined. If I combine MacAvoy's estimates for coal (-1.4) and natural gas (+8.6) from his Table 2 with my estimate for oil (7.5), petroleum import requirements in 1980, under constant real price regulation of crude oil, may not be anywhere near the 30 percent greater than 1973 levels, which MacAvoy finds. In fact, if that estimate of the elasticity of domestic crude supply is correct, then it seems likely that import requirements under the assumed regulatory policy could be below 1973 levels. All of this would suggest even lower costs to the U.S. economy of a future energy embargo than the small estimates that MacAvoy has found.

Finally, now that the real price of crude oil has been increased by the OPEC cartel, we are observing considerable stimulus to exploration in other foreign areas. Large fields such as the North Sea, and potentially large fields such as Mexico will be undergoing development during the remainder of the decade. As more and more countries become eligible for membership in the OPEC cartel, it seems less and less likely that they will be able to consistently agree on a joint effort. This will reduce the probability that the U.S. will face a successful embargo as time goes on.

Where does this leave us on the question of why regulation is likely to remain, even though we would prefer to see it removed? The point, I believe, is that regulation will never be overthrown by examining the potential costs that it suggests in the event of disruption of imports. Such costs are nickel and dime issues compared with the benefits accruing to those for whom the regulators regulate. [2] If we wish to make a serious effort at removing the regulation, then I think we must emphasize that there are welfare costs of the regulation in terms of distortions and inefficiencies, which go on year after year even if there are no embargoes. Research needs to be undertaken to quantify these costs, and these estimates could be used to present a case for the elimination of regulation of energy industries which has a considerable higher probability of winning public acceptance.

---

[2] Obviously one of the most important vested interest groups is the regulators themselves. They are faced with unemployment in the event that regulation is overthrown.